T0215338

Lecture Notes in Computer Science 14521

Founding Editors

Gerhard Goos
Juris Hartmanis

Editorial Board Members

Elisa Bertino, *Purdue University, West Lafayette, IN, USA*
Wen Gao, *Peking University, Beijing, China*
Bernhard Steffen ⓘ, *TU Dortmund University, Dortmund, Germany*
Moti Yung ⓘ, *Columbia University, New York, NY, USA*

The series Lecture Notes in Computer Science (LNCS), including its subseries Lecture Notes in Artificial Intelligence (LNAI) and Lecture Notes in Bioinformatics (LNBI), has established itself as a medium for the publication of new developments in computer science and information technology research, teaching, and education.

LNCS enjoys close cooperation with the computer science R & D community, the series counts many renowned academics among its volume editors and paper authors, and collaborates with prestigious societies. Its mission is to serve this international community by providing an invaluable service, mainly focused on the publication of conference and workshop proceedings and postproceedings. LNCS commenced publication in 1973.

Sascha Hunold · Biwei Xie · Kai Shu

Editors

Benchmarking, Measuring, and Optimizing

15th BenchCouncil International Symposium, Bench 2023
Sanya, China, December 3–5, 2023
Revised Selected Papers

Springer

Editors
Sascha Hunold 🆔
TU Wien
Vienna, Austria

Biwei Xie 🆔
Chinese Academy of Sciences
Beijing, China

Kai Shu 🆔
Illinois Institute of Technology
Chicago, IL, USA

ISSN 0302-9743   ISSN 1611-3349 (electronic)
Lecture Notes in Computer Science
ISBN 978-981-97-0315-9   ISBN 978-981-97-0316-6 (eBook)
https://doi.org/10.1007/978-981-97-0316-6

This Springer imprint is published by the registered company Springer Nature Singapore Pte Ltd.
The registered company address is: 152 Beach Road, #21-01/04 Gateway East, Singapore 189721, Singapore

Paper in this product is recyclable.

Preface

This volume contains the papers presented at the 15th BenchCouncil International Symposium on Benchmarking, Measuring and Optimizing (Bench 2023). The first nine events constituted the BPOE workshops, which were held in conjunction with ASPLOS, VLDB, and ICS. Since 2018, the Bench symposium, originating from the BPOE workshops, exhibits three defining characteristics: (1) it provides a high-quality, single-track forum for presenting results and discussing ideas that further the knowledge and understanding of the benchmark community; (2) it is a multi-disciplinary conference, attracting researchers and practitioners from different communities, including architecture, systems, algorithms, and applications; (3) the program features both invited and contributed talks.

The Bench symposium invites papers addressing pressing problems in benchmarking, measuring, and optimizing systems. The call for papers for the Bench 2023 conference attracted a number of high-quality submissions. These underwent a thorough review by at least four international experts. Ultimately, the program committee selected 11 papers for presentation at Bench 2023. The papers in this volume have been revised as per the program committee's recommendations.

At the conference, the International Open Benchmark Council (BenchCouncil) presented the BenchCouncil Achievement Award, recognizing a senior member for their enduring contributions to the field. Lieven Eeckhout from the Ghent University, Belgium, was named the 2023 recipient of the BenchCouncil Achievement Award. In the award's keynote address, Eeckhout emphasized the importance of rigorous performance evaluation. Eeckhout identified common pitfalls in both experimental design and data analysis, proposing potential solutions.

The Bench 2023 conference included a keynote lecture by Dhableswar K. Panda from Ohio State University, focusing on challenges and opportunities in designing middleware and benchmarks for HPC, AI, Big Data, and Data Science.

We are deeply thankful to all authors for their exceptional contributions to the Bench 2023 conference. Our gratitude extends to the invaluable support from the Bench 2023 Program Committee, and we express our sincere thanks to its members for their commitment and effort in maintaining the high standards of the Bench symposium.

December 2023

Sascha Hunold
Biwei Xie
Kai Shu

Organization

General Chairs

Rakesh Agrawal   Data Insights Laboratories, San Jose, CA, USA
Aoying Zhou   East China Normal University, China

Program Chairs

Sascha Hunold   TU Wien, Austria
Biwei Xie   Institute of Computing Technology, Chinese Academy of Sciences, China
Kai Shu   Illinois Institute of Technology, USA
Weining Qian   East China Normal University, China

Program Committee

Ahmad Ghazal   PingCAP, China
Bartlomiej Przybylski   Adam Mickiewicz University, Poland
Benson Muite   Kichakato Kizito, Kenya
Bin Ren   College of William & Mary, USA
Bo Wu   Colorado School of Mines, USA
Cheol-Ho Hong   Chung-Ang University, Republic of Korea
Chunjie Luo   Institute of Computing Technology, Chinese Academy of Sciences, China
David Boehme   Lawrence Livermore National Laboratory, USA
Florina M. Ciorba   University of Basel, Switzerland
Francieli Boito   University of Bordeaux, France
Guangli Li   Institute of Computing Technology, Chinese Academy of Sciences, China
Gwangsun Kim   POSTECH, Republic of Korea
Joseph Schuchart   University of Tennessee, Knoxville, USA
K. Selçuk Candan   Arizona State University, USA
Khaled Ibrahim   Lawrence Berkeley National Laboratory, USA
Lucas Mello Schnorr   Federal University of Rio Grande do Sul, Brazil
Mario Marino   Leeds Beckett University, UK
Miaoqing Huang   University of Arkansas, USA

Invited Talks

BenchCouncil Achievement Award Lecture: Essentially, All Models Are Wrong, but Some Are Useful

Lieven Eeckhout

Ghent University, Belgium

Abstract: Performance analysis and modeling is of critical importance to computer systems and architecture research and development. We must design and build our simulators, benchmarks, and analysis tools correctly, and we must measure and analyze our performance results rigorously, otherwise experimental research and development may lead to incorrect and misleading conclusions and ineffective optimizations. These tools are critical to our understanding of both the problems and the solutions. In this talk, I will revisit the importance of rigorous performance evaluation, and decompose the performance evaluation challenge into two sub-problems, experimental design and data analysis. I will discuss some of the (not so obvious) pitfalls in both experimental design and data analysis, and argue for potential solutions. I will also emphasize the importance of picking the right level of abstraction for steering performance analysis tool as there no one size fits all.

Biography: Lieven Eeckhout (PhD 2002) is a Senior Full Professor at Ghent University, Belgium, in the Department of Electronics and Information Systems (ELIS). His research interests include computer architecture, with specific emphasis on performance evaluation and modeling, dynamic resource management, CPU/GPU microarchitecture, and sustainability. He is the recipient of the 2017 ACM SIGARCH Maurice Wilkes Award and the 2017 OOPSLA Most Influential Paper Award, and he was elevated to IEEE Fellow in 2018 and ACM Fellow in 2021. Other awards include three IEEE Micro Top Pick selections (2007, 2010, and 2022), the ISPASS 2013 and MICRO 2023 Best Paper Awards, and Best Paper Nominations at PACT 2014, ISPASS 2012, ISPASS 2014, ISPASS 2015, ISPASS 2016, MICRO 2019, MICRO 2021, and ISCA 2023. He served as the Program Chair for ISCA 2020, HPCA 2015, CGO 2013, and ISPASS 2009, and has served or serves as General Chair for ISPASS 2010, IISWC 2023, and ASPLOS 2025. He served as the Chair of the IEEE Computer Society Technical Committee on Computer Architecture (TCCA) (2017–2018), Editor-in-Chief of IEEE Micro (2015–2018), Associate Editor of IEEE Transactions on Computers (2016–2018), IEEE Computer Architecture Letters (2013–2015), and ACM Transactions on Architecture and Code Optimization (2010–2017). He has served as technical program committee member for 50+ computer architecture conferences. He is the recipient of five European Research Council (ERC) grants, including a Starting Grant, an Advanced Grant, and three Proof-of-Concept Grants.

Designing High-Performance and Scalable Middleware and Benchmarks for HPC, AI, and Data Sciences

Dhabaleswar K. (DK) Panda

The Ohio State University

Abstract: This talk will focus on challenges and opportunities in designing middleware and benchmarks for HPC, AI (Deep/Machine Learning), Big Data, and Data Science. We will start with the challenges in designing runtime environments for MPI+X programming models by considering support for multi-core systems, high-performance networks (InfiniBand, RoCE, Slingshot), GPUs (NVIDIA and AMD), and emerging BlueField-3 DPUs. Features and sample performance numbers of using the MVAPICH2 libraries over a range of benchmarks will be presented. For the Deep/Machine Learning domain, we will focus on MPI-driven solutions (MPI4DL) to extract performance and scalability for popular Deep Learning frameworks (TensorFlow and PyTorch), large out-of-core models, and Bluefield-3 DPUs. MPI-driven solutions to accelerate Big Data applications (MPI4Spark) and data science applications (MPI4Dask) with appropriate benchmark results will be presented.

Biography: DK Panda is a Professor and University Distinguished Scholar of Computer Science and Engineering at the Ohio State University. He is serving as the Director of the ICICLE NSF-AI Institute (https://icicle.ai). He has published over 500 papers. The MVAPICH2 MPI libraries, designed and developed by his research group (http://mvapich.cse.ohio-state.edu), are currently being used by more than 3,300 organizations worldwide (in 90 countries). More than 1.74 million downloads of this software have taken place from the project's site. This software is empowering many clusters in the TOP500 list. High-performance and scalable solutions for Deep Learning frameworks and Machine Learning applications from his group are available from https://hidl.cse.ohio-state.edu. Similarly, scalable and high-performance solutions for Big Data and Data science frameworks are available from https://hibd.cse.ohio-state.edu. Prof. Panda is an IEEE Fellow and recipient of the 2022 IEEE Charles Babbage Award. More details about Prof. Panda are available at https://web.cse.ohio-state.edu/~panda.

Contents

ICBench: Benchmarking Knowledge Mastery in Introductory Computer Science Education

Zhenying Li[1,2]([🖂]) [ID], Zishu Yu[1,2] [ID], Lian Zhai[1,2] [ID], Xiaohui Peng[1] [ID], and Zhiwei Xu[1,2] [ID]

[1] Institute of Computing Technology, Chinese Academy of Sciences, Beijing 100190, China
{lizhenying20b,yuzishu19s,zhailian20s,pengxiaohui,zxu}@ict.ac.cn
[2] University of Chinese Academy of Sciences, Beijing 100049, China

Abstract. In computer science education, a fundamental challenge is to accurately assess a student's knowledge mastery. Inspired by Knuth's view that "the ultimate test of whether I understand something is if I can explain it to a compute", we introduce the Knuth test and construct ICBench for benchmarking knowledge mastery in introductory computer science education. Three metrics of knowledge coverage, Bloom's taxonomy, and traditional score are used in ICBench, where the former two assess the breadth and depth of a student's mastery, respectively. We present the Rule-Property-Crux-Cohesion (RPCC) model for modeling a knowledge point and the Encode-Construct-Personalize (ECP) method to generate a personalized question set for each student. By analyzing the data of over 1000 students in the UCAS CS101 course from 2021 to 2023, we find that ICBench improves both knowledge coverage and Bloom's taxonomy level. Furthermore, students who passed the test in ICBench outperformed their peers on final exams, scoring an average of 14% higher.

Keywords: Automatic Assessment · Benchmark · Introductory Computer Science Education · Knuth Test

1 Introduction

Accurate evaluation of a student's knowledge mastery is crucial to identifying shortcomings and improving the performance of the student. Automatic approaches have been employed, assessing intended learning contents [4] based on Bloom's taxonomy [5,17] or generating personalized question sets [1,23,28] to prevent cheating.

This project is partially funded by the National Natural Science Foundation of China under grant No. 62072434 and the Beijing Natural Science Foundation under grant No. 4212027.

S. Hunold et al. (Eds.): Bench 2023, LNCS 14521, pp. 1–17, 2024.
https://doi.org/10.1007/978-981-97-0316-6_1

Conducting an objective and comprehensive assessment of a student's knowledge mastery is challenging. The evaluation criteria should be free from teachers' subjective influences and uniformly applied across all students. Comprehensiveness requires coverage of key and difficult aspects of a knowledge point. Approaches that only focus on question personalization help prevent student cheating, neglecting the coverage of knowledge, which is usually completed by a teacher's manual selection [1,23,28]. Existing methodology that maps a question to a knowledge point fails to consider various aspects of a knowledge point [4], potentially leading to insufficient coverage.

Knuth proposed that "the ultimate test of whether I understand something is if I can explain it to a computer" [8], a viewpoint he emphasized in 1974 [14], 1995 [15], and 2020 [8]. Knuth pointed out that the notion of an algorithm or a computer program provides us with an extremely useful test for the depth of our knowledge about any given subject. Utilizing a computer as an assessment tool meets the requirements of objectivity and comprehensiveness. A computer strictly follows the instructions of programs or the statements of specifications, applying consistent standards across all students to yield objective evaluation results. Execution requires all necessary details; any grammatical or semantic errors could lead to erroneous outcomes.

Learning from the Turing test, Knuth's perspective needs to be operationalized into the Knuth test, serving as a methodology to assess a student's knowledge mastery. The development of the Knuth test presents the following two challenges:

- *Assessment Criteria*: How to describe the knowledge mastery level of a student?
- *Methodology Selection*: What is the process of the Knuth test? How can this methodology be scaled for a large number of students and prevent cheating?

This paper introduces the Knuth test, with which we construct a benchmark, ICBench, for assessing knowledge mastery in introductory computer science education. We construct question sets in ICBench, considering both knowledge coverage and Bloom's taxonomy levels, a set of hierarchical models used for the classification of educational learning objectives into different levels. Furthermore, we present three degrees of personalization. The contributions of this paper are:

1. Introduction of the benchmarking methodology. We propose evaluation metrics to assess the breadth and depth of a student's mastery, the Rule-Property-Crux-Cohesion (RPCC) model to model knowledge points, and the Encode-Construct-Personalize (ECP) method to generate a concise, personalized benchmark with satisfactory coverage.
2. Implementation of ICBench for introductory computer science courses. ICBench includes a prototype system and a set of seed questions, covering the four types of computational thinking: logical, algorithmic, systems, and network thinking. The prototype system produces ten thousand unique question sets within one second using just hundreds of kilobytes of storage, demonstrating scalability for a large number of students.

3. Analysis of the ICBench's effectiveness in real-world course data. ICBench improves knowledge coverage and Bloom's taxonomy level compared to the previous exercises. On average, students who passed the Knuth test in ICBench scored 14% higher on corresponding knowledge points in the final exam than those who did not.

2 Overview

2.1 The RPCC Model for Knowledge Points

A knowledge point is a set of problems relevant to a specific topic. To explain a knowledge point unambiguously to a computer, we express these problems as algorithmic problems, as demonstrated in Table 1. If a student can correctly explain all the problems to a computer, then mastery over a knowledge point is achieved. We refer to the tasks provided for students during an assessment as "questions", which are distinguished from "problems" in modeling a knowledge point. The questions provided for students can take multiple forms and variations during an assessment.

A knowledge point can be modeled using Rule-Property-Crux-Cohesion quadruples. Table 1 illustrates the RPCC model for *Truth Table*. Rule is the constructive definition of the knowledge point, such as the truth table definition. Property refers to the key characteristics related to a knowledge point. Crux denotes teaching challenges. Cohesion represents the interconnection of a knowledge point with others in the course, such as applying truth tables in the design of combinational circuits.

Table 1. RPCC model of *Truth Table*. All problems are designed to allow for automated computer grading.

RPCC Element	Problem
Rule	P1: Given one or more arbitrary Boolean expressions, compute the corresponding truth table
Property	P2: Given the number of input and output variables, compute the different numbers of truth tables
Crux	P3: Given Boolean expressions containing implication operators, compute the corresponding truth table
Cohesion	P4: Given a truth table as input, determine the Boolean expressions
	P5: Given a proposition or digital circuit, determine the Boolean expression and write the truth table

We only consider the knowledge points for which a computer can automatically evaluate the correctness of the solutions, such as the *Truth Table* provided in Table 1. Some knowledge points do not meet the automated computer grading requirement. For example, in the Introduction to Computer Science course (CS101) at the University of Chinese Academy of Sciences (UCAS), students design and implement a dynamic webpage as a personal artifact [27]. This project requires demonstrating creativity, and assessing creativity depends on teachers' judgment.

2.2   Metrics

We introduce three metrics: knowledge coverage, Bloom's taxonomy, and traditional score. Knowledge coverage and Bloom's taxonomy represent the breadth and depth of students' knowledge mastery, respectively. The assessment should provide a comprehensive set of questions to cover all important aspects of the knowledge points. Our primary goal is to assist teachers in ensuring their assessments comprehensively cover the content they expect their students to master. We specifically focus on the content and concepts emphasized and prioritized by the teacher within the course, rather than a complete exploration of the entire knowledge point without any context. The knowledge coverage is computed as the proportion of problems of a knowledge point in an assessment. For example, if 2 out of 5 problems in Table 1 are assessed, then the coverage of *Truth Table* is 40% in the assessment.

In Bloom's taxonomy, the cognitive domain is divided into six levels: Remember, Understand, Apply, Analyze, Evaluate, and Create [17]. In this paper, Apply, Analyze, Evaluate, and Create are collectively referred to as Create for simplicity. Currently, Bloom's taxonomy level of the question set depends on manual annotation. The annotation of question instances presented to students should align with the actual teaching context. For example, a task to design a Turing machine for binary addition would fall under the Remember level if rules for such a machine were taught. Students would simply recall and write down these rules. If not previously presented, the same task tests students' ability to create a new solution, thus falling under the Create level of Bloom's taxonomy.

2.3   The Process of the Knuth Test

The Knuth test involves three roles: teacher, student, and computer, as shown in Fig. 1. We define the Knuth test as follows:

- Objective: The test evaluates whether the student S has mastered knowledge point K.
- Process: During the interval [0, T], computer C asks any question q from the question set Q associated with the knowledge point K to the student S. The student S submits answer a to computer C, which determines the correctness.
- Result: If the accuracy of student S's responses is above 90%, student S is considered to have mastered the knowledge point K. The number 90% is an empirical number based on the experience in the UCAS CS101 course.

The Knuth test process shown in Fig. 1 consists of six steps:

1. Knowledge explanation: The teacher explains a knowledge point K to the student.

2. Knowledge modeling: The teacher inputs the RPCC model that describes K into the computer.
3. Problem annotation: The teacher associates the questions with K, annotates the levels of Bloom's taxonomy, and enters the annotated questions into the computer.
4. Question set generation: The teacher specifies the requirements of the question set, such as the knowledge points to be assessed, the desired level of Bloom's taxonomy, and the desired level of personalization. The computer generates a question set adhering to these specifications and forwards it to the teacher for review.
5. Question answering: The computer releases the teacher-reviewed questions to the student, who then provides answers within a time period T.
6. Results analysis: The computer determines whether the student has passed the Knuth test and provides feedback based on the student's answers.

Note that questions might take the form of programming exercises and fill-in-the-blanks instead of the single-choice questions to decrease the probability of students guessing the correct answer.

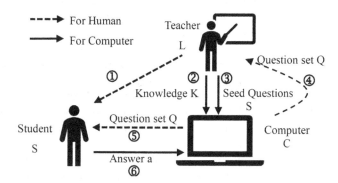

Fig. 1. The process of the Knuth test for a knowledge point.

3   Methodology

This section introduces the methodology for constructing a question set. The target question set should meet the following four requirements. (i) The question set should comprehensively cover the content and concepts that teachers emphasize within their course, spanning various levels of Bloom's taxonomy. (ii) The question set should contain various question types, including focused questions that assess specific aspects of the knowledge point and comprehensive questions that assess multiple aspects. (iii) The method should generate different degrees of personalized question sets according to the teacher's needs. (iv) The question set should be as concise as possible.

To construct a question set that fulfills the necessary requirements for knowledge point K, a teacher can use the three-step Encode-Construct-Personalize (ECP) method. The seed questions shown in Fig. 1 serve as templates and can be constructed with the help of a computer. A teacher encodes the questions mathematically, considering the knowledge content assessed and Bloom's taxonomy level. The computer identifies representative questions based on the teacher's requirements and creates a concise seed question set with the required coverage. After the teacher reviews the seed question set, the computer utilizes the seed question set as templates to generate a personalized question set for each student.

3.1 Encoding Questions

The key to automatically generating a question set with satisfactory coverage is to find a question representation that can be analyzed by a computer. Conventionally, teachers rely on their experience to select representative questions from various types including focused questions that assess specific aspects of the knowledge point and comprehensive questions that assess multiple aspects. This manual approach can be time-consuming. To address this, we propose a mathematical encoding of questions, enabling automatic analysis by a computer.

A question Q_i associated with knowledge point K can be encoded with a pair (C_i, L_i), where C_i and L_i respectively represent the knowledge content and the level in Bloom's taxonomy. C_i is a vector of length n (the total number of algorithmic problems in K). If Q_i assesses the j-th problem modeled in K, then C_{ij} is 1, otherwise C_{ij} is 0. L_i is scalar, with values 0, 1, or 2, representing the Remember, Understand, and Create levels, respectively. For a comprehensive question containing multiple sub-questions, Bloom's taxonomy level is set to the highest level among all sub-questions.

Take the following four questions for *Truth Table* as examples. The encoding of *Simple proposition* is $((1, 0, 0, 0, 0), 0)$. *Simple proposition* only assesses problem 1 of Table 1, and its truth table is given in the course, resulting in Remember level. The encoding of *Variables number* is $((0, 1, 0, 0, 0), 2)$. This question assesses problem 2 of the truth table and asks students to deduce the number of variables from a given truth table, which is not explained in the course, resulting in Create level. Similarly, the encoding of *Model sentence* and *Full Adder* is $((1, 0, 1, 0, 1), 1)$ and $((1, 0, 0, 1, 1), 2)$, respectively.

- *Simple proposition*: Write the truth table for the proposition $P \wedge Q$.
- *Model sentence*: Write the truth table for R with respect to P and Q. P: It's raining today. Q: The road will be wet today. R: If it rains today, then the road will be wet today.
- *Variables number*: Find the input variables in the given truth table (Table 2).

Table 2. Find the input variables.

P	Q	R	S	T	U	V
0	0	0	0	1	1	0
0	1	0	1	1	1	1
1	0	0	1	0	0	1
1	1	1	1	0	1	0

– *Full Adder*: A full adder is a single-bit adder with 3 inputs and 2 outputs. It has 5 Boolean variables: (1) a carry input variable C_{in} and two input variables, X and Y; (2) a sum output variable Z and a carry output variable C_{out}. Please write the truth table and the Boolean expressions of the output variables, Z and C_{out}.

The encoding for a question set Q can be derived from the encodings of the included questions. Suppose n is the total number of the algorithmic problems in the RPCC model of the Knowledge point K, $Q_S = \{Q_1, Q_2, \ldots, Q_m\} = \{(C_1, L_1), (C_2, L_2), \ldots, (C_m, L_m)\}$, then the encoding (C_S, L_S) of Q_S is defined as follows:

$$C_S = \bigvee_1^m C_i, \ where \ C_i \vee C_j = (C_{i1} \vee C_{j1}, C_{i2} \vee C_{j2}, \ldots, C_{in} \vee C_{jn}) \quad (1)$$

$$L_S = \max_{i=1}^m L_i \quad (2)$$

3.2   Constructing Seed Question Set

Inspired by the supercomputing community's benchmarking strategy of using spatial and temporal locality to select representative programs [27], this paper selects representative questions based on the comprehensiveness of the questions and the level of Bloom's taxonomy. We define a question's comprehensiveness as the total number of the knowledge point's algorithmic problems it assesses, represented by the sum of its knowledge vector C elements. For example, *Full Adder* covers three aspects, resulting in a score of 3, which is the maximum among all questions for *Truth Table* in the CS101 course.

The four questions in Subsect. 3.1 above form a representative question set Q_r, reflecting four distinct combinations of knowledge comprehensiveness and Bloom's taxonomy level, as shown in Fig. 2. The questions: *Full Adder*, *Model sentence*, *Variables number*, and *Simple proposition*, correspond to high-high, high-low, low-high, and low-low combinations, respectively. The four combinations encapsulate the spectrum of knowledge comprehensiveness and Bloom's taxonomy level observed in other questions.

The identification of the representative question set Q_r can be automatic through a computer algorithm. When looking for questions that balance both high knowledge coverage and Bloom's taxonomy levels, the algorithm searches based on the weighted importance of these two dimensions. To accommodate diverse teaching objectives, our system offers a user-friendly interface, allowing teachers to set the weights for these two dimensions, customizing the search according to their needs.

The representative question set Q_r can provide a coarse-grained evaluation of a student's mastery of knowledge. For instance, students who correctly answer all four questions can be considered to have mastered the truth table knowledge points up to the Create level. However, for a more fine-grained assessment of students for a complex knowledge point with a large number of problems, additional questions may need to be selected to thoroughly cover all content of the knowledge point.

To construct a question set that completely covers all aspects of a knowledge point, we need to ensure that, for each problem indexed by i in the RPCC model, the corresponding value of C_{Qi} is 1. We add constraint (3) as follows:

$$\forall i \in \{1,\ 2,\ \ldots,\ n\},\ C_{Qi} = 1 \tag{3}$$

it is imperative that the question set Q encompasses all questions in Q_r. To formalize this requirement, we introduce constraint (4):

$$Q \supseteq Q_r \tag{4}$$

To maintain the conciseness of the question set and save students' time, we aim to minimize the number of questions, m, as much as possible in constraint (5):

$$\min m \tag{5}$$

If these requirements cannot be met, the system is designed to prompt the teacher to add new questions, thereby enriching the question pool to comprehensively address all aspects of the knowledge point.

3.3   Personalizing Question Set

Depending on the degree of personalization, question sets can be non-personalized, personalized at the question-set level (assessing the same knowledge points), or personalized at the knowledge level (assessing different knowledge points according to the student's status). For routine homework, we can personalize the set to assess the same knowledge points, while for non-graded tests, we can customize the set to cover different knowledge points based on each student's needs.

A template-based method is employed for question variation. Questions are specified by Profile [26], a high-level specification language based on TLA$^+$ [19]. A question profile contains elements such as the question stem, variation parameters, scoring function, parameter generation function, and mathematical encoding. We define a series of variation operators, such as parameter substitution

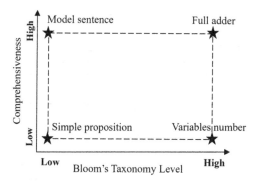

Fig. 2. Construct a representative question set covering the knowledge point and Bloom's taxonomy level.

and randomization. For personalization at the question set level, we can generate personalized question sets through parameter variation. For knowledge-level personalization, we can construct personalized question sets according to students' historical data of knowledge space [13].

4 Implementation

We have constructed the seed question sets in ICBench, utilizing the RPCC model and ECP method. These question sets comprise 12 weekly assignments and three programming projects, which evaluate logical, algorithmic, systems, and network thinking. All questions are designed to support automatic scoring. We have also implemented a prototype system that uses these seed question sets to generate personalized question sets for each student.

The prototype system can automatically grade and determine whether students pass the Knuth test. It supports teachers in adding new questions beyond those in the ICBench seed question sets to assess new knowledge points. The system should be scalable to handle a large number of students and extensible functionalities. The system is designed based on the Model-View-Controller (MVC) architecture [16]. In the subsequent discussion, a brief overview of the system's functionalities will be presented. As shown in Fig. 3. The resources layer provides annotated questions, knowledge points, and student data. The assessment engine implements core computational logic. The interface layer offers Web interfaces for both teachers and students.

The resources layer stores the RPCC models of knowledge points, annotated questions, and student data. Student data can contain multiple types of information, such as high-level Knuth test results, finer-grained descriptions of knowledge mastery based on knowledge space, and raw data like student-submitted answers and their scores. The system can construct personalized question sets based on student data.

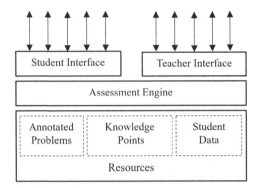

Fig. 3. The architecture of the prototype system.

The assessment engine manages tasks such as constructing and varying question sets, grading the submitted answers, and analyzing data. The engine is designed to be extensible in terms of functionalities. Take the question variation module as an example. This module utilizes three constraints for the variation operators implementation: uniform interface, pure function, and composability. The uniform interface allows for the extension of new variation operators. The pure function enables the caching of variation results, enhancing scalability. Composability allows the result of one variation operator to be passed to the next operator for further variation, enabling personalization for a larger number of students.

The interface layer offers Web interfaces for teachers and students. Teachers can specify RPCC models of knowledge points and questions in Profile [26]. The system then constructs, model checks, and varies the questions based on these specifications. Students provide answers according to the constraints described in the questions. Regarding the grading mechanism, the system employs string comparison for questions with single, unambiguous answers, such as multiple-choice or certain fill-in-the-blanks. For fill-in-the-blank questions that might have multiple valid answers, teachers can integrate custom grading scripts to evaluate student answers. For programming exercises, the system evaluates the correctness of student code using grading scripts against provided test cases. The system does not focus on the automatic grading of questions where standard answers are difficult to judge via computer algorithms. This approach ensures precise and flexible grading across various question types. After the system automatically grades the answers, it provides feedback to both teachers and students. For instance, for programming questions, students receive their total score and are informed of the test cases they did not pass. In addition to specific question feedback, all students are provided with a Cumulative Distribution Function (CDF) graph showing the performance of the entire class on that question.

5   Evaluation

ICBench has been used as the routine exercise for the UCAS CS101 course in 2023. We analyzed the student performance in UCAS CS101 across 2021, 2022, and 2023. The routine exercises in 2021 and 2022 emphasized personalization, leaving coverage to teacher manual selection. Traditional, face-to-face classroom instruction and exams were employed in 2021 and 2023. The course in 2022 adopted an online mode for both instruction and the final exam because of the COVID-19 pandemic. Over the three-year period, the CS101 course was taken by more than 1000 students.

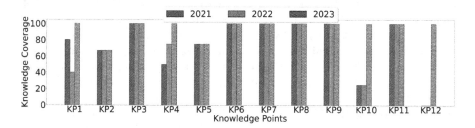

Fig. 4. Knowledge point coverage in routine exercise. Routine exercise consists of programming projects and assignments in the form of multiple-choice and fill-in-the-blank questions. The knowledge coverage is the proportion of RPCC problems assessed in the routine exercise.

Table 3. Bloom's Taxonomy levels of routine exercises for the 12 knowledge points.

Year	Create	Understand	Remember	Not Assessed
2023	25%	42%	33%	0%
2022	17%	42%	33%	8%
2021	17%	42%	33%	8%

We analyzed 12 key knowledge points that were assessed in the final exams at least twice over the three years. The 12 knowledge points were selected in the exams due to their comprehensive coverage of Bloom's taxonomy levels and the four types of computational thinking. We use numerical identifiers for the knowledge points to avoid revealing the final exam content. KP1-KP3 assess logical thinking, KP4-KP6 assess algorithmic thinking, KP7-KP10 assess systems thinking, and KP11 and KP12 assess network thinking.

ICBench improves both the coverage and the level of Bloom's Taxonomy compared to the routine exercises in 2021 and 2022. As shown in Fig. 4, 4 of the 12 knowledge points have improved in coverage. For example, ICBench improves the coverage of KP10 from 20% to 100% and includes KP12, which was previously overlooked in 2021 and 2022. ICBench does not fully cover KP2 and KP5. This was due to an emphasis on question set brevity, limiting each assignment to around ten questions and omitting some less crucial content. ICBench improves Bloom's Taxonomy levels on one-fourth of the knowledge points. The level of KP1 has been improved from Understand to Create, and KP10 has improved from Remember to Understand. The results in Fig. 4 and Table 3 underscore the necessity of computer-aided question set generation for comprehensive coverage. Manual construction of question sets can potentially lead to coverage shortfalls.

5.1 Student Performance

Figure 5 shows the pass rate in the Knuth test from 2021 to 2023, and most students passed the Knuth test. Figure 6 compares the exam performance of students who passed the Knuth test to those who did not. In 2023, those who passed the Knuth test in the fully covered knowledge points typically outperformed in the final exam, with an average improvement of 14% and a maximum of 21%. Data from 2021 and 2022 indicate that when question sets do not fully cover the knowledge points, assessment results may not accurately reflect a student's mastery of the knowledge. For instance, students who performed well in routine exercises for KP1 and KP10 only showed a final score increase of 7% and 6%, respectively, in 2022. In 2021, KP6 was presented as a group project, with all group members receiving the same score. Students with higher scores in the project did not perform better in the final exam than their peers. Note that the interval between exercises and the final exam may introduce inaccuracies. For example, students who initially passed might not perform as well in the exam due to forgetting. The performance in routine exercises in 2023 was not as good as in 2021 and 2022 in some Knowledge points, such as KP4 and KP5. A significant reason for this was that the 2023 questions predominantly adopted fill-in-the-blanks format, replacing the multiple-choice questions of the previous two years, which reduced the chances for students to guess answers correctly.

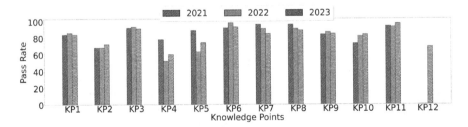

Fig. 5. Pass rate in the Knuth test. KP12 was not assessed in routine exercises in 2021 and 2022.

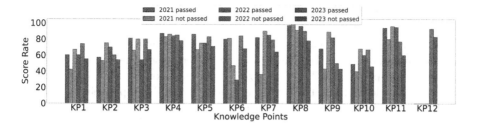

Fig. 6. Final exam performance: students who passed vs. did not pass the Knuth test. KP12 was not assessed in routine exercises in 2021 and 2022.

5.2   System Overhead

The prototype system generates personalized question sets for ten thousand students within one second, demonstrating its scalability with respect to the number of students. We conducted our experiments on a server equipped with 64 cores and 128 GB of memory. Take the example of the *Truth Table*: a personalized question set is created for each student by parameterizing the seed questions. Figure 7 shows the relationship between question set generation time, disk storage cost, and the number of distinct personalized question sets. The term "distinct personalized question sets" implies that any two sets differ from one another by at least one question. For a group of 1,000 students, the system requires only 7 milliseconds and 51 KB of disk space. The system's efficiency and low overhead in generating personalized question sets can be attributed to adopting the principle of separation of concerns. Instead of generating and storing a complete question set for each student, the system only maintains the question template, question parameters, and a mapping that links students to these parameters.

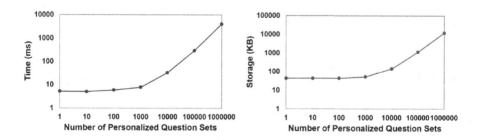

Fig. 7. Generation time and disk storage of the prototype system.

6   Related Work

This section categorizes related works on automatic assessment in terms of personalization and coverage. Depending on the degree of personalization, question sets can be non-personalized, personalized at the question-set level, or personalized at the knowledge level. For coverage, studies typically employ either manual selection or human-machine collaboration.

6.1   The Personalization of Question Set

Non-Personalization. ArTEMiS [18] is an interactive learning assessment system that emphasizes immediate feedback and scalability for a large number of students. While it efficiently provides instant feedback on programming errors, its primary focus isn't on creating personalized question sets for individual students. Ashraf Amria et al. [4] provided a framework for automatically generating exam questions based on Bloom's taxonomy. This work focused on the coverage of knowledge points instead of personalization. Other automatic assessments concentrated on managing the difficulty of questions or offering interactive guidance [11], yet they did not provide personalized question sets.

Question-Set-Level Personalization. Various works focused on personalized lab environment [20] and personalized exercise [1,6,10,24,25]. Jan Vykopal et al. [23] proposed a system to personalize the information security course's lab environment. Max Fowler et al. [12] developed a method for generating personalized basic programming questions by altering function names, the order of function parameters, and other features. The ontology-based approach is widely used for question variation [2,7,21,22]. Laura Zavala et al. [28] proposed a method that utilizes Linked Open Data (LOD) to modify programming question parameters. This approach combined template-based question generation with LOD to automatically generate context-specific programming exercises. This tool has been used in introductory programming courses to generate questions of equivalent difficulty for each student.

Knowledge-Level Personalization. Personalization at the knowledge level enables assessing different knowledge points according to the degree of knowledge mastery of students. Such approaches often model a student's current state of knowledge mastery based on their performance, represented in the form of a knowledge space [13]. Personalized question sets will be provided to students that correspond to their current learning state.

Unlike most of the aforementioned works, which lack the flexibility to specify the level of personalization, our work allows teachers to specify the degree of personalization and generate question sets that meet different levels of personalization requirements.

6.2   The Coverage of Question Set

Manual Control. In works [12, 18, 23, 28], the emphasis isn't on generating a question set that fully covers the knowledge being assessed. Teachers utilizing these systems are required to manually select questions or question templates that satisfy coverage needs. CodeMaster [3] considered coverage with manually selected 15 concepts for algorithmic programming and mobile applications.

Human-Machine Collaboration. Works based on knowledge space [13] and learning space [9] construct a knowledge space that covers domain knowledge via expert query. The system provides question sets to students based on this constructed knowledge space, ultimately facilitating comprehensive domain mastery. In contrast to our research, such studies typically do not concentrate on the personalized variation of questions.

7   Conclusion

We constructed ICBench for introductory computer science courses, utilizing the Knuth test. ICBench consists of seed question sets, a prototype system, and three benchmarking metrics. We analyzed data from over 1000 students in the UCAS CS101 course from 2021 to 2023 and derived the following three conclusions.

1. ICBench provides concise, personalized question sets for each student. The seed question sets include 12 weekly assignments and three programming projects, covering logical, algorithmic, systems, and network thinking. The prototype system can generate personalized question sets and evaluate a student's mastery of knowledge using the three metrics. We demonstrated the scalability of the system, which can generate personalized question sets for ten thousand students within one second.
2. We improved both the coverage of knowledge points and the levels of Bloom's Taxonomy in ICBench. From our analysis of 12 representative knowledge points, ICBench's questions improved the coverage for one-third of the knowledge points and improved the Bloom's Taxonomy levels for a quarter of them, compared to the routine exercises of 2021 and 2022.
3. An assessment with higher coverage can more accurately reflect the knowledge mastery level of students. In 2023, students who passed the Knuth test in the routine exercise outperformed their peers by 14% in the scores on relevant knowledge points. Data in 2021 and 2022 show that if the coverage of an assessment is low, students with higher scores on this assessment may not perform better in the final exam than their peers.

In practical education, the Knuth test not only serves for student evaluation but also aids in improving the effectiveness of teaching. In future work, we will focus on enhancing the automation of the Knuth test and undertake a more comprehensive analysis to further explore the effectiveness of ICBench and the Knuth test.

References

1. Agudo, I., Rios, R., Nieto, A.: Personalized computer security tasks with automatic evaluation and feedback. In: Proceedings of the 2019 AIS SIGED International Conference on Information Systems Education and Research, pp. 1–10 (2019)
2. Alsubait, T., Parsia, B., Sattler, U.: Ontology-based multiple choice question generation. KI - Künstliche Intell. **30**(2), 183–188 (2016)
3. Alves, N.D.C., Von Wangenheim, C.G., Hauck, J.C.R., et al.: A large-scale evaluation of a rubric for the automatic assessment of algorithms and programming concepts. In: Proceedings of the 51st ACM Technical Symposium on Computer Science Education, pp. 556–562. ACM, Portland (2020)
4. Amria, A., Ewais, A., Hodrob, R.: A framework for automatic exam generation based on intended learning outcomes. In: Proceedings of the 10th International Conference on Computer Supported Education, pp. 474–480. SCITEPRESS - Science and Technology Publications, Funchal (2018)
5. Bloom, B.S., Krathwohl, D.R.: Taxonomy of Educational Objectives: The Classification of Educational Goals. Book 1, Cognitive Domain. Longman, Harlow (1956)
6. Burket, J., Chapman, P., Becker, T.: Automatic problem generation for capture-the-flag competitions. In: 2015 USENIX Summit on Gaming, Games, and Gamification in Security Education (3GSE 15), pp. 1–8 (2015)
7. Cubric, M., Tosic, M.: Towards automatic generation of e-assessment using semantic web technologies. In: Proceedings of the 2010 International Computer Assisted Assessment Conference, pp. 1–9. University of Southampton (2010)
8. D'Agostino, S.: The computer scientist who can't stop telling stories. https://www.quantamagazine.org/computer-scientist-donald-knuth-cant-stop-telling-stories-20200416
9. Diana, O.: Learning Spaces. Educause, Washington, DC (2006)
10. Feng, W.: A scaffolded, metamorphic CTF for reverse engineering. In: 2015 USENIX Summit on Gaming, Games, and Gamification in Security Education (3GSE 15), pp. 1–8 (2015)
11. Foss, S., Urazova, T., Lawrence, R.: Automatic generation and marking of UML database design diagrams. In: Proceedings of the 53rd ACM Technical Symposium on Computer Science Education, pp. 626–632. ACM, Providence (2022)
12. Fowler, M., Zilles, C.: Superficial code-guise: investigating the impact of surface feature changes on students' programming question scores. In: Proceedings of the 52nd ACM Technical Symposium on Computer Science Education, pp. 3–9. ACM, Virtual Event (2021)
13. Jean-Paul Doignon, J.C.F.: Knowledge Spaces, 1 edn. Springer, Heidelberg (1999). https://doi.org/10.1007/978-3-642-58625-5
14. Knuth, D.E.: Computer programming as an art. Commun. ACM **17**(12), 667–673 (1974)
15. Knuth, D.E.: Foreword to A=B. A K Peters, Massachusetts (1995)
16. Krasner, G.E., Pope, S.T., et al.: A description of the model-view-controller user interface paradigm in the smalltalk-80 system. J. Object Orient. Program. **1**(3), 26–49 (1988)
17. Krathwohl, D.R.: A revision of bloom's taxonomy: an overview. Theory Pract. **41**(4), 212–218 (2002)
18. Krusche, S., Seitz, A.: ArTEMiS: an automatic assessment management system for interactive learning. In: Proceedings of the 49th ACM Technical Symposium on Computer Science Education, pp. 284–289. ACM, Baltimore (2018)

19. Lamport, L.: Specifying Systems: The TLA$^+$ Language and Tools for Hardware and Software Engineers. Addison-Wesley, Boston (2003)
20. Schreuders, Z.C., Shaw, T., Shan-A-Khuda, M., et al.: Security scenario generator (SecGen): a framework for generating randomly vulnerable rich-scenario VMs for learning computer security and hosting CTF events. In: 2017 USENIX Workshop on Advances in Security Education (ASE 17). USENIX Association, Vancouver (2017). https://www.usenix.org/conference/ase17/workshop-program/presentation/schreuders
21. Stasaski, K., Hearst, M.A.: Multiple choice question generation utilizing an ontology. In: Proceedings of the 12th Workshop on Innovative Use of NLP for Building Educational Applications, pp. 303–312. Association for Computational Linguistics, Copenhagen (2017)
22. Vinu, E.V., Kumar, P.S.: Improving large-scale assessment tests by ontology based approach. In: Improving Large-Scale Assessment Tests by Ontology Based Approach, pp. 1–6. AAAI Press, Palo Alto (2015)
23. Vykopal, J., Švábenský, V., Seda, P., Čeleda, P.: Preventing cheating in hands-on lab assignments. In: Proceedings of the 53rd ACM Technical Symposium on Computer Science Education, pp. 78–84. ACM, Providence (2022)
24. West, M., Herman, G.L., Zilles, C.: PrairieLearn: mastery-based online problem solving with adaptive scoring and recommendations driven by machine learning. In: 2015 ASEE Annual Conference & Exposition, Seattle, Washington, pp. 26.1238.1–26.1238.14 (2015)
25. Willert, N., Thiemann, J.: Template-based generator for single-choice questions. Technol. Knowl. Learn. (2023)
26. Xu, Z., Li, Z., Yu, Z., et al.: Information superbahn: towards a planet-scale, low-entropy and high-goodput computing utility. J. Comput. Sci. Technol. **38**(1), 103–114 (2023)
27. Xu, Z., Zhang, J.: Computational Thinking: A Perspective on Computer Science, 1 edn. Springer, Singapore (2023)
28. Zavala, L., Mendoza, B.: On the use of semantic-based AIG to automatically generate programming exercises. In: Proceedings of the 49th ACM Technical Symposium on Computer Science Education, pp. 14–19. ACM, Baltimore (2018)

Generating High Dimensional Test Data for Topological Data Analysis

Rohit P. Singh$^{(\boxtimes)}$ ⓘ, Nicholas O. Malott ⓘ, Blake Sauerwein, Neil Mcgrogan, and Philip A. Wilsey ⓘ

Department of ECE, University of Cincinnati, Cincinnati, OH 45221, USA
{singh2ro,malottno,sauerwba,mcgrognp}@mail.uc.edu

Abstract. *Topological Data Analysis (TDA)* characterizes data based on topological invariants present in the data. In general, TDA treats the data as a discrete sampling of an underlying manifold. While based in the field of topology, TDA is primarily vested in the three computational elements: *Persistent Homology, Euler Characteristic,* and *mapper.* The focus of this paper is on developing infrastructure to generate synthetic test data suitable to evaluate computational elements of TDA. The objective of this work is to generate test data with *known topological invariants.* While it is possible to use test data of known topological objects such as n-spheres and n-tori, these structures present limited opportunities to fully exercise TDA tools. This is especially true for high-dimensional and big data. This work supports the generation of test data with tools that use algebraic expressions of manifold structures to sample the data. The approach is augmented with additional tools to combine test data sets (possibly from various dimensions n_i) into an ambient dimension k ($k \geq n_i$) with rotations. The motivation for this work is to support verification of algorithms to implement TDA computational elements.

Keywords: Synthetic Test Data · High Dimensional Data · Topological Invariants · Persistent Homology · Topological Data Analysis

1 Introduction

Topological Data Analysis (TDA) extracts information about topological invariants present in data [16,21,49]. *Topological invariants* are measurable properties of a space, such as connectedness, cardinality, or homology; they are resilient to noise and continuous deformation of the data. TDA has demonstrated success in fields such as network analysis [36,38,48], images and movies [4,17,39,43,45,59], protein analysis [14,26,61], genomic sequencing [13,19,44,48] and many others.

In general, TDA treats data, $\mathcal{X}$, as a sampling of a manifold and reports the topological invariants found therein. One important invariant reported by TDA tools is the *persistence of homologies* in the data [30]. Unfortunately the computation of *Persistent Homology (PH)* exhibits exponential time and space complexities for increasing homology classes. This has motivated many optimizations

S. Hunold et al. (Eds.): Bench 2023, LNCS 14521, pp. 18–37, 2024.
https://doi.org/10.1007/978-981-97-0316-6_2

and approximations in the computation of PH [2,3,9,11,20,22,40,46,53,58]. Verification and characterization of these optimizations and approximations are performed on synthetic and real-world data and analyzed with respect to ground truth results. Unfortunately few data sets labeled with ground truth topological invariants are available; this is especially true of high-dimensional and big data.

While theoretical bounds on error are often established for TDA algorithms, the practical error of the methods are often well below the bound [6]; as such, experimental results can highlight the practical impact of a TDA algorithm beyond its formal limits. In the TDA community, synthetic test data generally comes from geometric objects in $\mathbb{R}^2$ and $\mathbb{R}^3$ [57]. While higher dimensional real-world test data is available from the data mining community [23], it is at best labeled for classification or clustering and seldom characterized by the topological features contained therein. In a few cases, general purpose k-dimensional test data with known topological properties are available [8,50,52].

This paper presents a method to generate k-dimensional test data with known topological features for verification and accuracy analysis of TDA algorithms. The approach is based on *Hamiltonian Markov Chain Monte Carlo (HMC)* [5,33] to generate samples from a posterior distribution using *algebraic varieties* [37] representing differentiable manifolds. This approach enables the generation of more unique and topologically interesting data sets. By representing the topological features as algebraic varieties the homology of the manifolds can be computed, mitigating non-trivial intersections found through feature placement of geometric objects. In general, the approach permits the generation of individual test data components (from this technique or other existing techniques) to be formed at any dimension n_i and combined and embedded into an ambient dimension k $(k \geq n_i)$. Thus, this work includes tools to combine, rotate, and embed test data into an ambient dimension.

The remainder of this paper is organized as follows. Section 2 contains background on TDA. Section 3 reviews some of the previous work on test data generation for TDA. Section 4 introduces the technical approach for generating synthetic test data using algebraic varieties. Section 5 reviews the challenges and mechanisms to establish ground truth validation for the topological invariants in the data. Section 6 contains examples of generating test data from this approach. Section 7 discusses the limitations and challenges of these test data generation techniques. Finally, Sect. 8 contains some concluding remarks.

2 Background

Several notable computational elements of TDA include: *Persistent Homology (PH)* [21,30,46], the *Euler Characteristic (EC)* [41,51], and *mapper* [54]. PH characterizes discrete data by the persistence of homological classes over a *filtration*. Topological invariants, such as the Euler Characteristic, are computed over a filtration as well. mapper filters the data (often through some clustering mechanism) to reduce the data and focus it into regions where significant topological information can be extracted. Each of these elements capture the existence of homological classes in the data with slightly different perspectives.

Homological classes are of interest as a topological invariant because they represent algebraic structure and can compare the structures of different spaces. For example, the H_0 homology group characterizes connected components, the H_1 homology group characterizes cycles or loops, H_2 characterizes voids, and so on to their higher dimensional analogues.

A key component in the computation of PH and EC is the construction of a *filtration* of the data. The filtration represents an ordered set of *complexes* arranged by their connectivity distances $\epsilon = (\epsilon_0, \epsilon_1, \cdots, \epsilon_\infty)$ s.t. $\forall i, j : i < j, \epsilon_i < \epsilon_j$. Each complex contains all edges and higher-order construction (simplices) less than the connectivity distance. Formally, PH constructs a *filtration*, $\mathcal{K}_\mathcal{F}$ of the data as a sequence of nested subcomplexes such that:

$$\emptyset \subseteq K_{\epsilon_0} \subseteq K_{\epsilon_1} \subseteq ... \subseteq K_{\epsilon_\infty} = \mathcal{K}_\mathcal{F}. \tag{1}$$

The filtrations are then examined to determine the persistence of homological classes found in the data, each individually referred to as a topological feature [21,32,49,62]. In general, PH examines the filtration to characterize the persistence of homologies in the data by the tuple: $\langle dim, \epsilon_{birth}, \epsilon_{death} \rangle$, where dim reports the dimension of the topological feature, ϵ_{birth} (and ϵ_{death}) records the connectivity distance where the topological feature first appears (disappears).

PH is a widely used tool for TDA, however, it suffers from exponential growth in memory and time. This exponential growth occurs both in the size of the data and dimension of homology classes to realize. Due to the computational complexity, the application of PH to big and high-dimensional data is impractical without significant constraints or approximations. As a result, a large body of research has been performed to develop techniques for optimizing and approximating the computation of PH [10,20,22,24,27,28,40–42,55,56,58]. An important complication of these methods is the need for testing data with known topological features. This is especially important in studies with higher dimensional homologies where no known real-world test data has been characterized and where no techniques to synthesize generalized manifold-based point cloud data exist. Finally, studies with algorithm scalability to data is highly limited without the ability to adequately generate scalable test data.

3   Related Work

Understanding and experimenting with TDA tools require diverse and significant topological data sets for testing and evaluation. Despite advancements in TDA tools, few widely available public bench-marking data sets suitable for TDA exist. This is especially true in dimensions above $\mathbb{R}^3$. That said, there are a few test data generators that can generate common topological shapes in any dimension n (although this ability is often limited to the generation of n-spheres).

One popular library for generating topological shapes is the Python TADASETS library, which can generate n-sphere, swiss roll, infinity sign, and torus samplings [52]. Each of these shapes is parameterized to change the scale and bounding of the generation. For example, the n-sphere of tadasets can be generated in any arbitrary dimension and rotated into an ambient dimension in a single call to the library. This functionality has proven useful in testing and validating lower-dimensional topological data analysis, however, high-dimensional interactions can be difficult to model and assess. In addition, there are several other libraries that can generate specific samplings or distributions of topological shapes. For example, FIBLAT is a python library capable of generating Fibonacci spheres in $\mathbb{R}^n$. Likewise, the data generation package TDA can sample uniformly from a n-sphere [31]. Finally, the package KODAMA is a spiral set generator [12].

Complementary to the equational based approach for generating manifolds outlined in this paper, Diaconis *et al* presents a method to generate datasets by manifold sampling [29]. Although related to this work, the approach suffers from various technical problems inherent to Markov Chain Monte Carlo (MCMC) simulations, in particular: non-convergence, low probability regions, and so on. These challenges are identified and rectified in this work to employ an MCMC sampling of algebraic varieties representing differentiable manifolds.

A topology assisted comparative study has demonstrated to improve the Monte Carlo Uncertainty Propagation(MCUP) models [47]. The approach has completely different motivation and was developed to topological compare the posterior distribution of probabilistic geological models and uncertainty index models to improve generation of plausible models. However, the approach does not provide capability to generate through algebraic varieties and validation of ground truth for topological characterization. This paper approaches test data generation to support the generation of benchmarking datasets with known topological features (and invariants) for TDA tool development and evaluation. In particular, the work in this paper exploits the algebraic origins of TDA to generate point clouds homotopic to manifolds with known topological properties.

4 Overview of the Approach

This paper details a technique for test data generation for verification and validation of TDA algorithms and approximations. The approach is based on the *Hamiltonian Markov Chain Monte Carlo (HMC)* method [5,33] to generate samples from a posterior distribution using *algebraic varieties* [37] representing differentiable manifolds. This approach enables the generation of unique and topologically interesting data sets. By representing the topological features as algebraic varieties the homology of the manifolds can be computed, mitigating non-trivial (unexpected) intersections that can arise among topological features in the manual placement of geometric objects.

In addition to this data generation component described here, the system also contains secondary components to generate simple geometric objects as well as manipulate, place, and embed objects (possibly from various dimension spaces) into a common ambient space to compose the test data. Furthermore, the generation components of this work can also be combined with other generators such as TADASETS [52]. The remainder of this section discusses: (i) data generation using algebraic varieties, (ii) a review of several design alternatives that were explored

---

Algorithm 1. Sampling a Manifold to Capture Test Data

1: **function** MANIFOLDSAMPLER(
        ss: Sample Size; dim: Dimension; av: Algebraic Variety; ϵ: Epsilon;
        disp: dispersion; step: Stddev of Step Size; maxHeat: Maximum Threshold)

2:     testData $\leftarrow \phi$

3:     indx, heat, stepS, onManifold $\leftarrow$ 0, 0, step, **False**

4:     C $\leftarrow \langle x_0, x_1, \cdots x_{dim-1} \rangle$ $\triangleright$ Begin with a random point from $\mathbb{R}^{dim}$

5:     **while True do**

6:         newC $\leftarrow$ C
            $\triangleright$ Move a coordinate value following a normal distribution

7:         newC[indx] $\leftarrow$ N(newC[indx], stepS)
            $\triangleright$ Using two acceptance functions

8:         tst$_{v1}$ $\leftarrow$ ACCEPTFN1(av, newC, ϵ, disp)

9:         tst$_{v2}$ $\leftarrow$ ACCEPTFN2(av, newC, ϵ, disp)

10:         **if** (tst$_{v1}$ **or** tst$_{v2}$) **and** SPARSETEST(testData, newC) **then**

11:             testData.append(newC)

12:             C $\leftarrow$ newC $\triangleright$ Move to less sampled region

13:             onManifold, heat, stepS $\leftarrow$ **True**, 0, step $\triangleright$ Reset

14:         **else**

15:             heat++ $\triangleright$ Count num of failures

16:             **if** heat $>$ maxHeat **and** stepS $<$ maxStep **then**

17:                 stepS $\leftarrow$ INCREASE(stepS)

18:                 heat $\leftarrow$ 0 $\triangleright$ Cool down as step is increased
                $\triangleright$ Find a starting point for C near the manifold

19:                 **if not** onManifold **then** C $\leftarrow$ newC

20:         **if** len(testData) $==$ ss **then break**

21:         indx $\leftarrow$ (indx $+$ 1) mod dim

22:     **return** testData $\triangleright$ Samples of a Smooth Manifold Surface

---

in the development of this work, and (iii) some of the sensitivities of the solution to user definable critical parameters. A python library of the test data generation techniques of this paper is available with the LHF code base [50].

4.1   HMC Sampling of Algebraic Varieties

The steps to sample points on algebraic varieties are captured in Algorithm 1. The algorithm begins at a random point in the dimensional space of interest, $\mathbb{R}^{dim}$ (Line: 4). Each iteration (Line: 5) of the algorithm moves about the region of the last point added to the test set. Since the algorithm begins with the random selection of a point in the target space, the algorithm must first determine if that point is within an acceptance distance of the manifold surface (discussed below). Once a point passes the acceptance test (it is sufficiently near the manifold surface) it is added to the test data set and the onManifold variable is set to **True**. Thereafter, the algorithm searches for another acceptable point near the surface of the manifold; that is, it moves around in the "nearby" region of the space to find additional points that pass the acceptance test. If no additional

---

Algorithm 2. Accepting Function for Points on a Manifold Surface

---

1: **function** ACCEPTFN1(av: Algebraic Variety; point; ϵ: Epsilon; disp: Dispersion)
2:   **if** $\epsilon < |\text{av(point)}|$ **then**
3:     **return** False
4:   **else**
5:     **if** av(point) > 0 **then** noise $\leftarrow (1 - \frac{\text{av(point)}}{\epsilon})^{-1}$
6:     **else** noise $\leftarrow (1 + \frac{\text{av(point)}}{\epsilon})^{-1}$
        ▷ ACCEPTSTRICT (default) or ACCEPTRELAXED (not shown)
7:     acceptProb $\leftarrow$ ACCEPTSTRICT(noise, disp)
8:     **return** (UNIFORM(0,1) $<$ acceptProb)

Algorithm 3. Accepting Function for Points on a Manifold Surface

---

1: **function** ACCEPTFN2(av: Algebraic Variety; point; ϵ: Epsilon; disp: Dispersion)
2:   pDV $\leftarrow \frac{\text{point} \times \epsilon}{|\text{point}|}$
3:   mag1 $\leftarrow av(\text{point} + pDV)$
4:   mag2 $\leftarrow av(\text{point} - pDV)$
5:   **if** $(\text{mag1} \times \text{mag2}) > 0$ **then**
6:     **return** False
7:   **else**
8:     mag1, mag2 $\leftarrow |\text{mag1}|, |\text{mag2}|$
9:     **if** mag2 $>$ mag1 **then** noise $\leftarrow \frac{mag2}{mag1}$
10:    **else** noise $\leftarrow \frac{mag1}{mag2}$
        ▷ ACCEPTSTRICT (default) or ACCEPTRELAXED (not shown)
11:    acceptProb $\leftarrow$ ACCEPTSTRICT(noise, disp)
12:    **return** (UNIFORM(0,1) $<$ acceptProb)

---

points are found or if the region becomes over-sampled, the nearby distance step size is increased (Line: 17) to grow the region of the search for new points. Finally the `heat` variable records the number of failed attempts to find a new point in the region. The algorithm will increase the size of the search region if the `heat` variable exceeds a maximum (`maxHeat`) (Line: 16). The regional walk for points and the point evaluation for inclusion in `testData` set are discussed below.

In each successive iteration, the algorithm adjusts the value of one of the coordinates using a normal distribution function N (Line: 7) to find the next point to test for inclusion into `testData`. This test is twofold: (a) is the point within the acceptable region of the manifold surface (Lines: 8 and 9), and (b) is the local region of the manifold underrepresented by the points in `testData` (Line: 10)? Parameters ϵ, `disp`, and `av` and functions (ACCEPTPT1 and ACCEPTPT2) determine if the new point is within the acceptable region of the manifold surface. Parameter ϵ defines a boundary distance (above and below) about the manifold surface that a point can be successfully drawn; `disp` defines how acceptable points are dispersed throughout the boundary (`disp` $= 1$ defines a uniform distribution; increasing values push the density of points closer to the manifold surface). The functions ACCEPTPT1 and ACCEPTPT2 use the algebraic variety

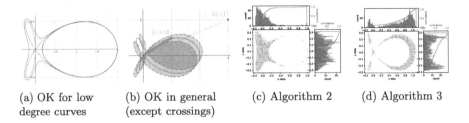

(a) OK for low
degree curves

(b) OK in general
(except crossings)

(c) Algorithm 2

(d) Algorithm 3

Fig. 1. Impact of Different Dilation Procedures (Color figure online)

and boundary parameters to determine if a new point is a candidate for inclusion in `testData` (Line: 11). These function are described below.

An acceptance test for each point considered by Algorithm 1 is performed by two functions, namely: ACCEPTFN1 (Algorithm 2) and ACCEPTFN2 (Algorithm 3). These algorithms consider the new point (`point`) and evaluates it against its "nearness" to the manifold surface. The manifold surface and the acceptance region about the manifold is defined by the `av` (the algebraic variety), ϵ and `disp` parameters. More precisely, ϵ determines a boundary distance above and below the manifold surface and `disp` describes the probability of acceptability for a point to lie at that distance from the manifold surface. The dispersion of points are more frequently positioned closer to the manifold surface as the dispersion parameter (`disp`) is increased. In some senses, the ϵ and `disp` parameters permit the characterization of "noise" in the generated data. The remainder of this paper will use the term ϵ-*dilation boundary* to characterize the region about the manifold surface defined by the ϵ and `disp` parameters.

Algorithm 2 (ACCEPTFN1) tests the ϵ-dilation boundary by offsetting the algebraic curve above and below the manifold surface by the ϵ factor. The impact of this test is shown by the purple and green Fish curves of Fig. 1a. This approach behaves differently for higher order curves; the fish curve is an order 4 curve and the offset between green and purple curves varies by the location on the Fish surface. The corresponding sampling effect is shown in Fig. 1c where the right side of the Fish curve suffers from a sparse sampling. The algorithm computes the noise of the ϵ-validated point at Lines: 5 and 6.

Algorithm 3 (ACCEPTFN2) overcomes the issue of Algorithm 2 (ACCEPTFN1) by approaching the dilation with respect to a fixed point, ideally the Barycentric point of the curve. Algorithm 3 evaluates two vectors within the neighborhood of the point to establish acceptance from the fixed point (Lines: 3 and 4). The orientation of the vectors with respect to the ϵ-dilation boundary is evaluated at Line: 5. If both of these vectors lie on same side of the manifold boundary the point is rejected (returning **False** at Line: 6). Conversely, if the two vectors lie on opposite sides, the surface passes between those two points. To identify the relative distance of the manifold surface from the two vectors, noise is computed at Lines: 9 and 10. Based on this noise, the algorithm decides whether to accept or reject this point by checking it against an acceptance function (Line: 11).

Algorithm 4. Strict Acceptance Rule

1: **function** ACCEPTSTRICT(noise, dispDegree)
2:     **return** $1 - \sqrt{(1 - \text{noise}^{-dispDegree})}$

Algorithm 5. Relaxed Acceptance Rule

1: **function** ACCEPTRELAXED(noise, dispDegree)
2:     **return** $(1 + (\text{noise} - 1)^{dispDegree})^{-1}$

In testing of this approach, two different acceptance functions were evaluated, namely: ACCEPTSTRICT (Algorithm 4) and ACCEPTRELAXED (Algorithm 5). These functions return a probability of acceptance for each point based on its location in the ϵ-dilation boundary. The acceptance probability curves corresponding to Algorithms 4 and 5 are shown in Fig. 2 for dispersion degree values $0, 1, 2, 3$, and 4. In testing, it was observed that the best results were found with ACCEPTSTRICT and thus, it is used in both Algorithms 2 and 3.

The final step of Algorithms 2 and 3 is to accept or reject the point with probability proportional to the acceptance score. Algorithm 1 accepts a new point if it passes the acceptance test from either ACCEPTFN1 or ACCEPTFN2. The acceptance rate for the algorithm vary with the selection of the sampling parameters. The acceptance rate varied between 0.25 to 0.62 for datasets generated in this paper indicating the number of iterations required for datasets in Sect. 6, in worst case is 4 times the sample size. For larger value of sample size, the approach can be parallelized with different starting locations to reduce generation time.

4.2 Sensitivity of HMC Parameters

As previously stated, this work uses a variant of the *Hamiltonian Markov Chain Monte Carlo (HMC)* method for generating a sampling from regions about a manifold surface that is characterized algebraically. Sampling from the region

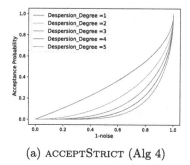
(a) ACCEPTSTRICT (Alg 4)

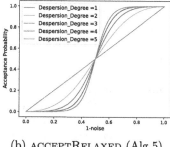
(b) ACCEPTRELAXED (Alg 5)

Fig. 2. Acceptance Functions

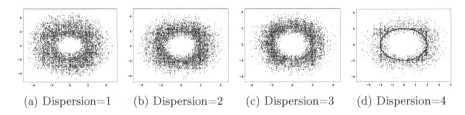

(a) Dispersion=1   (b) Dispersion=2   (c) Dispersion=3   (d) Dispersion=4

Fig. 3. Dispersion impact for Circle in $\mathbb{R}^2$ with $N = 5000$ and inverse-crowding $= 0.00001$

about a manifold surface has been studied earlier [29] but their approach is unrealistic for surfaces with higher algebraic degrees and spatial dimensions. One of the major issues that sampling algorithms face in higher dimensions occurs when a change in a dimension parameter significantly affects other dimensions. This impact can be mitigated by sampling from dilated/inflated surfaces.

The algorithm of this work (Algorithm 1) uses a collection of parameters that are crucial to generate points on and about the surface of a manifold. These parameters collectively manage the search for points that are evaluated for inclusion into a test data set. The remainder of this section discusses some of the key concepts of this approach and describes how some of the parameters impact the overall operation of the algorithm.

ϵ-dilation boundary: Constructing test data strictly from the surface of a manifold represents an overly simplistic construction of test data; this is especially true if the data is to mimic properties such as noise of real-world data. The outlined approach addresses this by constructing an ϵ-dilation boundary about the manifold surface to collect data. More interestingly, the ϵ-dilation boundary does not simply define a fixed region about the surface from which test data can be sampled. Instead this boundary includes a dispersion factor that establishes a probabilistic profile spanning this boundary from which points can be selected. An example of the ϵ-dilation boundary is illustrated in Fig. 3. The sampled points are more frequently closer to the manifold surface as the dispersion parameter is increased (here the value of ϵ is held constant).

The ϵ-dilation boundary forms a neighborhood to control sampling noise at distances from the surface; however, this can result in a significant number of rejected samples. For example, Fig. 1 illustrates how a surface experiences different dilations. Figure 1a depicts the offset (purple, green) of the parametric equation (red). The interior of these curves represent the sampling region. This results in a variable sampling based on the surface complexity and can result in an incomplete sampling as shown in Fig. 1c. A second approach (Fig. 1b) overcomes this issue with a second acceptance criteria (Sect. 4). The approach illustrates a mechanism where an object is rotated around a sphere with radius equal to ϵ and its barycentric coordinates to identify a stable ϵ-dilation for uniform sampling. Unfortunately, this approach suffers from low sampling near intersection points (Fig. 1d). Since each approach has complementary sampling issues, a solution is to incorporate both for acceptance testing.

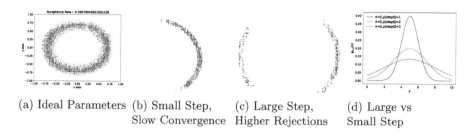

(a) Ideal Parameters (b) Small Step,   (c) Large Step,   (d) Large vs
                     Slow Convergence Higher Rejections   Small Step

Fig. 4. Variable Step Size Impact on Performance

Step Size: The `step` parameter controls the maximum distance of each jump to the next point in a testing region. That is, Algorithm 1 draws a new point from a normal distribution with the mean corresponding to the current coordinate value and the standard deviation equal to the step size (Line: 7). The mean ensures that the new sample is drawn around the last successful draw of the coordinate and the standard deviation enables a jump within the vicinity. This approach ensures a higher acceptance probability of a newly drawn point. This concept is illustrated in the images of Fig. 4. For example, Fig. 4a shows an idealized sampling of a circle. However, if the step size is too small, the algorithm might not walk the entire surface (*e.g.*, the half circle of Fig. 4b). In contrast, a large step size can cause the walk to skip large portions of the surface (*e.g.*, the missing parts of the circle in Fig. 4c). Even worse, for highly convoluted surfaces a constant step size is not always suitable and thus an adjustable step size is utilized in this adaptation of the *HMC* method. The normal distribution for various step sizes is shown in Fig. 4d. The *HMC* based frog-leaping approach enables sampling by changing step size dynamically using a heating and cooling mechanism embedded in Algorithm 1.

Dispersion and the Acceptance Functions: As previously discussed, the dispersion parameter characterizes a probability profile of points expected in the test data based on their distance from the manifold surface. Higher dispersion values cause Algorithms 4 and 5 to accept points closer to the manifold surface with higher probability. The impact that dispersion has on the acceptance probability is illustrated in Fig. 2. The strict acceptance curve has a higher acceptance probability for points with less noise (Fig. 2a); the relaxed acceptance curve, has higher probability for even lower noise (Fig. 2b), resulting in more accepted points than the strict curve. While both methods provide some degree of success in use, the generation of test data in higher dimensions is generally best served with the AcceptStrict function (Algorithm 4) and therefore it is used in the acceptance functions shown in Algorithms 2 and 3.

Inverse-Crowding: The `sparseTest` function (Line: 10 of Algorithm 1) is used to ensure that a region of the manifold surface is not over represented (over crowded) by the points in the final test set. That is, the current testing infrastructure is designed to ensure a fairly uniform representation of points in any particular region of the final test data. The parameter controlling this (not shown in Algorithm 1) limits overcrowding by rejecting points within close vicinity of already sampled points. This step also ensures that, for large enough sample space, the points are uniformly sampled irrespective of surface curvature.

4.3   Combine, Rotate, and Embed Constructions

Most existing TDA test generators operate by sampling test data from known geometric objects (n-spheres, n-tori, and so on). Data sampled from geometric objects can then be composed together provided they are placed into an ambient dimension space in a way that controls their respective positioning. For example, combining two spheres of different radii centered at the origin will create a different result than shifting one of the spheres to lie outside of the other.

This tool suite includes capabilities to support embedding, rotations, and shifting of test data (sampled from geometric objects or a manifold surface) into an ambient space in an expected manner. To embed objects in a higher-dimensional ambient space, trailing zeros are added to pad the dimensions to the higher-dimensional embedding. Embedding, combined with a rotation into the ambient space, distributes the lower dimensional data through the dimensions to create more complexity of the test data.

Due to non-trivial intersections, neither geometric or algebraic variety generated data is immune to creating unexpected homology classes. However, the geometric approaches lose the equational definitions of each separately constructed data; with the algebraic varieties the polynomial manifold equations can be transposed, rotated, or embedded using linear algebra that retains the manifold definition. In summary, the final equations from the algebraic varieties can be used to determine the homology of the manifolds (Sect. 5).

5   Ground Truth Validation

Although high-dimensional test data exist for use with TDA tools, few are labeled with their true homology classes. Those few that are labeled are typically for low dimension homology classes ($H_d, d \leq 3$) and are generally trivial in their analysis. This work is interested in creating complex, labeled, high-dimensional homology class test data that can validate and characterize TDA tools.

Homology classes (H_d) are defined as connected components (H_0), loops (H_1), voids (H_2), and higher-dimensional voids identified in the data. More specifically, a homological class in a mathematical object is a topological structure which prevents the space from being continuously deformed to a point. Formally, a subspace $\mathbb{Y}$ of a space $\mathbb{X}$ can be categorized as a homology if either:

- $\mathbb{Y}$ has no boundary (*e.g.*, a loop has no end points, represents a hole in $\mathbb{R}^2$).
- $\mathbb{Y}$ is not a boundary of anything else (*e.g.*, a empty/hollow spherical surface does not bound anything, represents a void in $\mathbb{R}^3$).

An equivalent definition for a homology class comes from the study of nice and smooth surfaces. In differential topology, a form is *closed* if its derivative is 0, and a form is *exact* if it is the derivative of something else [35]. This is analogous to following statements:

- $\mathbb{Y}$ is closed.
- $\mathbb{Y}$ is not exact.

This manner of measuring homology classes is called de-Rham cohomology: the k-dimensional de-Rham cohomology of a space is the quotient of the space of closed k-forms by the space of exact k-forms. For smooth differential manifolds, the simplicial, singular, and de-Rham co-homologies are isomorphic and yield the same homology groups [60].

The algebraic computation of homology provides a manner to label datasets with known homology groups from algebraic varieties. Fortunately, various software implementations exist to perform commutative algebra and compute de-Rham cohomology groups [1,25,34]. These platforms provide a method to compute de-Rham cohomology classes for a set of polynomials. Data generation from algebraic varieties representing differential manifolds are defined by a set of n polynomials of degree d. The number of polynomials, n, impacts the combinatorial complexity and the degree of polynomials, d, defines the algebraic complexity of the space. The algebraic varieties are used to generate data and can be simultaneously evaluated to establish the manifold's homology using de-Rham cohomology. This concept is illustrated with the deRham.lib library to compute co-homology classes for polynomial algebraic varieties in *Singular* [25]:[1]

2-Torus   ring r $= 0, (x, y, z), dp$;

list L $= (x^2 + y^2 - 5)^2 + z^2 - 9$;

output H_n : 1 1 1 2

3-Sphere   ring r $= 0, (x, y, z, w), dp$;

list L $= (x^2 + y^2 + z^2 + w^2 - 1)$;

output H_n : 1 1 0 0 1

3-Roman surface or Steiner surface

$$\text{ring r} = 0, (x, y, z), dp; \tag{2}$$

$$\text{list L} = (x^2 * y^2 + z^2 * y^2 + x^2 * z^2 - 10xyz); \tag{3}$$

$$\text{output } H_n : 1\ 1\ 0\ 4 \tag{4}$$

The Roman surface depicted in Fig. 5c is defined by the polynomial in Eq. 3 over a ring r determines by ground field 0, ring variables x, y, z and monomial ordering dp in Eq. 2. The de-Rham cohomology groups are captured in Eq. 4. From the output, it can be observed that the surface encloses a 4-void (H_3) in $\mathbb{R}^3$ as depicted in Fig. 5c. This provides a basis to generate point cloud from the manifolds described by these algebraic varieties and extract their known homology groups.

---

[1] The output is a list, where the ith entry is the $(i-1)^{th}$ de-Rham cohomology group of the complement of the complex affine variety given by the polynomials in L.

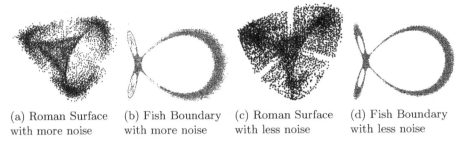

(a) Roman Surface
with more noise

(b) Fish Boundary
with more noise

(c) Roman Surface
with less noise

(d) Fish Boundary
with less noise

Fig. 5. Roman Surface $(a = 1)$ $(\mathbb{R}^3)$ and Fish Surface $(a = 1)$ $(\mathbb{R}^2)$

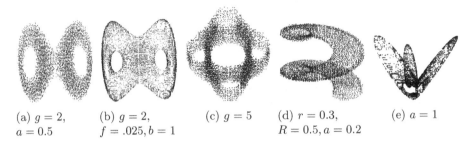

(a) $g = 2$,
$a = 0.5$

(b) $g = 2$,
$f = .025, b = 1$

(c) $g = 5$

(d) $r = 0.3$,
$R = 0.5, a = 0.2$

(e) $a = 1$

Fig. 6. Pretzel, Bretzel2, Bretzel5, Spiral Tube and Boys Surfaces in $\mathbb{R}^3$

6   Examples of Data Generation

This section is focused on data generation from algebraic varieties representing differentiable manifolds using the HMC approach detailed in Sect. 4. These constructions are topologically interesting structures and are provided to show coverage and examples. Initially, data generation in $\mathbb{R}^2$ and $\mathbb{R}^3$ is demonstrated in Sect. 6.1. Examples of higher-dimensional generations are presented in Sect. 6.2. Examples used in these sections are validated against their known homological classes and source equations are included for reproduction.

6.1   Data Generation in $\mathbb{R}^2$ and $\mathbb{R}^3$

This section illustrates surfaces generated using HMC sampling of algebraic varieties. The approach requires several parameters to achieve the desired sampling distribution (Sect. 4). For example, the user can choose how close the samples should be from the manifold surface; using more strict parameters may lead to longer sampling times as the acceptance region can be reduced significantly.

Figure 5a depicts a sampling from a Roman Surface (Eq. 7) with a relaxed noise parameter. This leads to fast generation of samples, but results in a rough surface in $\mathbb{R}^3$. Likewise, the Fish curve (Eq. 5) in $\mathbb{R}^2$ is shown in Fig. 5b with a rough surface. An improved sampling distribution can be achieved with stricter acceptance controlled by parameters at the cost of longer sampling times; this impact is depicted in Figs. 5c and 5d.

Surfaces with different genus (holes) can be generated from corresponding algebraic polynomials [7]. Figures 6a and 6b depict a surface of a Pretzel and a Bretzel with genus 2, respectively; Fig. 6c shows a surface in $\mathbb{R}^3$ with genus 5. These surfaces are constructed from the polynomials in Eqs. 8, 9, and 10.

Another class of datasets that are useful in the study of TDA tools is the spiral. Spirals come in different flavors; one such spiral is shown in Fig. 6d corresponding to Eq. 11. The samples from the Spiral tube are more uniformly distributed when compared to the Boys surface captured by Fig. 6e and Eq. 12. The result is due to the *inverse crowding* parameter. This parameter prevents overcrowding by rejecting valid samples that are too close, thereby forcing the algorithm to sample uniformly through the manifold surface.

$$Fish : (x^2 + y^2)^2 - ax(x^2 - y^2) = 0 \tag{5}$$

$$Salmon : (x^2 - a^2)^2 + (y^2 - a^2)^2 - b^4 = 0 \tag{6}$$

$$Roman : x^2y^2 + z^2y^2 + x^2z^2 - r^2xyz = 0 \tag{7}$$

$$Pretzel : (((x-1)^2 + y^2 - a^2)((x+1)^2 + y^2 - a^2))^2 + z^2 = 0 \tag{8}$$

$$Bretzel2 : (x^2(1-x^2) - y^2)^2 + \frac{1}{2}z^2 - f(1 + b(x^2 + y^2 + z^2)) = 0 \tag{9}$$

$$Bretzel5 : ((x^2 + \frac{y^2}{4} - 1)(\frac{x^2}{4} + y^2 - 1))^2 + \frac{z^2}{2} = 0 \tag{10}$$

$$Spiral : (x - Rcos(\frac{z}{a}))^2 + (y - Rsin(\frac{z}{a}))^2 - r^2 = 0 \tag{11}$$

$$Boys : \begin{aligned} &64(a-z)^3z^3 - 48(a-z)^2z^2(3y^2 + 3y^2 + 2z^2) \\ &+12(1-z)z(27(y^2 + y^2)^2 - 24z^2(y^2 + y^2) + \\ &36\sqrt{2}yz(y^2 - 3y^2) + z^4) + (9y^2 + 9y^2 - 2z^2) \\ &(-81(y^2 + y^2)^2 - 72z^2(y^2 + y^2) + 108\sqrt{2} \\ &yz(y^2 - 3y^2) + 4z^4) = 0 \end{aligned} \tag{12}$$

6.2   Data Generation in $\mathbb{R}^n$ for $n > 3$

The HMC technique can efficiently generate data in higher dimensions. In high dimensions most topological surfaces can be created using the surgery technique on finite manifolds: when combined in a controlled manner they generate another manifold [15]. This paper limits the scope of the discussion to higher-dimensional surfaces that can be created from other manifolds by the surgery theorem.

Surgery can be performed on n-spheres (denoted by $\mathbb{S}^{n-1}$) and n-tori (denoted by $\mathbb{T}^{n-1}$) to obtain manifolds as self products or cross products. For example, a n-Clifford torus here on $\mathbb{C}^{n-1}$ is a product of *two* $\mathbb{S}^{\frac{n-1}{2}}$ or *three* $\mathbb{S}^{\frac{n-1}{3}}$ spheres, or in general j- $\mathbb{S}^{\frac{n-1}{j}}$ spheres. Other interesting surfaces can be constructed by products of different factors on n-spheres to obtain Clifford manifolds (*e.g.*, $\mathbb{S}^m * \mathbb{S}^n$ gives a Clifford surface $\mathbb{C}^{m+n}$).

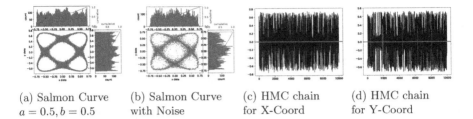

(a) Salmon Curve
$a = 0.5, b = 0.5$

(b) Salmon Curve
with Noise

(c) HMC chain
for X-Coord

(d) HMC chain
for Y-Coord

Fig. 7. Stationarity and Probability Distributions

Toratopic Notation and Spheration is an encoded representation of torus-like objects constructed in higher-dimensional spaces [18]. Genus-1 ((II)II)-toratope manifold from Eq. 13 in $\mathbb{R}^4$; Genus-2 ((II)(II))-toratope manifold from Eq. 14 in $\mathbb{R}^4$; and Genus-1 ((II)III)-toratope manifold from Eq. 15 in $\mathbb{R}^5$ can be represented.

$$S^2.S^1 : (\sqrt{x^2 + y^2} - R)^2 + z^2 + w^2 = r^2 \tag{13}$$

$$S^1.C^2 : (\sqrt{x^2 + y^2} - R_a)^2 + \sqrt{z^2 + w^2} - R_b)^2 = R^2 \tag{14}$$

$$S^3.S^1 : (\sqrt{x^2 + y^2} - R)^2 + z^2 + w^2 + v^2 = r^2 \tag{15}$$

This process can be applied to teratopes in higher-dimensional spaces with more combinatorial possibilities, but with increasing computational complexities.

7   Limitations and Challenges

Algorithm 1 is sensitive to the parameters that impact the sampling distribution. There are several ways to infer values for these parameters which will be a focus of future research to better understand their use for arbitrary algebraic varieties. The sampling from a manifold depends on several factors, including:

- $n \propto surface\ area(S)$: the sample size n must be sufficient to cover the surface S
- $IC \propto \frac{surface\ area(S)}{sample\ size(n)}$: inverse crowding should be selected based on sample size and surface area
- $sharpness \propto Degree(d)$: the degree of acceptance defines the boundary sharpness
- $step\ Size \propto inter\ Component\ Distance$: the step size must be adaptively adjusted for disconnected surfaces

As shown in Fig. 7, the Salmon curve (Eq. 6) with different parameters generates significantly different test data. The probability distribution provides insight into how the different coordinates are distributed across the sampling space. Visual inspection is sufficient for surfaces up to $\mathbb{R}^3$ to verify the sampling quality. In high dimensions visual inspection becomes insufficient. The HMC chain of samples drawn as shown in Fig. 7c and 7d can provide significant information about the distribution of points. Despite this, the surface generated can not be fully verified from these parameters.

Unfortunately, in higher dimensions the sampling quality is not easily established. Multiple runs with different parameters can provide estimates for the surface complexity and can aid in the selection of appropriate parameters. Fortunately, one can determine the sampling quality by PH computation using TDA tools and verify it with de-Rham cohomology computations.

8 Conclusions

This paper presents a novel data generation tool to sample algebraic varieties representing differentiable manifolds. The method introduces a technique to randomly walk the surface about a differentiable manifold to sample points, resulting in topologically interesting constructs for verification and characterization of TDA tools. The experimental results demonstrate the efficacy of a generalized approach and can cater to generation of complex topological spaces, enabling further analysis of high-dimensional homological classes and their constructions.

Acknowledgements. Support for this work was provided in part by the National Science Foundation under grant IIS-1909096.

References

1. Abbott, J., Bigatti, A.M.: CoCoA and CoCoALib: fast prototyping and flexible C++ library for computations in commutative algebra. In: Ábrahám, E., Davenport, J.H., Fontaine, P. (eds.) Proceedings of the 1st Workshop on Satisfiability Checking and Symbolic Computation co-located with 18th International Symposium on Symbolic and Numeric Algorithms for Scientific Computing. CEUR Workshop Proceedings, vol. 1804, pp. 1–3. CEUR-WS.org (2016)
2. Bauer, U.: Ripser: efficient computation of vietoris-rips persistence barcodes. J. Appl. Comput. Topol. **5**, 391–423 (2021). https://doi.org/10.1007/s41468-021-00071-5
3. Bauer, U., Kerber, M., Reininghaus, J.: Clear and compress: computing persistent homology in chunks. In: Bremer, P.-T., Hotz, I., Pascucci, V., Peikert, R. (eds.) Topological Methods in Data Analysis and Visualization III. MV, pp. 103–117. Springer, Cham (2014). https://doi.org/10.1007/978-3-319-04099-8_7
4. Bendich, P., Edelsbrunner, H., Kerber, M.: Computing robustness and persistence for images. IEEE Trans. Visual Comput. Graphics **16**(6), 1251–1260 (2010). https://doi.org/10.1109/TVCG.2010.139
5. Betancourt, M., Byrne, S., Livingstone, S., Girolami, M.: The geometric foundations of Hamiltonian Monte Carlo. Bernoulli **23**(4A), 2257–2298 (2017). https://doi.org/10.3150/16-BEJ810
6. Bingham, E., Mannila, H.: Random projection in dimensionality reduction: applications to image and text data. In: Knowledge Discovery and Data Mining, KDD 2001, pp. 245–250. ACM Press (2001). https://doi.org/10.1145/502512.502546
7. Bloomenthal, J., Wyvill, B. (eds.): Introduction to Implicit Surfaces. Morgan Kaufmann (Jul 1997)
8. Board, G.E.: GUDHI datasets manual. https://gudhi.inria.fr/python/latest/datasets.html

9. Bobrowski, O., Kahle, M.: Topology of random geometric complexes: a survey. J. Appl. Comput. Topol. **1**, 331–364 (2018). https://doi.org/10.1007/s41468-017-0010-0

10. Boissonnat, J.D., Karthik, C.S.: An efficient representation for filtrations of simplicial complexes. ACM Trans. Algorithms **14**(4), 1–21 (2018). https://doi.org/10.1145/3229146

11. Boissonnat, J.D., Pritam, S., Pareek, D.: Strong collapse for persistence. In: Azar, Y., Bast, H., Herman, G. (eds.) 26th Annual European Symposium on Algorithms (ESA 2018). Leibniz International Proceedings in Informatics (LIPIcs), vol. 112, pp. 67:1–67:13. Schloss Dagstuhl-Leibniz-Zentrum fuer Informatik, Dagstuhl (2018). https://doi.org/10.4230/LIPIcs.ESA.2018.67

12. Cacciatore, S., Tenori, L., Luchinat, C., Bennett, P.R., MacIntyre, D.A.: Kodama: an R package for knowledge discovery and data mining. Bioinformatics **33**(4), 621–623 (2016). https://doi.org/10.1093/bioinformatics/btw705

13. Camara, P.G., Rosenbloom, D.I.S., Emmett, K.J., Levine, A.J., Rabadan, R.: Topological data analysis generates high-resolution, genome-wide maps of human recombination. Cell Syst. **3**(1), 83–94 (2016). https://doi.org/10.1016/j.cels.2016.05.008

14. Cang, Z., Mu, L., Wu, K., Opron, K., Xia, K., Wei, G.W.: A topological approach for protein classification. Mol. Based Math. Biol. **3**(1), 140–162 (2015). https://doi.org/10.1515/mlbmb-2015-0009

15. Cappell, S., Ranicki, A., Rosenberg, J. (eds.): Surveys on Surgery Theory: Papers Dedicated to C.T.C. Wall (AM-145). Annals of Mathematics Studies, vol. 1. Princeton University Press (2000)

16. Carlsson, G.: Topology and data. Bull. Am. Math. Soc. **46**(2), 255–308 (2009). https://doi.org/10.1090/S0273-0979-09-01249-X

17. Carlsson, G., Ishkhanov, T., de Silva, V., Zomorodian, A.: On the local behavior of spaces of natural images. Int. J. Comput. Vision **76**(1), 1–12 (2008). https://doi.org/10.1007/s11263-007-0056-x

18. Chakour, E.: An exploration of higher dimensional objects (2018)

19. Chan, J.M., Carlsson, G., Rabadan, R.: Topology of viral evolution. Proc. Natl. Acad. Sci. **110**(46), 18566–18571 (2013). https://doi.org/10.1073/pnas.1313480110

20. Chazal, F., Fasy, B.T., Lecci, F., Michel, B., Rinaldo, A., Wasserman, L.: Subsampling methods for persistent homology. In: International Conference on Machine Learning, ICML 2015, Lille, France, vol. 37, pp. 2143–2151 (2015)

21. Chazal, F., Michel, B.: An introduction to topological data analysis: fundamental and practical aspects for data scientists. Front. Artif. Intell. **4** (2021). https://doi.org/10.3389/frai.2021.667963

22. Chen, C., Kerber, M.: Persistent homology computation with a twist. In: Proceedings 27th European Workshop on Computational Geometry (EuroCG 2011), pp. 197–200 (2011)

23. Ciarelli, P.M., Oliveira, E.: UCI machine learning repository. http://archive.ics.uci.edu/ml/datasets/CNAE-9

24. de Silva, V., Carlsson, G.: Topological estimation using witness complexes. In: Gross, M., Pfister, H., Alexa, M., Rusinkiewicz, S. (eds.) Eurographics Symposium on Point-Based Graphics, pp. 157–166. SPBG 2004. The Eurographics Association, Goslar, DEU (2004). https://doi.org/10.2312/SPBG/SPBG04/157-166

25. Decker, W., Greuel, G.M., Pfister, G., Schonemann, H.: Singular 4.3.0 – a computer algebra system for polynomial computations (2022). http://www.singular.uni-kl.de

26. Dey, T.K., Mandal, S.: Protein classification with improved topological data analysis. In: 18th International Workshop on Algorithms in Bioinformatics, WABI 2018, vol. 113, pp. 6:1–6:13. Schloss Dagstuhl-Leibniz-Zentrum fuer Informatik, Dagstuhl (2019). https://doi.org/10.4230/LIPIcs.WABI.2018.6

27. Dey, T.K., Shi, D., Wang, Y.: SimBa: an efficient tool for approximating rips-filtration persistence via simplicial batch-collapse. In: Sankowski, P., Zaroliagis, C. (eds.) 24th Annual European Symposium on Algorithms (ESA 2016). Leibniz International Proceedings in Informatics (LIPIcs), vol. 57, pp. 35:1–35:16. Schloss Dagstuhl-Leibniz-Zentrum fuer Informatik, Dagstuhl (2016). https://doi.org/10.4230/LIPIcs.ESA.2016.206

28. Dey, T.K., Wang, Y.: Reeb graphs: approximation and persistence. Discrete Comput. Geom. $49(1)$, 46–73 (2013). https://doi.org/10.1007/s00454-012-9463-z

29. Diaconis, P., Holmes, S., Shahshahani, M.: Sampling from a manifold. In: Advances in Modern Statistical Theory and Applications: A Festschrift in honor of Morris L. Eaton, vol. 10, pp. 102–125 (2013). https://doi.org/10.1214/12-IMSCOLL1006. (also published in arXiv Statistics Theory)

30. Edelsbrunner, H., Harer, J.: Persistent homology – a survey. Surv. Discrete Comput. Geom. 453, 257–282 (2008)

31. Fasy, B.T., Kim, J., Lecci, F., Maria, C., Millman, D.L., Rouvreau, V.: TDA: statistical tools for topological data analysis (2019). https://CRAN.R-project.org/package=TDA. R package version 1.6.9

32. Fugacci, U., Scaramuccia, S., Iuricich, F., Floriani, L.D.: Persistent homology: a step-by-step introduction for newcomers. In: Pintore, G., Stanco, F. (eds.) Smart Tools and Apps for Graphics - Eurographics Italian Chapter Conference, pp. 1–10. The Eurographics Association (2016). https://doi.org/10.2312/stag.20161358

33. Girolami, M., Calderhead, B.: Riemann manifold Langevin and Hamiltonian Monte Carlo methods. J. Roy. Stat. Soc.: Ser. B (Stat. Methodol.) $73(2)$, 123–214 (2011). https://doi.org/10.1111/j.1467-9868.2010.00765.x

34. Grayson, D.R., Stillman, M.E.: Macaulay2, a software system for research in algebraic geometry (2002)

35. Greene, P.: De Rham cohomology, connections, and characteristic classes (2009)

36. Hajij, M., Wang, B., Scheidegger, C.E., Rosen, P.: Visual detection of structural changes in time-varying graphs using persistent homology. In: IEEE Pacific Visualization Symposium, pp. 125–134. PacificVis 2018. IEEE Computer Society, USA (2018). https://doi.org/10.1109/PacificVis.2018.00024

37. Hartshorne, R.: Algebraic Geometry. Graduate Texts in Mathematics. Springer, New York (1977). https://doi.org/10.1007/978-1-4757-3849-0

38. Horak, D., Maletić, S., Rajković, M.: Persistent homology of complex networks. J. Stat. Mech: Theory Exp. $2009(3)$, P03034 (2009). https://doi.org/10.1088/1742-5468/2009/03/p03034

39. Kaczynski, T., Mischaikow, K., Mrozek, M.: Computational Homology. Applied Mathematical Sciences, vol. 157. Springer, New York (2004). https://doi.org/10.1007/b97315

40. Malott, N.O., Chen, S., Wilsey, P.A.: A survey on the high-performance computation of persistent homology. IEEE Trans. Knowl. Data Eng. $35(5)$, 4466–4484 (2022). https://doi.org/10.1109/TKDE.2022.3147070

41. Malott, N.O., Lewis, R.R., Wilsey, P.A.: Homology-separating triangulated Euler characteristic curve. In: IEEE International Conference on Data Mining. ICDM 2022 (2022)

42. Malott, N.O., Wilsey, P.A.: Fast computation of persistent homology with data reduction and data partitioning. In: 2019 IEEE International Conference on Big Data, Big Data 2019, pp. 880–889 (2019). https://doi.org/10.1109/BigData47090.2019.9006572

43. Mischaikow, K., Nanda, V.: Morse theory for filtrations and efficient computation of persistent homology. Discrete Comput. Geom. **50**(2), 330–353 (2013). https://doi.org/10.1007/s00454-013-9529-6

44. Moitra, A., Malott, N.O., Wilsey, P.A.: Persistent homology on streaming data. In: 2020 International Conference on Data Mining Workshops (ICDMW), ICDMW 2020, pp. 636–643. IEEE, USA (2020). https://doi.org/10.1109/ICDMW51313.2020.00090

45. Nanda, V.: Discrete Morse theory for filtrations. Ph.D. thesis, Department of Mathematics, Rutgers University (2012). http://people.maths.ox.ac.uk/nanda/source/Thesis.pdf

46. Otter, N., Porter, M.A., Tillmann, U., Grindrod, P., Harrington, H.A.: A roadmap for the computation of persistent homology. EPJ Data Sci. **6**(1) (2017). https://doi.org/10.1140/epjds/s13688-017-0109-5

47. Pakyuz-Charrier, E., Jessell, M., Giraud, J., Lindsay, M., Ogarko, V.: Topological analysis in Monte Carlo simulation for uncertainty propagation. Solid Earth **10**(5), 1663–1684 (2019). https://doi.org/10.5194/se-10-1663-2019, https://se.copernicus.org/articles/10/1663/2019/

48. Petri, G., Scolamiero, M., Donato, I., Vaccarino, F.: Topological strata of weighted complex networks. PLoS One **8**(6), 1–8 (2013). https://doi.org/10.1371/journal.pone.0066506

49. Pun, C.S., Xia, K., Lee, S.X.: Persistent-homology-based machine learning and its applications - a survey (2018). https://doi.org/10.2139/ssrn.3275996

50. Researchers at The High Performance Computing Laboratory: LHF: Lightweight homology framework (2020). https://github.com/wilseypa/lhf

51. Richardson, E., Werman, M.: Efficient classification using the Euler characteristic. Pattern Recogn. Lett. **49**, 99–106 (2014). https://doi.org/10.1016/j.patrec.2014.07.001

52. Saul, N.: TaDAsets. https://pypi.org/project/tadasets/

53. Sens, A.: Topology preserving data reductions for computing persistent homology. Master's thesis, Department of Electrical Engineering and Computer Science, University of Cincinnati (2021)

54. Singh, G., Memoli, F., Carlsson, G.: Topological methods for the analysis of high dimensional data sets and 3D object recognition. In: Botsch, M., Pajarola, R., Chen, B., Zwicker, M. (eds.) Eurographics Symposium on Point-Based Graphics. The Eurographics Association (2007). https://doi.org/10.2312/SPBG/SPBG07/091-100

55. Singh, R.P., Wilsey, P.A.: Persistence homology of proximity hyper-graphs for higher dimensional big data. In: IEEE International Conference on Big Data, BigData 2022 (2022). https://doi.org/10.1109/BigData55660.2022.10020926

56. Singh, R.P., Wilsey, P.A.: Polytopal complex construction and use in persistent homology. In: IEEE ICDM Workshop on High Dimensional Data Mining, HDM 2022 (2022). https://doi.org/10.1109/ICDMW58026.2022.00087

57. Sumner, R.W., Popovic, J.: Mesh data from deformation transfer for triangle meshes (2004). https://people.csail.mit.edu/sumner/research/deftransfer/data.html

58. Verma, R.R., Malott, N.O., Wilsey, P.A.: Data reduction and feature isolation for computing persistent homology on high dimensional data. In: Workshop on Applications of Topological Data Analysis to Big Data, pp. 3860–3864. IEEE, USA (2021). https://doi.org/10.1109/BigData52589.2021.9671839
59. Wagner, H., Chen, C., Vuçini, E.: Efficient computation of persistent homology for cubical data. In: Peikert, R., Hauser, H., Carr, H., Fuchs, R. (eds.) Topological Methods in Data Analysis and Visualization II: Theory, Algorithms, and Applications. Mathematics and Visualization, pp. 91–106. Springer, Heidelberg (2012). https://doi.org/10.1007/978-3-642-23175-9_7
60. Walther, U.: Algorithmic computation of de Rham cohomology of complements of complex affine varieties. J. Symb. Comput. **29**(4–5), 795–839 (2000). https://doi.org/10.1006/jsco.1999.0328
61. Xia, K., Wei, G.W.: Persistent homology analysis of protein structure, flexibility, and folding. Int. J. Numer. Methods Biomed. Eng. **30**(8), 814–844 (2014). https://doi.org/10.1002/cnm.2655
62. Zhu, X.: Persistent homology: An introduction and a new text representation for natural language processing. In: Twenty-Third International Joint Conference on Artificial Intelligence, IJCAI 2013, pp. 1953–1959. AAAI Press (2013). https://doi.org/10.5555/2540128.2540408

Does AI for Science Need Another ImageNet or Totally Different Benchmarks? A Case Study of Machine Learning Force Fields

Yatao Li[1,2,3(✉)], Wanling Gao[1], Lei Wang[1], Lixin Sun[3], Zun Wang[3], and Jianfeng Zhan[1,2]

[1] Institute of Computing Technology Chinese Academy of Science, No. 6 Kexueyuan South Road, Haidian, Beijing 100190, China
{gaowanling,wanglei_2011,zhanjianfeng}@ict.ac.cn
[2] University of Chinese Academy of Sciences, No. 19(A) Yuquan Road, Shijingshan, Beijing 100049, China
[3] Microsoft Research, No. 5 Dan Ling Street, Haidian, Beijing 100080, China
{yatli,lixinsun,zunwang}@microsoft.com

Abstract. AI for science (AI4S) is an emerging research field that aims to enhance the accuracy and speed of scientific computing tasks using machine learning methods. Traditional AI benchmarking methods struggle to adapt to the unique challenges posed by AI4S because they assume data in training, testing, and future real-world queries are independent and identically distributed, while AI4S workloads anticipate out-of-distribution problem instances. This paper investigates the need for a novel approach to effectively benchmark AI for science, using the machine learning force field (MLFF) as a case study. MLFF is a method to accelerate molecular dynamics (MD) simulation with low computational cost and high accuracy. We identify various missed opportunities in scientifically meaningful benchmarking and propose solutions to evaluate MLFF models, specifically in the aspects of sample efficiency, time domain sensitivity, and cross-dataset generalization capabilities. By setting up the problem instantiation similar to the actual scientific applications, more meaningful performance metrics from the benchmark can be achieved. This suite of metrics has demonstrated a better ability to assess a model's performance in real-world scientific applications, in contrast to traditional AI benchmarking methodologies. This work is a component of the SAIBench project, an AI4S benchmarking suite. The project homepage is https://www.computercouncil.org/SAIBench.

1 Introduction

Benchmarks are extensively utilized in computer science research and the IT industry to assess and compare the performance patterns of various types of entities, from abstract and mathematically specified problem definitions and

S. Hunold et al. (Eds.): Bench 2023, LNCS 14521, pp. 38–52, 2024.
https://doi.org/10.1007/978-981-97-0316-6_3

algorithms to fully materialized software + hardware systems [6, 20]. The term "benchmark" originated from land measurement practices, where marks were carved onto a stone, creating a "fixture" for mounting measurement equipment. Modern computer science benchmarks follow a similar concept. To measure performance metrics, a "fixture" is created by instantiating the target problem into a standardized set of computing resources and tasks. For instance, in machine learning benchmarks, problem instantiation is achieved by mapping high-level goals (e.g., image classification) to a concrete dataset, such as ImageNet [9]. A critical factor in benchmarking is to ensure that the problem instantiation aligns with the stakeholders' interests. In the context of machine learning benchmarks, this means that the chosen dataset should cover all typical scenarios implied by the high-level goals. Consequently, if a machine learning model performs well on the dataset, it is expected to perform well in real-world applications.

AI for science (AI4S) is an emerging research field that focuses on leveraging machine learning methods to improve accuracy and speed in scientific computing tasks [16, 23]. Benchmarking AI4S is crucial, as it allows scientific researchers to evaluate the quality of an AI4S machine learning model and ensure its successful integration into the scientific computing pipeline.

The ultimate goal of AI4S is to assist scientific researchers in exploring the unknown, which often challenges fundamental assumptions in machine learning. For instance, traditional machine learning assumes that the training and testing instances share the same distribution, and so do instances from any future queries. While this assumption works well with traditional workloads such as object recognition in ImageNet, where the dataset is indeed randomly sampled from all possible objects "in the wild", a scientific computing pipeline is well expected to encounter entirely new instances. In other words, the "in-distribution" assumption fails in AI4S scenarios, where encountering "out-of-distribution" data is anticipated.

Consequently, traditional AI benchmarking methods struggle to adapt to the AI4S context due to this "out-of-distribution" challenge. Good performance in training and simple testing no longer guarantees that the model will perform well when integrated into a real-world scientific computing pipeline. Adhering to conventional AI benchmarking practices will invariably result in a biased problem instantiation that is misaligned with the objectives of AI4S.

This ponders the question: do we need to carry over the practices from conventional AI benchmarking by collecting a comprehensive dataset like ImageNet, or do we need a completely different approach to benchmark AI for science effectively? In this paper, we study a particular example in AI for science, molecular dynamics (MD) simulations. MD simulation serves as a crucial tool that is extensively employed in chemical physics, materials science, biophysics, and related fields. MD simulation models the motion of atoms and molecules within a chemical system and how it evolves over time. Machine learning was proposed to accelerate MD simulation. At the core of the machine learning acceleration lies the machine learning force field (MLFF), which computes the forces applied to each atom in the chemical system.

We identify numerous missed opportunities in scientifically meaningful benchmarking MLFF models, and we propose solutions that allow us to investigate the behavior of MLFF models in greater detail. Our contribution is as follows. 1. We propose an evaluation of the sample efficiency of MLFF models, specifically focusing on their performance in scenarios with sparse data. This is in contrast to conventional AI workloads, such as large-scale language models and image recognition tasks, which often have access to vast amounts of data. 2. While conventional AI benchmarks assume that the samples in the dataset are independent and identically distributed, we propose to take advantage of the fact that the MD simulation produces time-series data, and we furthermore evaluate the time domain sensitivity of the models. 3. Contrasting to conventional AI benchmarks that typically treat different datasets as separate entities, we propose the development of cross-dataset generalization tests for MLFF models. 4. While our primary objective is to evaluate the performance of MLFF models, we also uncover an intriguing correlation between the test results and a similarity metric known as Smooth Overlap of Atomic Positions (SOAP). This discovery can, in turn, help us to improve the simulation pipeline.

2 Preliminaries

MD simulation is an essential tool that simulates atomic motions within chemical systems, providing key insights for computational chemistry, biology, and physics to unravel thermodynamic and kinetic phenomena. The key of an MD simulation is to integrate atomic motion by applying computed forces to each atom and subsequently displacing atoms following Newton's Second law $\boldsymbol{f}_i = m_i \boldsymbol{a}_i$, where $\boldsymbol{f}_i$, m_i, a_i are the force, mass, and acceleration of atom i. Traditionally, the atomic forces are computed with empirical inter-atomic potentials or with *ab initio* methods as the negative gradient of potential energy (Eq. 1).

$$\boldsymbol{f}_i = -\frac{\partial}{\partial \boldsymbol{x}_i} E(\boldsymbol{x}_1, \boldsymbol{x}_2, \ldots, \boldsymbol{x}_n) \tag{1}$$

In empirical potentials, the potential energy functionals are relatively simple analytical equations, such as in Lennard-Jones potential [15]. They often assume that each atom is only affected by its neighboring atoms,

$$\boldsymbol{f}_i = -\frac{\partial}{\partial \boldsymbol{x}_i} E_i(\boldsymbol{x}_i, \boldsymbol{x}_{j_1}, \boldsymbol{x}_{j_2}, \ldots, \boldsymbol{x}_{j_{n_i}}) \tag{2}$$

where j_k are atoms that are close to the atom i with $|\boldsymbol{x}_{j_k} - \boldsymbol{x}_i| < r_{\text{cut}}$. This locality assumption leads to an $O(N_{\text{atom}})$ complexity for classical force fields. On the other hand, the *ab initio* methods solve Schrödinger's equation to obtain potential energy, with a complexity of $O(N_{\text{electron}}^K)$, $K = 3 - 5$. Even though the empirical potentials are easy to compute and often scale linearly with the number of atoms N_{atom}, they are limited to systems without the formation and breaking of chemical bonds. In contrast, *ab initio* MD (AIMD) methods incorporate quantum mechanic effects, providing a more precise representation of the potential in chemical reactions, albeit at the expense of prohibitive computation time. This accuracy-cost trade-off makes it prohibitive to use MD simulation to model systems with chemical reactions.

Machine learning enables a new solution, MLFF, to solve this accuracy-cost trade-off problem. It uses neural networks [5] or Gaussian Process [2] for the potential energy functional. The functional is more complicated than empirical force fields but keeps the $O(N_{atom})$ scaling. Hence MLFF can scale up to large molecular systems that were previously impossible to simulate with empirical force fields while maintaining an acceptable level of accuracy [14].

As mentioned before, MD simulation is an iterative process where each step computes the forces applied to each atom in the system. Based on the force field, the algorithm iteratively updates the velocities and positions of the atoms over time steps, generating a trajectory of the molecular system that illustrates the evolution of the system over time. Given a chemical system of N_{atom} atoms, the force field takes the cartesian coordinates and atomic numbers as input and outputs the potential energy and forces as written in Eq. 1.

The construction and training of MLFF constitute the following steps.

1. Obtain training data from *ab initio* methods, which contains cartesian coordinate $x_1, x_2, \ldots, x_N$, atomic numbers $z_1, z_2, \ldots, z_N$, total potential E, and forces $f_1, f_2, \ldots, f_N$. For simplicity, all the variables can be written as matrices: $\mathbf{x}, \mathbf{F} \in \mathbb{R}^{N \times 3}$, $\mathbf{Z} \in \mathbb{R}^{N \times 3}$, $E \in \mathbb{R}$, where $\mathbf{F} = -\frac{\partial}{\partial \mathbf{X}} E$.
2. construct a machine learning model

$$\widetilde{E}, \widetilde{\mathbf{F}} = \mathcal{F}(\mathbf{X}, \mathbf{z}) \tag{3}$$

where $\mathcal{F}$ can be a neural network or a Gaussian Process model.
3. Design a loss function $\mathcal{L}$ over both the forces and the energy. An example is to use mean square error.

$$\mathcal{L} = \sum_{\text{batch}} [\alpha(E - \widetilde{E})^2 + \beta \sum_i \sum_{u=x,y,z} (f_{i,u} - \widetilde{f}_{i,u})^2] \tag{4}$$

4. Optimize the functional $\mathcal{F}$ over the training data, to minimize $\mathcal{L}$.
5. Evaluate the performance of the trained model.

3 Related Works

The rapid development of MLFF models [3,18,21] has garnered significant interest in various applications, such as drug discovery and material design. These applications require high numerical accuracy from MD simulations, making the quality of a trained MLFF model crucial for successful deployment. As highlighted by [10,22], a suboptimal MLFF model can introduce errors in the predicted potential energy and forces, which accumulate throughout the iterative simulation steps. These accumulated errors can result in simulation failures, manifesting as non-physical conformations of the chemical system or numerical runaway conditions.

Numerous benchmarking suites have been developed to evaluate machine learning workloads [11,13,17]. The evaluation metrics chosen by each benchmark correspond to the interests of the stakeholders. For instance, machine learning model benchmarks emphasize convergence rate and accuracy and focus on metrics such as the validation and test loss function performance, while industrial AI benchmarks prioritize cost-efficient model deployment [12] and concentrate on performance metrics such as model throughput and hardware resource utilization. Recently, benchmarks specifically targeting AI for science are also proposed [19], which carries over the methodologies of conventional AI benchmarking.

In the context of MLFF, the primary interest of stakeholders lies in the successful integration of the MLFF model into MD simulations. However, conventional benchmarking methods encounter difficulties in accurately reflecting this objective. Traditional AI evaluation metrics primarily concentrate on statistical performance across the entire dataset; however, Tong et al. [22] observed that failures in MD simulations with MLFFcan likely be traced back to a few poor force predictions, resulting in irrecoverable error accumulation. Moreover, conventional AI evaluation metrics are derived directly from the difference between model output and ground truth data, while Tian et al. [10] pointed out that stability in simulation does not align with training and testing performance. Therefore, we argue that conventional benchmarking methods are not well suited for evaluating MLFF.

Despite the efforts in existing works, it remains desirable to characterize MLFF better. This motivates us to develop a novel benchmark specifically for MLFF, aiming to ensure MLFF quality.

4   Benchmarking MLFF

The benchmark uses focuses on evaluating NequIP [4], an equivariant graph neural network architecture specifically designed for learning MLFF from ab-initio calculations. NequIP emerges as a prominent representative of the state-of-the-art in this field, distinguished by its exceptional data efficiency and superior performance when compared to previous HDNN-style neural networks [5] and kernel-based methods [2]. NequIP's remarkable data efficiency enables accurate modeling of MLFF with minimal training data, making it an appealing choice for scenarios where data availability is limited or costly to obtain.

To assess the performance of the machine learning model, we utilize a benchmarking fixture created from the revised MD17 (rMD17) dataset [8]. The original MD17 dataset [7] comprises data points obtained from MD simulation trajectories based on density functional theory (DFT), encompassing a predefined set of molecules. The rMD17 dataset further enhances the MD17 dataset by employing a more accurate level of theory, thereby mitigating numerical noise and improving data quality. It is important to call out that we adopt a different fixture setup compared to conventional machine-learning-style practices. In a conventional machine-learning-style setup, it would assume that the data points (from both the MD17 and rMD17 datasets) are randomly sampled from the ground

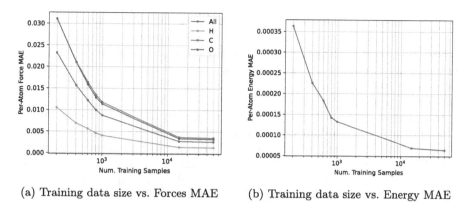

(a) Training data size vs. Forces MAE   (b) Training data size vs. Energy MAE

Fig. 1. Sample Efficiency Benchmarks

truth problem space. Training and testing are subsequently conducted by randomly partitioning the data into subsets. However, MD17 data points are drawn from simulated trajectories, resulting in inherent correlations in the time domain. Consequently, randomly sampling training and test subsets can lead to the interleaving of data points from different time steps. While this scenario aligns with the ideal situation in MLFF-powered MD, where simulated data covers a wide range of molecule conformation space, we argue that it is not the case for the MD17/rMD17 dataset, which will be demonstrated in the forthcoming experimental results. The rMD17 dataset is often consumed in a random train/test split manner, as mentioned before because the data points are not ordered as a trajectory time series. This can be mitigated by sorting the data with the "old_index" field, which maps the data points back to the original MD17 and restores temporal order in the data. Our benchmarking fixture is established on this calibrated dataset by splitting out the last 10% data in the time series as the test subset.

4.1 Sample Efficiency

We evaluate the sample efficiency of the model by fixing the training data window to the first 90% of the trajectory simulated on an aspirin molecule and progressively sample more data (200, 400, 600, 800, 1000, 15000, and 50000 samples, respectively) from the window into different training subsets, and compare the performance of trained models on the test subset. The training process for each subset is given a fixed wall time budget, allowing all to converge properly. We compare both per-atom force mean average error (MAE) and per-atom energy MAE for the trained models. The benchmarking results are illustrated in Fig. 1.

We can see that the model has good sample efficiency, achieving per-atom energy MAE of less than 4 meV over the test data given only 200 training samples. More specifically, given a fixed training data window, the performance of the trained models progressively improves with more training data points. Both the performance on energy and forces follow a similar trend, where increasing the number of samples results in proportional improvements up to 1000 samples, but the gain decreases exponentially afterward, where the benefit of increasing the size of the training set from 1K to 15K samples is not as good as increasing from 200 to 400, albeit at the cost of much longer computational cost spent in each training epoch.

In conventional AI benchmarking, it is not practical to evaluate the performance on parts of each data point, such as the first ten tokens generated from a model or the accuracy of prediction about the top-left part of an image. However, the structural and composable nature of molecular data allows for a more versatile projection of performance results, providing a unique opportunity to evaluate AI performance in multiple dimensions and giving more insights into the model's behavior and capabilities. For example, Fig. 1a additionally presents per-atom forces MAE for each species of atoms (Hydrogen, Carbon, and Oxygen). The analysis reveals that the error on different species generally follows the same trend, and the error on Hydrogen is significantly lower than the others due to its low atomic charge. Interestingly, the errors are not strictly proportional to the atomic charge of each species, as one might expect the errors of Oxygen to be proportionally higher than that of Carbon, but the data shows otherwise.

This observation suggests that force prediction is sensitive to the structural configuration of the molecule in addition to the invariant features of each atom. Moreover, it indicates that the model captures more structural information to reflect the steepness in the potential energy surface than an empirical potential energy equation.

4.2   Time-Series Extrapolation

The previous benchmark evaluates the model performance when the entire range of trajectory up to the test window is available to the training process. That is, the model is trained on data sampled from 9 times more time steps (90%) to predict the immediately upcoming steps (10%). In real-world MLFF-powered MD simulations, it is expected that the MLFF model should be able to support longer runs with more time steps, where the training window might not cover a large number of time steps compared to the inference steps and may not be immediately adjacent to the inference window. To evaluate the model's performance under such conditions, multiple variations of benchmarks are created using a grid-scan method to vary the size of the training window and its starting point. The training window sizes are set to 30%, 45%, 60%, 75%, and 90% of the whole trajectory, while the starting points are set to 0%, 15%, 30%, 45%, and 60% of the whole trajectory. For each of these training window variants, two models are trained with 1K and 15K data points sampled from the window, respectively, and their performance is tested on the final 10% of the trajectory.

Figure 2 presents the time-series extrapolation benchmarking results. Each horizontal line segment in the left part of the chart represents a training window variant, with starting/ending points in the 0%-90% range. The bar on the right corresponds to the per-atom force MAE evaluated on the test window

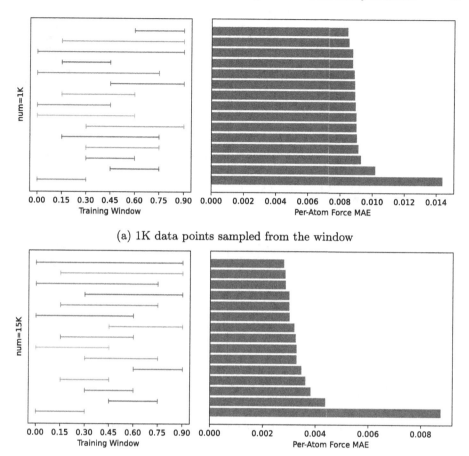

(a) 1K data points sampled from the window

(b) 15K data points sampled from the window

Fig. 2. Time-Series Extrapolation Benchmarks

for the model trained on this specific training window. The data is sorted by test performance, with the training window on the first row having the best test performance. The data shows that the test performance varies significantly with different training windows, and the patterns differ for 1K and 15K training samples. For the 1K samples, the best window is the one closest to the test window, with the narrowest range (60%-90%). In contrast, for the 15K samples, the best window is the widest (0% to 90%). This observation suggests that, even though the model demonstrates excellent sample efficiency, 1K samples still lead to underfitting when a large window is used. The reason is that there is not enough data within each subsection of the window for the model to generalize to similar cases effectively.

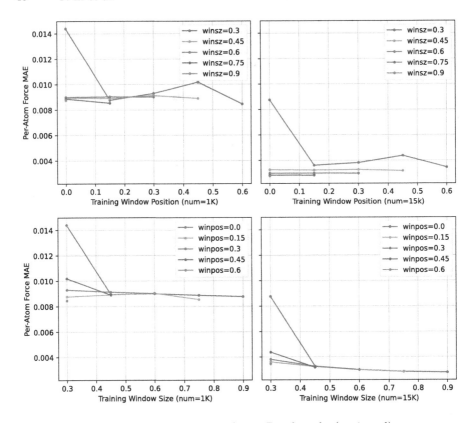

Fig. 3. Time-Series Extrapolation Benchmarks (projected)

Both the 1K and 15K charts show that a small window temporally distant from the test window (0%–30%) results in the worst performance. This observation suggests that maintaining the model's accuracy over a long trajectory is challenging, as it may not have enough information from distant data to generalize effectively to the test window.

In order to better evaluate the models trained on different windows, it is a good idea to project the results by grouping the data by window size and plotting each group to show the performance changes based on different window positions. Similarly, we can analyze how the performance changes with different window sizes for each starting position. This approach is visualized in Fig. 3. From the data, it is observed that both 1K and 15K models exhibit a pattern where, given a fixed window starting position (in short, winpos), the performance increases monotonically with the window size, except for 1K samples with a winpos of 0.15. However, given a fixed window size, the performance does not monotonically increase as the training window moves closer to the testing window. To understand why this occurs, the SOAP (Smooth Overlap of Atomic Positions) descriptor [1] is leveraged. The SOAP descriptor computes a high-dimensional feature vector for a given molecular system, allowing for the comparison of different molecular configurations. The correlation between two molecular configurations can be calculated by computing the cosine similarity of their corresponding SOAP descriptors. By computing all pairwise correlations between the training windows with a 30% range and the testing window, the mean average values are used to represent the similarity of the training windows to the test window. This information is visualized in Fig. 4.

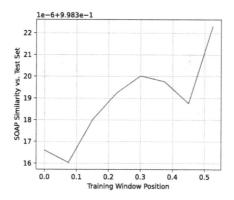

Fig. 4. Training data window vs. Test window SOAP similarity

The similarity curve presented in the figure demonstrates that similarity does not monotonically increase as the training window moves closer to the testing window. This result has two significant implications. First, the finding suggests that the trajectory does not constantly move away from the initial molecular configuration. Instead, it occasionally "bounces back" into the data distribution of earlier trajectories. This behavior indicates that the MD simulation may exhibit a certain degree of periodicity or recurring patterns in the molecular configurations, which can be essential in understanding the system's underlying behavior. Second, the result shows a clear relationship between the window similarity metric and the test performance. This relationship suggests that a real-world MLFF-powered MD system could leverage this metric as an accuracy indicator. When the similarity drops below a certain threshold, it signals that the MLFF-powered MD loop is heading towards out-of-distribution space. In such cases, the model may require further fine-tuning to maintain accuracy and stability.

4.3 Cross-Molecule Generalization Benchmarks

The revised MD17 dataset consists of multiple MD simulation trajectories for a fixed set of molecules. Traditionally, separate benchmarking fixtures are created for different molecules because cross-molecule performance is poor and considered impractical for simulation purposes.

However, it is important to consider this as an opportunity to evaluate the out-of-distribution generalization capabilities of a target machine learning model. While the results may not be practical for direct simulation purposes, they can provide valuable insights into the relationship between the potential energy surfaces of different molecules and the fine local structures within these molecules.

Table 1. Dataset Builds For Generalization Benchmarks

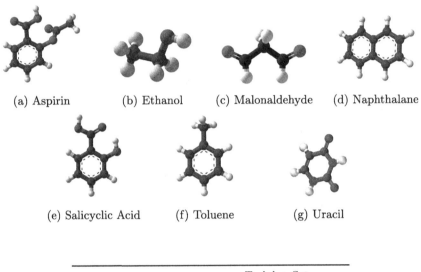

(a) Aspirin   (b) Ethanol   (c) Malonaldehyde   (d) Naphthalane

(e) Salicyclic Acid   (f) Toluene   (g) Uracil

	Training Set
Train on 1 molecule	f, b, a
Train on 2 molecules	ab, bc, de
Train on 3 molecules	abg, abd, cef
Train on 4 molecules	abeg, bcdf, abce
Train on 5 molecules	abceg, abcde, bcdef

First, we deterministically sample 1000 data points from each trajectory. These datasets are designated 'a' to 'g' and will be combined to create datasets that consist of multiple types of molecules. We select three different combinations of these datasets for one to five types of molecules. The dataset builds are shown in Table 1. As shown in the table, the datasets are selected to create overlaps between combinations of the same number of molecule types (for example, abg vs. abd), and between the combinations of different numbers of molecule types (for example, ab vs. abg). This allows us to analyze the performance impact of progressively adding more trajectories to the datasets.

It is important to note that various molecular systems exhibit significantly different potential energy levels. When merging distinct trajectories into a single dataset, we normalize the energy levels by conducting a linear regression across the entire dataset to calculate the reference energy for each type of atom.

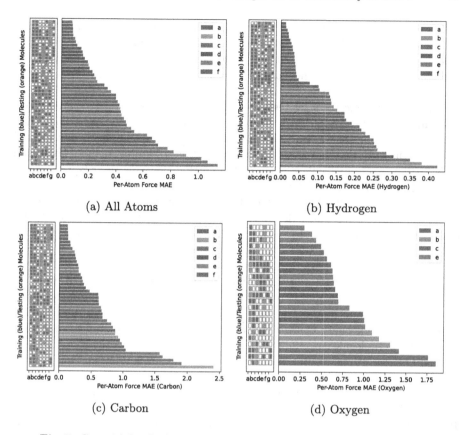

(a) All Atoms   (b) Hydrogen

(c) Carbon   (d) Oxygen

Fig. 5. Cross-Molecule Generalization Benchmarks (Color figure online)

After constructing the fixtures, we proceed to train a model for each combined training set and individually evaluate their performance on the trajectories not present in the combined training set. We intentionally design the test set in this manner because when trajectory data for a known molecule is being tested, its performance will be significantly better than that of unseen molecules. Consequently, this would statistically obscure the performance patterns of the latter. We also remove molecules with a completely unseen species of atom (for example, Nitrogen in molecule g) in the training set from the test sets.

Furthermore, it is important to note that even if the partial energy contributions of all atoms are normalized by the reference energy points, the combined output should still be considered biased. This bias arises because the reference energy itself contains a high error margin, which would consequently offset the predicted potential energy level towards the most seen configurations. As a result, our primary focus lies on the forces where the offset bias is eliminated by the gradient operator.

Figure 5 illustrates the cross-molecule generalization evaluation results. Similar to previous experiments, we present per-atom force MAE both over all the atoms and over different atom species. Each row in a plot represents training conducted on a specific combined dataset and testing conducted on one individual unseen molecule. The left side of each plot presents the training (blue) and testing (orange) molecules, and the horizontal bar on the right presents the per-atom force MAE.

Upon sorting the rows by testing performance, a distinct pattern emerges, revealing that certain molecules (such as f and d) are easier to generalize than others, while some (like c) prove difficult to generalize. Intriguingly, molecules d and f are the only two that consist of just two types of atoms, namely Hydrogen and Carbon, while molecule c is the only one that contains two Oxygen atoms arranged in a symmetrical configuration.

The charts also reveal that different atom species do not consistently generalize best on the same molecule. While molecule f exhibits the overall best generalization, the top-performing molecule for each atom species varies: molecule d for Hydrogen, molecule f for Carbon, and molecule e for Oxygen.

This observation implies that the generalization performance is highly sensitive to the local structure and symmetries of the molecules. Although molecule d is the only one containing two Benzene rings and thus exhibits unique global structure features, its symmetries and the proximity around each atom resemble those of other molecules. Conversely, while the inter-atomic distances and dihedral angles in molecule c resemble other molecules, the symmetrical arrangement of dual Oxygen atoms results in configurations that are largely unseen in other molecules.

Counter-intuitively, expanding the training data to include a new molecule does not always enhance the model's ability to generalize onto a specific molecule. Rather, we observe that the quality of generalization largely depends on the similarity between the training and testing molecules. Expanding the training set to include a molecule with low similarity to the testing molecule will most likely decrease generalization performance.

This finding suggests that although neural networks excel at processing a large number of training samples with diverse characteristics, for the specific application of MD, if generalization over unseen molecules is a required capability, it may be more effective to consider the similarities of the molecules instead of feeding conflicting data into a single model. By partitioning the training data, training separate models, and dynamically routing the inference to the most compatible model, we can potentially achieve better generalization performance across a range of molecular structures.

5   Conclusion

Benchmarking on AI for Science requires careful design to combine the benchmarking steps for machine-learning-based AI methods and scientific computing. When the combined approach encounters conflicting assumptions, we override the conventional AI benchmarking settings with the scientific computing settings, for example, to embrace out-of-distribution problem instances. The end result is an interleaved procedure that closely follows the conventional AI benchmarking practices by creating datasets, training AI models, and evaluating the performance on the test set but prioritizes scientifically meaningful setups in each step. More concretely, we demonstrate how this procedure is designed for MLFF-powered MD, a computational chemistry tool that plays a significant role in many scientific research applications. Conventionally, MLFF evaluation adopts methodologies from AI benchmarking. This approach treats data points within the same trajectory as independent and identically distributed (i.i.d.), while data points in different trajectories of distinct molecules are considered to be completely differently distributed, often resulting in separate evaluations. However, we argue that the evaluation of MLFFs should be tailored to accurately represent real-world MD computations. This would enable the time-domain correlation of trajectory data to be exploited in order to assess the generalization capabilities of an MLFF model when predicting future time steps. Additionally, incorporating configurations from various molecules would test the model's adaptability to previously unseen spatial structures, which are common in chemical reaction simulations. As a result, this leads to a realistic setup in the context of MLFF applications. Taking advantage of the scientific research application setup, we can produce more scientifically meaningful performance metrics from the benchmark compared to conventional AI benchmarking methods, and contribute to the development of more robust and generalizable AI4S machine learning models.

References

1. Bartók, A.P., Kondor, R., Csányi, G.: On representing chemical environments. **87**(18), 184115. https://doi.org/10.1103/PhysRevB.87.184115
2. Bartók, A.P., Payne, M.C., Kondor, R., Csányi, G.: Gaussian approximation potentials: the accuracy of quantum mechanics, without the electrons. **104**(13), 136403. https://doi.org/10.1103/PhysRevLett.104.136403
3. Batatia, I., Kovacs, D.P., Simm, G.N.C., Ortner, C., Csanyi, G.: MACE: Higher Order Equivariant Message Passing Neural Networks for Fast and Accurate Force Fields. https://openreview.net/forum?id=YPpSngE-ZU
4. Batzner, S., et al.: E(3)-equivariant graph neural networks for data-efficient and accurate interatomic potentials. **13**(1), 2453. https://doi.org/10.1038/s41467-022-29939-5. https://www.nature.com/articles/s41467-022-29939-5
5. Behler, J., Parrinello, M.: Generalized neural-network representation of high-dimensional potential-energy surfaces. **98**(14), 146401. https://doi.org/10.1103/PhysRevLett.98.146401
6. Bischl, B., et al.: ASlib: a benchmark library for algorithm selection. **237**, 41–58. https://doi.org/10.1016/j.artint.2016.04.003. https://www.sciencedirect.com/science/article/pii/S0004370216300388
7. Chmiela, S., Tkatchenko, A., Sauceda, H.E., Poltavsky, I., Schütt, K.T., Müller, K.R.: Machine learning of accurate energy-conserving molecular force fields. **3**(5), e1603015. https://doi.org/10.1126/sciadv.1603015. https://www.science.org/doi/10.1126/sciadv.1603015
8. Christensen, A.S., von Lilienfeld, O.A.: On the role of gradients for machine learning of molecular energies and forces. http://arxiv.org/abs/2007.09593

9. Deng, J., Dong, W., Socher, R., Li, L.J., Li, K., Fei-Fei, L.: ImageNet: a large-scale hierarchical image database. In: 2009 IEEE Conference on Computer Vision and Pattern Recognition, pp. 248–255. https://doi.org/10.1109/CVPR.2009.5206848

10. Fu, X., et al.: Forces are not enough: benchmark and critical evaluation for machine learning force fields with molecular simulations. https://doi.org/10.48550/arXiv.2210.07237

11. Gao, W., et al.: AIBench: towards scalable and comprehensive datacenter AI benchmarking. In: Zheng, C., Zhan, J. (eds.) Bench 2018. LNCS, vol. 11459, pp. 3–9. Springer, Cham (2019). https://doi.org/10.1007/978-3-030-32813-9_1

12. Gao, W., et al.: AIBench: An Industry Standard Internet Service AI Benchmark Suite. http://arxiv.org/abs/1908.08998

13. Gao, W., et al.: AIBench scenario: scenario-distilling AI benchmarking. In: 2021 30th International Conference on Parallel Architectures and Compilation Techniques (PACT), pp. 142–158. IEEE. https://doi.org/10.1109/PACT52795.2021.00018. https://ieeexplore.ieee.org/document/9563026/

14. Jia, W., et al.: Pushing the limit of molecular dynamics with ab initio accuracy to 100 million atoms with machine learning. http://arxiv.org/abs/2005.00223

15. Jones, J.E., Chapman, S.: On the determination of molecular fields.-I. From the variation of the viscosity of a gas with temperature. **106**(738), 441–462. https://doi.org/10.1098/rspa.1924.0081. https://royalsocietypublishing.org/doi/10.1098/rspa.1924.0081

16. AN Laboratory: AI for Science Report. https://publications.anl.gov/anlpubs/2020/03/158802.pdf

17. Mattson, P., et al.: MLPerf Training Benchmark, p. 14

18. Musaelian, A., et al.: Learning local equivariant representations for large-scale atomistic dynamics **14**(1), 579. https://doi.org/10.1038/s41467-023-36329-y. https://www.nature.com/articles/s41467-023-36329-y

19. Thiyagalingam, J., Shankar, M., Fox, G., Hey, T.: Scientific machine learning benchmarks. **4**(6), 413–420. https://doi.org/10.1038/s42254-022-00441-7. https://www.nature.com/articles/s42254-022-00441-7

20. Wang, L., et al.: BigDataBench: a big data benchmark suite from internet services. In: 2014 IEEE 20th International Symposium on High Performance Computer Architecture (HPCA), pp. 488–499. https://doi.org/10.1109/HPCA.2014.6835958

21. Wang, Y., et al.: ViSNet: a scalable and accurate geometric deep learning potential for molecular dynamics simulation. https://arxiv.org/abs/2210.16518v1

22. Wang, Z., et al.: Improving machine learning force fields for molecular dynamics simulations with fine-grained force metrics. **159**(3), 035101. https://doi.org/10.1063/5.0147023

23. Zhang, X., et al.: Artificial Intelligence for Science in Quantum, Atomistic, and Continuum Systems. https://doi.org/10.48550/arXiv.2307.08423

MolBench: A Benchmark of AI Models for Molecular Property Prediction

Xiuyu Jiang[1], Liqin Tan[1], Jianhuan Cen[1], and Qingsong Zou[1,2($\boxtimes$)]

[1] School of Computer Science and Engineering, Sun Yat-sen University,
Guangzhou 510006, China
mcszqs@mail.sysu.edu.cn
[2] Guangdong Province Key Laboratory of Computational Science,
Sun Yat-sen University, Guangzhou 510006, China

Abstract. In recent years, there has been a growing demand for the prediction of complex molecular properties in the fields of drug design, material science, and biotechnology. Compared to traditional laboratory methods, the deep learning method has many advantages such as saving enormously time and money. The deep learning method achieves revolutionary success in predicting molecular properties and many models based on the deep learning method has been developed in this field. However, there still lacks reliable and multidimensional benchmarks for evaluating these artificial intelligence (AI) models. In this paper, we develop a general method to evaluate AI models for predicting molecular properties. More precisely, we design multiple evaluation metrics based on the MoleculeNet datasets and introduce an extensible API interface to benchmark three types of AI models: molecular fingerprint based models, graph-based models, and pre-trained models. The purpose of the work is to establish a fair and reliable benchmark for future innovation in the field of molecular property prediction, emphasizing the importance of multidimensional perspectives.

Keywords: Molecular Property Prediction · Metric · Bench · MoleculeNet

1 Introduction

In recent years, the demand for high-quality molecular characterization in the fields of drug design, material science and biotechnology is growing. In addition to the traditional wet lab method, researchers have also developed numerous AI models for predicting molecular properties. While traditional wet lab experiments can accurately predict molecular properties, they are known to be time-consuming and costly [9,18]. In contrast, deep learning technology can overcome these shortcomings by enabling researchers to quickly predict molecular properties, significantly accelerating the drug development process and reducing costs [13,17,27,38].

S. Hunold et al. (Eds.): Bench 2023, LNCS 14521, pp. 53–70, 2024.
https://doi.org/10.1007/978-981-97-0316-6_4

Generally speaking, in order to steadily develop AI models in a certain field, it is necessary to establish standardized benchmarks. For example, ImageNet has driven the development of the field of image classification [8], while PDEBench has promoted the advancement of AI models for solving partial differential equations (PDEs) [42]. In the field of molecular property prediction, a robust benchmark should guarantee the availability and reliability of datasets, encompass a comprehensive range of current AI models, and offer a multidimensional evaluation of a model's performance and functionality through diverse metrics. While existing benchmarks like MoleculeNet provide well-recognized datasets [47], they only evaluate supervised models and utilize limited metrics. In addition, a common problem in the evaluation of current AI models is that researchers tend to directly compare their experimental results with classic models in the literature, which ignores differences in experimental conditions, such as hyperparameters. Researchers often carefully tune hyperparameters for their models and report only the best results, leading to potentially unfair comparisons and reducing the credibility of their findings. Therefore, it is necessary to establish a universal benchmark to evaluate existing molecular property prediction models. Only when the benchmark is fair and credible can it be more conducive to our further research and innovation.

In this paper, we propose MolBench, a novel benchmark designed for the evaluation of AI models aimed at predicting molecular properties, which has the following distinctive features: (1) Different from the simple machine learning (ML) models selected by MoleculeNet, our MolBench selects more advanced AI models, including not only molecular fingerprint-based models, but also graph-based models and pre-trained models. The pre-trained models in this paper are mainly based on three types of self supervised learning (SSL) strategies: predictive [20], contrastive [41,44]and denoising [21,26,52]. (2) Our evaluations are based on the MoleculeNet datasets, which are currently the most widely recognized datasets, with approximately 2,000 citations. (3) In order to evaluate these molecular property prediction models, MolBench sets up multidimensional evaluation indicators, including analyzing model stability, ranking model best performance and calculating task coverage. (4) Create an extensible API interface for evaluation services.

The rest of this paper is organized as follows. Section 2 presents an overview of existing benchmark evaluation efforts in the field of molecular property prediction. Section 3 describes the benchmark datasets and models that we have chosen in the MolBench. In Sect. 4, we conduct a series of experiments to evaluate the performance of the benchmark models using multiple indicators. Section 5 concludes this paper and outlines our insights and considerations for future work.

2   Related Work

To the best of our knowledge, three benchmark methods for molecular property prediction are presented below.

MatBench [10] introduces a benchmark testing suite and an automated ML procedure to evaluate models designed for supervised machine learning to predict the properties of bulk inorganic materials. This benchmark includes 13 distinct ML tasks, including the prediction of properties based on the composition and/or crystal structure of materials.

MoleculeNet [47] is a large-scale benchmark for molecular machine learning. MoleculeNet compiles multiple public datasets, establishes evaluation metrics, and provides implementations of previously proposed molecular characterizations and algorithms. It shows that learnable representations can provide superior performance for molecular representation learning compared to fixed representations.

MUBen [25] is a benchmark evaluation of uncertainty in pre-trained models for molecular representation learning. By meticulously fine-tuning different backbone molecular representation models, utilizing various molecular descriptors as input, and integrating uncertainty quantification(UQ) methods from different classes, MUBen provides a rigorous examination of the impact of architectural decisions and training strategies.

The above three benchmarks have made outstanding contributions in their respective fields. It should be noted that MatBench is aimed at evaluating supervised models of inorganic materials, MUBen focuses on the uncertainty of pre-trained models for molecular property prediction tasks, and MoleculeNet does not include evaluation of the latest deep learning models due to its earlier publication year. We attempt to establish a benchmark for deep learning models for molecular property prediction tasks based on MoleculeNet, which includes supervised models and pre-trained models.

3   Methodology

In this section, we first provide a detailed description of the pre-training datasets used in MolBench and the datasets selected from MoleculeNet for molecular property prediction. Then we present the following three types of AI models used in MolBench: Extended Connectivity Fingerprint (ECFP)-based models, graph-based models, and pre-trained models. Finally, we provide multidimensional evaluation metrics that explain model results, including widely accepted performance, stability, and task coverage metrics.

3.1   Datasets

In this part, we describe the pre-training dataset used in MolBench and the dataset selected from MoleculeNet for molecular property prediction.

Pre-training Datasets

Considering the highly recognized datasets utilized by popular pre-trained models, we have selected ZINC15 [39] and ChEMBL [14] as our pre-training datasets, and the benchmark models in MolBench are pre-trained using subsets of these datasets. (1) **ZINC15** is a freely accessible virtual screening database that includes over 230 million purchasable compounds [39]. (2) **ChEMBL** is a manually curated database of bioactive molecules with drug-like properties containing over 2 million compound records [14].

MoleculeNet Datasets

At present, MoleculeNet datasets are the most widely used and most highly recognized in the field of molecular property prediction, so we choose some MoleculeNet datasets as benchmark datasets for MolBench [11,53]. These benchmark datasets contain classification tasks and regression tasks, covering the domains of quantum mechanics, physical chemistry, biophysics, and physiology.

The Quantum Mechanics category comprises three datasets: QM7, QM8, and QM9. (1) **QM7 dataset**: determines the three-dimensional Cartesian coordinates and electronic properties of the most stable conformation of each molecule [3,31,37]. (2) **QM8 dataset**: applies more methods than QM7 on a set of molecules with up to eight heavy atom [33]. (3) **QM9 dataset**: provides properties in geometry, energy, electronics, and thermodynamics [32].

The Physical Chemistry category comprises three datasets: ESOL, FreeSolv and Lipo. (1) **Estimated Solubility (ESOL) dataset**: contains the solubility values of a series of compounds in water [7]. (2) **Free Solvation (FreeSolv) datast**: includes the hydration free energy data of a series of organic compounds obtained through experiments and computations [29,30]. (3) **Lipophilicity (Lipo) dataset**: contains the lipophilic affinity data of a series of compounds [15].

The Biophysics category comprises two datasets: HIV and BACE. (1) **HIV dataset**: is derived from the antiviral screening of the Drug Therapy Program (DTP)[1]. The screening tests the compounds' ability to inhibit the replication of the HIV virus. (2) **Beta-secretase 1 (BACE) dataset**: provides a set of quantitative and qualitative binding results for human β-secretase (BACE-1) inhibitors [40].

The Physiology category comprises five datasets: BBBP, Tox21, Toxcast, SIDER and Clintox. (1) **Blood-Brain Barrier Penetration (BBBP) dataset**: As a membrane separating circulating blood and brain extracellular fluid, the blood-brain barrier blocks most drugs, hormones, and neurotransmitters [28]. (2) **Toxicology in the 21st Century (Tox21) dataset**: aims to create a public database for compound toxicity[2]. (3) **Toxicity Forecaster (ToxCast) dataset**: provides toxicology data for a large compound library for high-throughput in vitro screening [34]. (4) **Side Effect Resource (SIDER) dataset**: classifies drug side effects according to MedDRA [24]. (5) **Clinical Toxicity (ClinTox) dataset**: compares FDA-approved drugs and drugs that failed in clinical trials due to toxicity reasons [2,16].

---

[1] https://wiki.nci.nih.gov/display/NCIDTPdata/AIDS+Antiviral+Screen+Data.
[2] https://tripod.nih.gov/tox21/challenge/.

3.2   Models

In this part, we succinctly outline the diverse set of models employed for conducting our rigorous benchmark evaluation on chosen datasets. Our selections encompass traditional ML techniques based on ECFP, such as Support Vector Machines (SVM) [6], Random Forests (RF) [4], XGBoost [5], and Multi-Layer Perceptron (MLP) [12], along with an array of graph-based models including Graph Convolutional Network (GCN) [23], Graph Attention Network (GAT) [50], Graph Isomorphism Network (GIN) [43], AttentiveFP [49], and Directed Message Passing Neural Network (D-MPNN) [51]. We also employ pre-trained models such as PretrainGNN [20], MolCLR [45], GROVER [36], and Uni-Mol [53]. These models are carefully chosen to cover molecular representations comprehensively, as well as to encompass both supervised and self-supervised learning methods. Moreover, each is highly recognized and widely utilized in current research, serving as a reputable baseline for our analysis.

ECFP-Based Models

ECFP is a widely used molecular characterization method in cheminformatics, providing an efficient way for machine learning [35]. ECFP takes into account the topological environment of the atoms in the molecule, encoding this information as a binary vector, typically 1024 or 2048 dimensional. Furthermore, ECFP is highly flexible and adaptable, with its radius parameter allowing for a balance between specificity and generality in the encoded information.

Traditional ML methods, such as SVM, RF, and XGBoost, have made significant contributions to molecular property prediction. Based on fixed molecular representations, these methods offer remarkable computational efficiency, interpretability, and the ability to handle high-dimensional data. Thus, while deep learning continues to make progress in this field, the unique strengths of traditional machine learning methods underscore their continued importance.

SVM: is a supervised learning technique predominantly employed for classification and regression tasks, aiming to discern the optimal hyperplane for separating different data classes in a high-dimensional space [6].

RF: is an ensemble learning method composed of multiple decision trees. Each decision tree is trained on a random subset of the data, and a random subset of features is used at each split point in the tree [4].

XGBoost: is a high-performance gradient boosting framework for supervised learning, which iteratively builds weak prediction models to improve accuracy and reduce errors from previous iterations [5].

MLP: is a kind of artificial neural network with a minimum of three layers: input, one or more hidden, and output layers [12].

Graph-Based Models

A molecule graph is a natural graph structure data where each molecule can be transformed into an undirected graph $G(V, E)$. Here, $V = (x_1, \cdots, x_N)$ represents the set of atom nodes, and E represents the set of chemical bond edges [22]. In our experiments, we initialize node features and edge features in the molecular graph using the properties of the molecule itself.

Graph Neural Networks (GNNs) are transformative in molecular property prediction [48]. Through end-to-end training, GNNs capture atomic and bond-level relationships within molecular structures and can adaptively learn task-specific molecular features to more accurately understand chemical properties. This combination of features has led to superior performance in a diverse range of prediction tasks, making GNNs a crucial tool in fields such as drug design and material science.

GCN: is a neural network model designed to handle graph data [23]. GCN extends convolutional operations to graphs, enabling the model to share parameters between a node and its neighbors, thereby capturing the local structure of the graph.

GAT: is a model that introduces the attention mechanism into graph neural networks to compute the weights of a node and its neighbors [50]. When aggregating neighbor information, GAT takes into account the importance of neighbors, assigning greater weights to important neighbors.

GIN: works through a special aggregation mechanism that allows the network to distinguish between different graphs even if these graphs are structurally isomorphic [43].

AttentiveFP: is a graph neural network model specifically designed to handle molecular structures [49]. AttentiveFP utilizes a self-attention mechanism to capture the topological structure of molecules and aggregates graph information through Gated Recurrent Unit (GRU) and virtual nodes.

D-MPNN: is a powerful graph neural network that handles directed graph data [51]. D-MPNN adopts a directed message passing mechanism that can distinguish edge directionality, thereby capturing more complex and detailed graph structure information.

Pre-trained Models

Pre-trained models have brought significant advances in molecular property prediction tasks. They efficiently leverage the vast amounts of unlabeled data in the biological domain, allowing for transfer learning and enrichment of the feature representations. Furthermore, these models save computational resources and time by minimizing the necessity for task-specific training from scratch. Consequently, they not only expedite model deployment but also foster the discovery of novel chemical entities, thereby revolutionizing predictive modeling in fields like medicinal chemistry and material science.

PretrainGNN: introduces a suite of methods for node-level and graph-level pre-training of GNNs, such as context prediction, masking, and graph-level prediction [20]. These methods leverage both unlabeled and labeled data derived from relevant auxiliary supervised tasks.

MolCLR: is a self-supervised learning framework [45]. In the pre-training phase, it employs three molecular graph augmentation techniques: atom masking, bond deletion, and subgraph removal. A contrastive estimator is then utilized to maximize the agreement between augmentations of the same molecule and minimize the coherence of distinct molecules.

GROVER: A novel framework to collect rich structural and semantic information from a wide range of unlabeled molecular data using well-designed self-supervised tasks at the node, edge, and graph levels [36]. To efficiently encode such complex information, GROVER incorporates MPNN into a Transformer-style architecture, resulting in a more expressive class of molecular encoders.

Uni-Mol: is capable to directly accept and generate 3D locations as input and output [53]. It consists of three main components: backbone, pre-training, and fine-tuning. During the pre-training stage, in addition to the masked atom prediction task, a 3D position denoising task is also utilized to learn a 3D spatial representation.

3.3 Metrics

In this part, we provide a comprehensive explanation of the metrics used for evaluating models, including widely accepted performance, stability metrics, and task coverage metrics for multidimensional evaluation.

Performance Metric

Following the recommendations of MoleculeNet and authoritative articles published to date, our MolBench employs a range of metrics for various tasks:

Receiver Operating Characteristic (ROC) Curve and Area Under Curve (AUC): For classification tasks, we rely on the AUC of the ROC curve, which is currently the most widely used metric for molecular property prediction tasks [11,53]. The ROC curve is a graphical representation of the true positive rate (sensitivity) against the false positive rate (1-specificity) across different threshold values. The AUC measures the entire two-dimensional area underneath the curve and provides an aggregate measure of performance across all possible classification thresholds. The calculation formula of AUC value is:

$$\text{AUC} = \int_0^1 \text{True Positive Rate (TPR)} d(\text{False Positive Rate (FPR)}). \quad (1)$$

Mean Absolute Error (MAE): For quantum mechanics datasets, we utilize the MAE. It's a measure of the absolute differences between predictions and actual values. The formula for MAE is:

$$\text{MAE} = \frac{1}{n} \sum_{i=1}^{n} |y_i - \hat{y}_i|, \tag{2}$$

where y_i is the actual value, $\hat{y}_i$ is the predicted value, and n is the number of observations.

Root Mean Square Error (RMSE): To evaluate other regression tasks, RMSE is used. RMSE indicates the square root of the second sample moment of the differences between predicted values and observed values or the quadratic mean of these differences. The formula for RMSE is:

$$\text{RMSE} = \sqrt{\frac{1}{n} \sum_{i=1}^{n} (y_i - \hat{y}_i)^2}, \tag{3}$$

where y_i is the actual value, $\hat{y}_i$ is the predicted value, and n is the number of observations.

It is important to note that for datasets encompassing multiple tasks, we report the average metric value across all tasks.

Stability Metric

After running the model multiple times on each task, we calculate the standard deviation and mean of the model's performance for each task. The Coefficient of Variation (CV) is then computed for each task by dividing its standard deviation by its mean performance [1]. Finally, we determine the average CV across both classification and regression tasks. This average CV is used as a stability metric for the model to provide insight into the consistency and reliability of the model's performance.

Task Coverage Metric

A benchmark for a given task is set by computing the average performance of all benchmark models on a single dataset. A model is considered competent for the task if it exceeds the average performance for a certain dataset. Otherwise, it is considered incompetent.

4   Experiments

In this section, we present the performance, stability, and task coverage of the selected benchmark models on various datasets. The ECFPs we used are all 1024-dimensional, which is a common choice because it provides a good balance of capturing sufficient information about the molecule while maintaining relatively low computational and storage overhead [19,46]. It should be noted that for the pre-trained model, we load the pre-trained model from the original paper and use it for the molecular property prediction tasks.

When evaluating the model, we performed three independent runs using the same random seed (0, 1, 2). We employed an NVIDIA GeForce RTX2080 Ti graphics card, which features 11 GB of memory and 4,352 CUDA cores, and the CUDA version is 12.2. No model is allowed to train for more than 24 h. Using multiple GPUs can indeed reduce computation time and expand accessible memory. However, it may simultaneously inject more complexity into the implementation process. We set time boundaries for the model to improve its efficiency and ensure reproducible experiments. It should be noted that the experimental results we provide do not cover the performance of all benchmark models on all benchmark datasets, because some models may run for too long or consume too much memory, resulting in a lack of experimental results for some tasks. For subsequent research, strategies such as optimized data loading and preprocessing, cumulative gradients, and model parallelism can be explored to reduce computational time. We hope that future researchers can achieve more comprehensive and detailed evaluation results based on ours.

4.1 Results

To present the results in a more intuitive and clear manner, we have divided the datasets into classification and regression tasks. The classification task consists of seven datasets: BACE, BBBP, ClinTox, HIV, SIDER, Tox21, and ToxCast. The performance of the models is evaluated using the ROC-AUC metric. Additionally, the regression task is divided into two parts based on the evaluation metrics. The first part includes three datasets: ESOL, FreeSolv, and Lipo, with the models' performance evaluated using the RMSE metric. The second part includes the datasets QM7, QM8, and QM9, with the evaluation based on the MAE metric.

Classification Tasks

In this part, we present the results of various classification tasks shown in Fig. 1, and all evaluation indicators are ROC-AUC values.

For the BACE dataset, RF, SVM, XGBoost, and pre-trained methods exhibit better performance. This can be attributed to the limited size of the data, which constrains the ability of graph networks to extract task-relevant representations from such a small amount of data.

For the BBBP dataset, D-MPNN and pre-trained models perform better, indicating that incorporating 3D information and pre-training enriches the models' capacity to extract valuable insights.

For the ClinTox dataset, despite its limited number of molecules, the models generally perform well, particularly the GNNs and pre-trained models. This

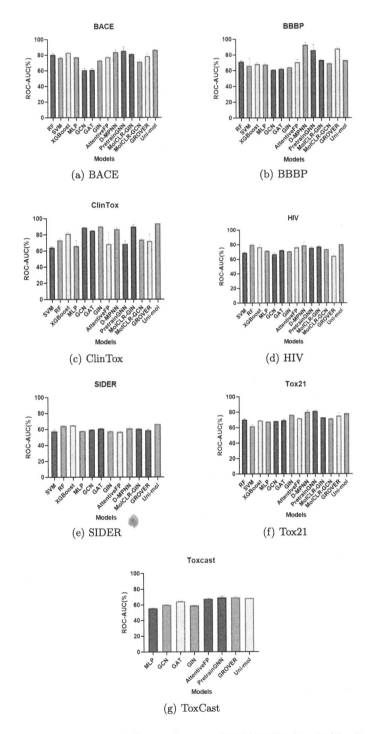

Fig. 1. Results of BACE/BBBP/ClinTox/HIV/SIDER/Tox21/ToxCast.

could be due to the dataset having fewer key functional groups representing toxicity. After performing scaffold splitting, the differences between the training, validation, and test subsets are not significantly large.

For the HIV dataset, all models generally perform well. This can be attributed to the large data volume and its single-task nature. GNNs, given an abundance of training data, can effectively demonstrate their advanced capabilities, even comparable to pre-trained models.

For the SIDER dataset, all models generally perform poorly. This is likely due to the dataset's limited size, consisting of only 1,427 molecules but encompassing 27 classification tasks. Extracting a representation capable of identifying multiple distinct features from such a small number of molecules has proven to be a difficult task.

For the Tox21 dataset, GNNs and pre-trained models outperform RF, SVM, and XGBoost. With relatively abundant training data, graph networks capable of learning molecular representation vectors exhibited superior performance compared to traditional machine learning methods based on ECFPs, even comparable to pre-trained models.

For the ToxCast dataset, all models generally perform poorly, and the pre-trained models are slightly outperforming the other two types of models. This can be attributed to ToxCast encompassing over 600 tasks, posing a considerable challenge for limited-length molecular representation vectors. Pre-trained models, having acquired domain knowledge from vast unlabeled datasets, offer an advantage in tackling such multifaceted tasks.

Regression Tasks

In this part, we present the results of various regression tasks in Fig. 2 and Fig. 3, with RMSE as the evaluation metric for the ESOL, FreeSolv, and Lipo datasets, and MAE as the evaluation metric for the QM7, QM8, and QM9 datasets.

For the ESOL and Lipo datasets, the graph networks models and pre-trained models outperform RF/SVM/XGBoost. When there is sufficient training data, the graph network, which can learn molecular representation vectors, demonstrates superior performance compared to traditional machine learning methods like ECFPs. However, it still falls short of the performance achieved by pre-trained models. For the FreeSolv dataset, the performance of each model is slightly different, possibly due to the limited amount of data, and the specific reason remains to be analyzed. It is worth noting that the results of MolCLR are better than those of the untrained GIN and GCN models, proving that pre-training does improve model performance to a certain extent.

For the QM datasets, Uni-Mol achieves the best performance. This can be attributed to the fact that Uni-Mol introduces the three-dimensional coordinates of molecules during the pre-training stage, which directly relates to the various properties of quantum mechanics.

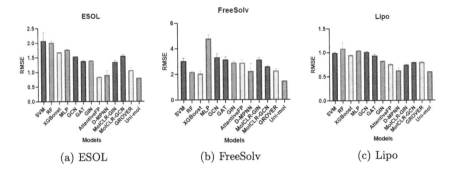

(a) ESOL   (b) FreeSolv   (c) Lipo

Fig. 2. Results of ESOL/FreeSolv/Lipo.

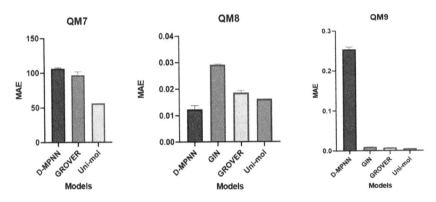

Fig. 3. Results of QM7/QM8/QM9

Since the selected datasets cover multiple domains and include both classification and regression tasks, it is difficult for a single model to achieve optimal performance on all tasks. In order to better quantify the performance of the model in molecular property prediction tasks, we propose a scoring method. The specific steps of this method are as follows: taking the top three as an example, calculate and rank the performance of each model on the aforementioned 13 datasets, tally the number of times each model achieves first, second, and third place. If the model comes first it gets three points, for second it gets two points, for third it gets three points, and finally the total score is calculated. Similarly, the top five scores and the top ten scores can also be calculated. This article only takes the top five scores as an example, because the top three scores may cause most models to score. The results are shown in Table 1.

Table 1. Model Evaluation Scores

Models	No.1	No.2	No.3	No.4	No.5	Score
SVM	0	0	0	0	0	0
RF	0	1	2	0	0	10
XGBoost	0	2	0	1	1	11
MLP	0	0	0	0	0	0
GCN	0	0	0	1	0	2
GAT	0	0	0	0	2	2
GIN	0	1	1	0	0	7
AttentiveFP	0	1	0	1	1	7
D-MPNN	1	2	3	2	1	**27**
PretrainGNN	1	2	1	0	0	16
MolCLR-GCN	0	0	0	0	0	0
MolCLR-GIN	0	0	1	3	3	12
GROVER	1	1	0	2	1	14
Uni-Mol	7	0	2	0	1	**_42_**

According to the results shown in Table 1, we can see that the model with the highest top five score is Uni-Mol, the second is D-MPNN, and the third is PretrainGNN. Based on these findings, we can infer that pre-training and incorporating 3D information are beneficial for molecular representation learning.

4.2   Stability

Since the datasets originate from different fields, it is impossible to determine their relative importance, and there is no appropriate theoretical basis for assigning weights to them. Therefore, we consider them to have equal weight. In this part, we initially computed the average performance of each model on classification and regression tasks, and the results are shown in Fig. 4. For classification tasks, higher values are better, and for regression tasks, lower values are better. It is should be noted that due to computational constraints, we only consider three datasets (ESOL, FreeSolv, and Lipo) to compute the regression task.

For classification tasks, the models with the best average performance are Uni-Mol, PretrainGNN and D-MPNN. Uni-Mol and PretrainGNN are robust pre-trained models that provide beneficial influence for downstream tasks through extensive unlabeled datasets and rich pre-training tasks. On the other hand, D-MPNN incorporates comprehensive three-dimensional information into the traditional MPNN model, significantly enriching the molecular information extracted by the graph network.

For regression tasks, graph network models demonstrate superior performance. However, since we only analyzed three regression datasets, this metric should be considered as a preliminary indication. Future studies should include additional regression datasets to thoroughly evaluate the models' capability in handling regression tasks.

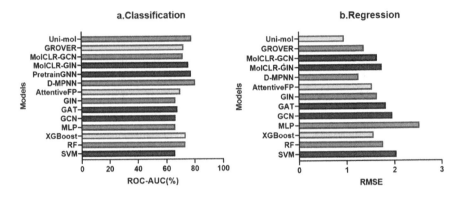

Fig. 4. Average Performance of Models on Classification and Regression Tasks

During the experiment, we simultaneously computed the standard deviation and determined the average CV of the model across all tasks. The results are depicted in Fig. 5, illustrating the stability of the models.

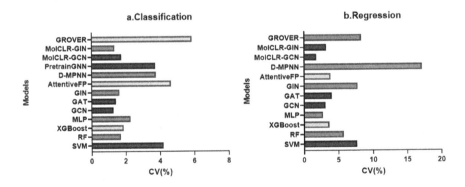

Fig. 5. CV of Model Performance on Classification and Regression Tasks

For classification tasks, models that performed well in terms of stability include GCN, MolCLR-GIN and GAT.

For regression tasks, the models that exhibited better performance are MolCLR-GCN, MLP and GCN.

4.3   Task Coverage

In this part, according to the calculation method of task coverage, we present the results in Table 2.

Based on this evaluation criterion, the top five performing models are Uni-Mol, D-MPNN, GROVER, MolCLR-GIN, and AttentiveFP. Uni-Mol, GROVER, and MolCLR-GIN are all pre-trained models that can achieve better generalization and prediction performance, thereby exceeding the average on multiple tasks. D-MPNN combines three-dimensional information with typical MPNN models, and AttentiveFP is improved on the basis of GAT.

4.4 API

We provide an extensible API that allows researchers to leverage the models and datasets mentioned in this article. At the same time, other data sets are also available, and researchers only need to upload them in the specified format and determine the model used to obtain the results. We hope that this API can facilitate subsequent research in related fields. The relevant code will be made publicly available at https://github.com/xiuyuJ/MolBench.

Table 2. Statistics on Task Coverage

Models	Task Coverage	Tasks
SVM	10%	BACE
RF	40%	BACE/HIV/SIDER/FreeSolv
XGBoost	40%	BACE/HIV/SIDER/FreeSolv
MLP	10%	BACE
GCN	10%	ClinTox
GAT	40%	ClinTox/SIDER/ToxCast/ESOL
GIN	40%	ClinTox/Tox21/ESOL/Lipo
AttentiveFP	60%	BACE/HIV/Tox21/ToxCast/ESOL/Lipo
D-MPNN	**90%**	Except ToxCast
MolCLR-GIN	70%	BACE/BBBP/ClinTox/HIV/Tox21/ESOL/Lipo
MolCLR-GCN	30%	HIV/FreeSolv/Lipo
GROVER	70%	BACE/BBBP/Tox21/ToxCast/ESOL/FreeSolv/Lipo
Uni-Mol	**100**%	All

5   Concluding Remarks

In this paper, we propose MolBench, a novel benchmark specifically designed for the evaluation of AI models in the domain of molecular property prediction. MolBench reveals the advantages and limitations of SOTA AI models, which helps to better understand and use these models. Furthermore, MolBench serves as a reference for future research on molecular property prediction. Despite significant progress made by deep learning models in this field, further enhancements are necessary to meet the increasing demand in current applications. On one hand, existing models generally perform poorly on datasets with small data volumes but multi-tasks, thus a possible important future direction is to improve model performance on such datasets. On the other hand, traditional machine learning models may still outperform existing advanced pre-trained models in certain tasks, so traditional machine learning models cannot be ignored. How to combine traditional machine learning models with advanced deep learning models is an issue worth further research.

Acknowledgements. The research was supported in part by the National Key Research and Program of China (2022ZD0117805), by the National Natural Science Foundation of China under grants 12071496 and 92370113, and by the Natural Science Foundation of the Guangdong Province under the grant 2023A1515012079.

References

1. Abdi, H.: Coefficient of variation. Encycl. Res. Des. **1**(5) (2010)
2. Artemov, A.V., Putin, E., Vanhaelen, Q., Aliper, A., Ozerov, I.V., Zhavoronkov, A.: Integrated deep learned transcriptomic and structure-based predictor of clinical trials outcomes. BioRxiv, p. 095653 (2016)
3. Blum, L.C., Reymond, J.L.: 970 million druglike small molecules for virtual screening in the chemical universe database GDB-13. J. Am. Chem. Soc. **131**(25), 8732–8733 (2009)
4. Breiman, L.: Random forests. Mach. Learn. **45**, 5–32 (2001)
5. Chen, T., Guestrin, C.: Xgboost: a scalable tree boosting system. In: Proceedings of the 22nd ACM SIGKDD International Conference on Knowledge Discovery and Data Mining, pp. 785–794 (2016)
6. Cortes, C., Vapnik, V.: Support-vector networks. Mach. Learn. **20**, 273–297 (1995)
7. Delaney, J.S.: ESOL: estimating aqueous solubility directly from molecular structure. J. Chem. Inf. Comput. Sci. **44**(3), 1000–1005 (2004)
8. Deng, J., Dong, W., Socher, R., Li, L.J., Li, K., Fei-Fei, L.: Imagenet: a large-scale hierarchical image database, pp. 248–255 (2009)
9. Dowden, H., Munro, J.: Trends in clinical success rates and therapeutic focus. Nat. Rev. Drug Discov. **18**(7), 495–496 (2019)
10. Dunn, A., Wang, Q., Ganose, A., Dopp, D., Jain, A.: Benchmarking materials property prediction methods: the matbench test set and automatminer reference algorithm. NPJ Comput. Mater. **6**(1), 138 (2020)
11. Fang, X., et al.: Geometry-enhanced molecular representation learning for property prediction. Nat. Mach. Intell. **4**(2), 127–134 (2022)
12. Gardner, M.W., Dorling, S.: Artificial neural networks (the multilayer perceptron)-a review of applications in the atmospheric sciences. Atmos. Environ. **32**(14–15), 2627–2636 (1998)
13. Gasteiger, J., Groß, J., Günnemann, S.: Directional message passing for molecular graphs. arXiv preprint arXiv:2003.03123 (2020)
14. Gaulton, A., et al.: ChEMBL: a large-scale bioactivity database for drug discovery. Nucleic Acids Res. **40**(D1), D1100–D1107 (2012)
15. Gaulton, A., et al.: A large-scale crop protection bioassay data set. Sci. Data **2**(1), 1–7 (2015)

16. Gayvert, K.M., Madhukar, N.S., Elemento, O.: A data-driven approach to predicting successes and failures of clinical trials. Cell Chem. Biol. **23**(10), 1294–1301 (2016)
17. Gilmer, J., Schoenholz, S.S., Riley, P.F., Vinyals, O., Dahl, G.E.: Neural message passing for quantum chemistry. In: International Conference on Machine Learning, pp. 1263–1272. PMLR (2017)
18. Hay, M., Thomas, D.W., Craighead, J.L., Economides, C., Rosenthal, J.: Clinical development success rates for investigational drugs. Nat. Biotechnol. **32**(1), 40–51 (2014)
19. Hirohara, M., Saito, Y., Koda, Y., Sato, K., Sakakibara, Y.: Convolutional neural network based on smiles representation of compounds for detecting chemical motif. BMC Bioinform. **19**, 83–94 (2018)
20. Hu, W., et al.: Strategies for pre-training graph neural networks. arXiv preprint arXiv:1905.12265 (2019)
21. Jiao, R., Han, J., Huang, W., Rong, Y., Liu, Y.: Energy-motivated equivariant pretraining for 3D molecular graphs. arXiv preprint arXiv:2207.08824 (2022)
22. Kearnes, S., McCloskey, K., Berndl, M., Pande, V., Riley, P.: Molecular graph convolutions: moving beyond fingerprints. J. Comput. Aided Mol. Des. **30**, 595–608 (2016)
23. Kipf, T.N., Welling, M.: Semi-supervised classification with graph convolutional networks. arXiv preprint arXiv:1609.02907 (2016)
24. Kuhn, M., Letunic, I., Jensen, L.J., Bork, P.: The sider database of drugs and side effects. Nucleic Acids Res. **44**(D1), D1075–D1079 (2016)
25. Li, Y., et al.: MUBen: benchmarking the uncertainty of pre-trained models for molecular property prediction. arXiv preprint arXiv:2306.10060 (2023)
26. Liu, S., Guo, H., Tang, J.: Molecular geometry pretraining with se (3)-invariant denoising distance matching. arXiv preprint arXiv:2206.13602 (2022)
27. Liu, Y., Wang, L., Liu, M., Zhang, X., Oztekin, B., Ji, S.: Spherical message passing for 3D graph networks. arXiv preprint arXiv:2102.05013 (2021)
28. Martins, I.F., Teixeira, A.L., Pinheiro, L., Falcao, A.O.: A Bayesian approach to in silico blood-brain barrier penetration modeling. J. Chem. Inf. Model. **52**(6), 1686–1697 (2012)
29. Mobley, D.L., Guthrie, J.P.: Freesolv: a database of experimental and calculated hydration free energies, with input files. J. Comput. Aided Mol. Des. **28**, 711–720 (2014)
30. Mobley, D.L., Wymer, K.L., Lim, N.M., Guthrie, J.P.: Blind prediction of solvation free energies from the sampl4 challenge. J. Comput. Aided Mol. Des. **28**, 135–150 (2014)
31. Montavon, G., et al.: Machine learning of molecular electronic properties in chemical compound space. New J. Phys. **15**(9), 095003 (2013)
32. Ramakrishnan, R., Dral, P.O., Rupp, M., Von Lilienfeld, O.A.: Quantum chemistry structures and properties of 134 kilo molecules. Sci. Data **1**(1), 1–7 (2014)
33. Ramakrishnan, R., Hartmann, M., Tapavicza, E., Von Lilienfeld, O.A.: Electronic spectra from TDDFT and machine learning in chemical space. J. Chem. Phys. **143**(8) (2015)
34. Richard, A.M., et al.: Toxcast chemical landscape: paving the road to 21st century toxicology. Chem. Res. Toxicol. **29**(8), 1225–1251 (2016)
35. Rogers, D., Hahn, M.: Extended-connectivity fingerprints. J. Chem. Inf. Model. **50**(5), 742–754 (2010)
36. Rong, Y., et al.: Self-supervised graph transformer on large-scale molecular data. Adv. Neural Inf. Process. Syst. **33**, 12559–12571 (2020)

37. Rupp, M., Tkatchenko, A., Müller, K.R., Von Lilienfeld, O.A.: Fast and accurate modeling of molecular atomization energies with machine learning. Phys. Rev. Lett. **108**(5), 058301 (2012)
38. Schütt, K., Kindermans, P.J., Sauceda Felix, H.E., Chmiela, S., Tkatchenko, A., Müller, K.R.: Schnet: a continuous-filter convolutional neural network for modeling quantum interactions. Adv. Neural Inf. Process. Syst. **30** (2017)
39. Sterling, T., Irwin, J.J.: Zinc 15-ligand discovery for everyone. J. Chem. Inf. Model. **55**(11), 2324–2337 (2015)
40. Subramanian, G., Ramsundar, B., Pande, V., Denny, R.A.: Computational modeling of β-secretase 1 (BACE-1) inhibitors using ligand based approaches. J. Chem. Inf. Model. **56**(10), 1936–1949 (2016)
41. Suresh, S., Li, P., Hao, C., Neville, J.: Adversarial graph augmentation to improve graph contrastive learning. Adv. Neural Inf. Process. Syst. **34**, 15920–15933 (2021)
42. Takamoto, M., et al.: Pdebench: an extensive benchmark for scientific machine learning. Adv. Neural Inf. Process. Syst. **35**, 1596–1611 (2022)
43. Veličković, P., Cucurull, G., Casanova, A., Romero, A., Lio, P., Bengio, Y.: Graph attention networks. arXiv preprint arXiv:1710.10903 (2017)
44. Wang, Y., Wang, J., Cao, Z., Farimani, A.: MolCLR: molecular contrastive learning of representations via graph neural networks. arxiv 2021. arXiv preprint arXiv:2102.10056
45. Wang, Y., Wang, J., Cao, Z., Barati Farimani, A.: Molecular contrastive learning of representations via graph neural networks. Nat. Mach. Intell. **4**(3), 279–287 (2022)
46. Watanabe, N., Ohnuki, Y., Sakakibara, Y.: Deep learning integration of molecular and interactome data for protein-compound interaction prediction. J. Cheminformatics **13**(1), 36 (2021)
47. Wu, Z., et al.: Moleculenet: a benchmark for molecular machine learning. Chem. Sci. **9**(2), 513–530 (2018)
48. Xia, J., et al.: Mole-BERT: rethinking pre-training graph neural networks for molecules. In: The Eleventh International Conference on Learning Representations (2022)
49. Xiong, Z., et al.: Pushing the boundaries of molecular representation for drug discovery with the graph attention mechanism. J. Med. Chem. **63**(16), 8749–8760 (2019)
50. Xu, K., Hu, W., Leskovec, J., Jegelka, S.: How powerful are graph neural networks? arXiv preprint arXiv:1810.00826 (2018)
51. Yang, K., et al.: Analyzing learned molecular representations for property prediction. J. Chem. Inf. Model. **59**(8), 3370–3388 (2019)
52. Zaidi, S., et al.: Pre-training via denoising for molecular property prediction. arXiv preprint arXiv:2206.00133 (2022)
53. Zhou, G., et al.: Uni-Mol: a universal 3D molecular representation learning framework (2023)

Cross-Layer Profiling of IoTBench

Fan Zhang[1] [ID], Chenxi Wang[1,2] [ID], Chunjie Luo[1,3] [ID], and Lei Wang[1,2,3([envelope])] [ID]

[1] Institute of Computing Technology, Chinese Academy of Sciences,
Beijing 100190, China
{zhangfan,wangchenxi21s,luochunjie,wanglei_2011}@ict.ac.cn
[2] School of Computer Science and Technology,
University of Chinese Academy of Sciences, Beijing 100049, China
[3] International Open Benchmark Council (BenchCouncil), Beijing, China

Abstract. The rapid expansion of the Internet of Things (IoT) industry highlights the significance of workload characterization when evaluating microprocessors tailored for IoT applications. The streamlined yet comprehensive system stack of an IoT system is highly suitable for synergistic software and hardware co-design. This stack comprises various layers, including programming languages, frameworks, runtime environments, instruction set architectures (ISA), operating systems (OS), and microarchitecture. These layers can be bucketed into three primary categories: the intermediate representation (IR) layer, the ISA layer, and the microarchitecture layer. Consequently, conducting cross-layer workload characterization constitutes the initial stride in IoT design, especially in co-design. In this paper, we use a cross-layer profiling methodology to conduct an exhaustive analysis of IoTBench-an IoT workload benchmark. Each layer's key metrics, including instruction, data, and branch locality, were meticulously examined. Experimental evaluations were performed on both ARM and X86 architectures. Our findings revealed general patterns in how IoTBench's metrics fluctuate with different input data. Additionally, we noted that the same metrics could demonstrate varied characteristics across different layers, suggesting that isolated layer analysis might yield incomplete conclusions. Besides, our cross-layer profiling disclosed that the convolution task, characterized by deeply nested loops, significantly amplified branch locality at the microarchitecture layer on the ARM platform. Interestingly, optimization with the GNU C++ compiler (G++), intended to boost performance, had a counterproductive effect, exacerbating the branch locality issue and resulting in performance degradation.

Keywords: IoT · Benchmark · Cross-layer profiling

1 Introduction

IoT enables us to connect to the internet using a wide range of devices, greatly enhancing our daily lives. The IoT industry is experiencing rapid growth, as highlighted in a report by IoT Analytics [2]. It states that the number of IoT

© The Author(s), under exclusive license to Springer Nature Singapore Pte Ltd. 2024
S. Hunold et al. (Eds.): Bench 2023, LNCS 14521, pp. 71–86, 2024.
https://doi.org/10.1007/978-981-97-0316-6_5

devices increased by 18% in 2022, reaching 14.3 billion, projected to reach 16.7 billion in 2023. The IoT devices span from simple thermometers to sophisticated smartphones and self-driving cars. Furthermore, IoT applications encompass diverse scenarios, including cloud and fog computing [10]. Consequently, selecting appropriate processors for specific IoT applications becomes crucial, and IoT benchmarks serve as an effective tool in this process.

IoT system always has a streamlined but comprehensive system stack, which is highly suitable for synergistic software and hardware co-design. And workload characterization plays a crucial role in exploring co-design. There are three main layers in the workloads' system stack for characterization: the IR, ISA, and microarchitecture layers. The IR layer, which is ISA-independent, includes programming languages and programming frameworks. The ISA layer, which is microarchitecture-independent, consists of runtime environments and the ISA, such as the GNU C Library (glibc) and the X86 ISA. The microarchitecture layer is where the actual execution of machine code occurs on a processor, and its performance can be measured using hardware performance counters.

Existing IoT benchmarks commonly employ performance metrics based on the microarchitecture layer for evaluation. For example, IoTBench [5] incorporates metrics such as iterations per second and cycle per instruction (CPI). In addition to IoT benchmarks, other general workload analyses also primarily focus on microarchitecture layer [3,7,8,12,13,15,17]. Except for the microarchitecture layer, the IR and ISA layers are also important and allow researchers to do analysis before running the workloads on the specific hardwares [9,16]. All those researches only focus on the characteristics of one layer, but focusing solely on a single layer may result in an incomplete understanding of workload characteristics and potentially biased conclusions [18]. Our experiments on IoTBench also support this observation, highlighting the need for comprehensive cross-layer profiling to better understand workload characteristics.

This paper proposes a cross-layer profiling approach to comprehensively analyze IoTBench for the first time. We deconstruct the system stack into three layers: the IR, ISA, and microarchitecture layers. Subsequently, we investigate instruction, data, and branch locality across these three layers. Our experiments cover both ARM and X86 architectures to provide a comprehensive analysis. The details of our evaluation methodology are shown in Sect. 3. The contributions of our study are as follows:

- We conducted a novel cross-layer profiling of IoTBench, which yielded insightful results. Our findings revealed significant correlations between the IR and ISA layers, while a weaker correlation was observed between the ISA and microarchitecture layers. Furthermore, we observed that different configurations of input data had varying impacts on the metrics. The size of the data had a significant impact on data locality, specifically at the IR and ISA layers. When the data size doubled, the data locality also doubled. However, there were no linear rules for the microarchitecture layer. The dimension of the data predominantly influenced instruction locality. For each increase in dimension by one, the instruction reuse distance at the IR layer increased by approximately 20%, and at the ISA layer, it increased by about 10%. Branch locality was mainly affected by the data dimension. Whenever the dimension increased by one, the branch locality increased by around 5% at both the IR and ISA layers. However, the data type also influenced the branch locality at the microarchitecture layer. When the dimension was one, and the type was integer, it had the smallest values.

– We conducted a comparative experiment between typical ARM (Kunpeng 920) and X86 (Intel Xeon Gold 5120T) platforms. Our cross-layer profiling revealed that the convolution task of IoTBench, characterized by deeply nested loops, significantly increased branch locality at the microarchitecture layer on the typical ARM platform. Surprisingly, the G++ '-O3' optimization worsened this issue. With '-O3', branch locality moderately increased at the ISA layer (1.4 times), but significantly increased at the microarchitecture layer (485.6 times). As a result, the typical ARM platform had a much higher branch locality and lower instructions per cycle (IPC) compared to the typical X86 platform. This suggests a mismatch between G++'s optimization capabilities (the ISA layer optimization) and the branch predictor implementation (the microarchitecture layer design) on the tested ARM platform. To address this, we use G++'s '-O1' optimization for the convolution task on Kunpeng 920, which reduced branch locality by 0.45 times and increased execution speed by 1.5 times.

2   Background and Related Work

2.1   IoT Benchmarks

There are several commonly used IoT benchmarks available. Dhrystone [19], developed by Reinhold P. Weicker in 1984, is a synthetic computing benchmark widely used for general processors. However, Dhrystone only focuses on integer operations and has limitations, including its susceptibility to compiler influence. In 2009, the Embedded Microprocessor Benchmark Consortium (EEMBC) introduced CoreMark [6] as an improved alternative to address the shortcomings of Dhrystone. CoreMark eliminates the impact of compilation optimization on results and incorporates specific rules for execution and reporting. Despite these advancements, both Dhrystone and CoreMark have fixed input data formats, which may not meet the requirements of diverse scenarios. To address this limitation, IoTBench [5] was developed in 2022, offering three tasks: list operation, matrix processing, and convolution. IoTBench's key advantage lies in its ability to easily adjust input data, including data scales, dimensions, and types. The detailed information on workloads and configuration space is shown in Table 1.

2.2   Workload Characterizations

Each workload execution encompasses multiple layers, which can generally be categorized into three main layers: the IR layer, the ISA layer, and the microarchitecture layer. The IR layer incorporates programming languages and frameworks and is independent of the ISA layer. For instance, when the Javac compiler

Table 1. IoTBench workloads

Workload	Data size	Data dimension	Data type
List search/sort	Any	1/2/3	INT/Float32/Double64
Matrix add/multiply	Any	1/2/3	INT/Float32/Double64
Convolution	Any	1/2/3	INT/Float32/Double64

compiles a Java file, it is transformed into bytecodes and packaged as a Java archive (JAR) file. The JAR file is associated with the IR layer. The ISA layer comprises runtime environments and the ISA itself. Examples include the GNU C Library (glibc) library and the X86 ISA. Finally, the machine codes are instantiated as an OS process, executing on the processor as an instruction stream specific to the underlying microarchitecture. In summary, the IR layer encompasses programming languages and frameworks, the ISA layer includes runtime environments and the ISA itself, and the microarchitecture layer involves the actual execution of machine codes on the processor, facilitated by the OS.

Existing research has predominantly focused on individual layers. Shao et al. [16] were the first to propose an ISA-independent method for workload characterization. They utilized computing, control, and memory indicators to quantify program characteristics. Their findings revealed that including ISA-related elements in workload behavior analysis resulted in significant deviations due to limitations in the number of registers, making it challenging to effectively reflect the program's essential characteristics. Hoste et al. [9] introduced a microarchitecture-independent workload characterization approach to mitigate the impact of microarchitecture defects. By instrumenting the binary instruction stream of a program, they analyzed 47 indicators, including instruction proportion, data span, and misprediction rate. A significant body of research has concentrated on the microarchitecture layer [3,7,12,13], where characteristics are measured based on hardware performance counters. Although the time overhead is relatively small, the analysis results are closely tied to the specific microarchitecture being studied. In summary, while some approaches have aimed to be ISA-independent or microarchitecture-independent, a considerable amount of research has focused on the microarchitecture layer, leveraging hardware performance counters for workload characterization.

However, focusing solely on the characteristics of a single layer may result in biased conclusions. To address this limitation, Wang et al. [18] introduced a comprehensive methodology called Whole-Picture Workload Characterization (WPC). This methodology incorporates three layers and aims to identify the proportional contributions of critical components to specific bottlenecks. Drawing inspiration from WPC [18], this paper adopts a cross-layer profiling approach to investigate IoTBench, enabling a more comprehensive understanding of its behavior and performance. By considering multiple layers, we can uncover the inter-dependencies and inter-actions among different components, leading to a more accurate assessment of the workload's characteristics.

3 Evaluation Methodology

Workload profiling is the basis and premise for guiding system design and co-optimization of software and hardware. Most of the existing workload profiling only focuses on the performance of the microarchitecture layer, and lacks consideration of the essential behavioral characteristics of the workload, dependent libraries, runtime environment, etc. Drawing inspiration from WPC, this paper uses a cross-layer profiling method to comprehensively analyze the characteristics of IoTBench.

3.1 Methodology

The workload under investigation is IoTBench, which comprises three tasks: list, matrix, and convolution. IoTBench offers three configurable input parameters: data size, data dimension, and data type. By varying the values of these parameters, we can observe the impact of input data on program characteristics. Regarding the data size parameter, we explore values that cover the L1 data cache size. For the data dimension parameter, we conduct tests using one, two, and three-dimensional data. Additionally, we evaluate different data types, including integer, float, and double. To obtain cross-layer metrics, we divide the system stack into three layers: IR, ISA, and microarchitecture. Given our focus on memory access and control behavior, we select three key metrics across these layers: instruction locality, data locality, and branch locality. Further details about these metrics are provided in Sect. 3.2. Next, we perform the profiling in the following steps:

- Analyze raw data. We analyze the mean and standard deviation of the raw data to identify cross-layer variation trends for different tasks under varied data input configurations.
- Do fusion analysis. We utilize two metrics: Z-Score [1] and Pearson coefficient [14], to explore the relationships among the three layers. The Z-Score is employed to mitigate discrepancies resulting from different data units across the layers. It is a statistical measure, calculated by the formula: $Z = (X - \mu)/\sigma$, where X is the raw data point, μ is the mean of the data set, and σ is the standard deviation. The resulting Z-Score indicates how many standard deviations a particular data point is away from the mean. It is employed in the analysis to mitigate discrepancies resulting from different data units across the layers. On the other hand, the Pearson coefficient is utilized to quantify the linear dependency between the layers. It is computed based on the covariance of the two variables divided by the product of their standard deviations. It ranges from -1 to 1, where a value of 1 indicates a perfect positive linear relationship, -1 represents a perfect negative linear relationship, and 0 indicates no linear relationship between the variables.
- Draw conclusions and insights.

3.2 Metric

As presented in Table 2, this paper utilizes three key metrics to investigate the characteristics of IoTBench: instruction locality, data locality, and branch locality. These metrics provide insights into the memory access behavior (instruction and data locality) and control behavior (branch locality) exhibited by the workloads. Instruction locality reflects the front-end pauses of the pipeline and the better the instruction locality, the less front-end pauses. Data locality reflects the back-end pauses of the pipeline and the better the data locality, the less back-end pauses. Branch locality reflects the complexity of branch prediction and the better the branch locality, the easier it is to predict branch results. To analyze these metrics across different layers of the system stack, specific counterparts are selected at IR, ISA, and microarchitecture layers. At the IR and ISA layers, the metrics chosen are instruction reuse distance, data reuse distance, and branch entropy. Instruction reuse distance measures the average number of instructions between two consecutive accesses to the same instruction address. A higher value indicates poorer instruction locality. Similarly, data reuse distance calculates the average number of data accesses between two consecutive accesses to the same data address, with a higher value indicating poorer data locality. For branch locality, the linear branch entropy metric is adopted, as introduced by Yokota et al. [20]. The formula for linear branch entropy is defined as $H(X) = 2 \cdot \min(p(x), 1 - p(x))$, where $p(x)$ represents the probability of taking the branch x. At the microarchitecture layer, the corresponding metrics are instruction MPKI, data MPKI, and branch MPKI. These metrics provide insights into the cache misses or mispredictions associated with instructions, data accesses, and branches, respectively.

Table 2. Metrics

Layer	Instruction locality	Data locality	Branch locality
IR	Instruction reuse distance	Data reuse distance	Branch entropy
ISA	Instruction reuse distance	Data reuse distance	Branch entropy
Microarchitecture	L1I MPKI	L1D MPKI	Branch MPKI

3.3 Tool

Table 3 enumerates the tools utilized in this study. The LLVM compiler [11] is utilized to obtain the IR code of the workload. By incorporating instrumentation code and compiling it alongside the tested code, we can extract the instrumentation analysis code of the program. To obtain the ISA code of the workload, we employ DynamoRIO [4]. DynamoRIO is also based on instrumentation techniques, but it offers a comprehensive interface and pre-built tools. By leveraging these tools, we collect the metric values associated with the ISA layer. For metrics pertaining to the microarchitecture layer, we utilize Perf. Perf is a native tool integrated into Linux that retrieves metric values by accessing the hardware performance counters.

Table 3. Tools

Layer	Tool
IR	LLVM 9.0
ISA	DynamoRIO 9.0.1
Microarchitecture	Perf 5.4.235 (X86), Perf 4.18.0 (ARM)

4   Experiment and Result

Our experiments involved testing the workload on two platforms: ARM and X86. ARM is a widely used platform in IoT, while X86 served as a comparative experiment platform for analysis and comparison purposes. For each platform, we conducted a profiling of three metrics for IoTBench tasks across different layers. The IoTBench tasks were compiled using the G++9.4 compiler with the optimization level set to 3. More configurations of the platforms are provided in Table 4.

Table 4. Configuration details

	ARM	X86
Processor	Kunpeng920	Intel(R) Xeon(R) Gold 5120T CPU @ 2.20 GHz
L1D Cache	64 KB	32 KB
L1I Cache	64 KB	32 KB
L2 Cache	512 KB	1024 KB
L3 Cache	32768 KB	19712 KB
Memory	382 GB	376 GB
G++ Compiler	9.4	9.4
G++ Optimization	-O3	-O3

4.1   Experiment on ARM Platform

4.1.1   Instruction Locality

In Fig. 1a, the instruction locality of three tasks from IoTBench on the ARM platform is depicted across three layers. We varied the configurations of the input data, represented on the x-axis of Fig. 1b, and calculated the average and standard deviation of the three tasks: list, matrix, and convolution. It is evident that the instruction locality remains relatively consistent across all three layers for the three tasks. The observed differences are within a factor of two, indicating that variations in input data configurations have minimal impact on instruction locality. Among the three configuration variables (data size, data dimension, and data type), experiments indicate that instruction locality is closely associated with data dimension. Figure 1b provides the instruction locality of IoTBench across three layers with varied configurations of the input data, revealing the following trends: (i) At the IR and ISA layers, instruction locality increases as the data dimension grows. Specifically, there is approximately a 20% increase in instruction locality from one-dimensional data to two-dimensional data, and a 10% increase from two-dimensional data to three-dimensional data. This can be attributed to the increased calculation of array subscripts and the presence of nested for loops resulting from higher data dimensions. These additional instructions contribute to the observed rise in instruction locality. (ii) In the microarchitecture layer, the changing trend of instruction locality is more complex, and no clear rule can be discerned. However, on the whole, instruction locality exhibits relative stability, with a CoV of less than 17%.

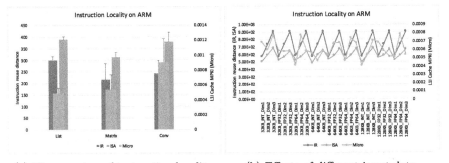

(a) The overview of instruction locality.   (b) Effects of different input data.

Fig. 1. Instruction locality of IoTBench on ARM platform.

Figure 2 illustrates the correlation analysis of instruction locality across three layers. Several observations can be made: (i) The analysis results vary among the three layers. In Fig. 2a, it can be observed that the trends of IR and ISA are consistent, whereas microarchitecture exhibits a different pattern. Specifically, for the list task, the instruction locality values are above average at the IR and ISA layers, but below average at the microarchitecture layer. For the matrix task, the values consistently remain below average across all three layers. In the case of the convolution task, the values are below average at the IR layer but above average at the ISA and microarchitecture layers. (ii) A strong linear relationship (Pearson correlation coefficient of 0.76) exists between the IR and ISA layers. However, the values between the ISA and microarchitecture layers exhibit linear independence (Pearson correlation coefficient of -0.13). This observation suggests that compared to the IR and ISA layers, the microarchitecture layer becomes more complex and relies heavily on specific implementations.

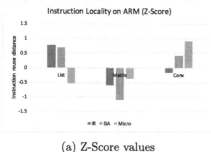

Task	IR-ISA	ISA-Micro
List	0.53	0.16
Matrix	0.81	-0.49
Conv	0.95	-0.05
IoTBench	0.78	0.08

(a) Z-Score values   (b) Pearson's coefficients

Fig. 2. Correlation analysis of instruction locality among three layers.

4.1.2   Data Locality

Figure 3a presents the data locality of three tasks from IoTBench on ARM across three layers. Several observations can be made: Firstly, the data localities of the three tasks exhibit significant variance across all three layers, indicating that different configurations of input data have a substantial impact on data locality. Additionally, the change in data locality is predominantly influenced by the size of the input data, as depicted in Fig. 3b. This figure illustrates that data locality increases as the data size grows across all three layers. Specifically: (i) At the IR and ISA layers, doubling the data size leads to a doubling of data locality. (ii) At the microarchitecture layer, there is an approximately 1.4-fold increase in data locality from 32 KB to 64 KB. However, the increase is more substantial, approximately 3.9-fold, from 64 KB to 128 KB. This discrepancy can be attributed to the fact that the L1D cache of the ARM platform has a size of 64 KB. Consequently, when the data size exceeds the L1D cache capacity, the L1D cache MPKI experiences a significant increase.

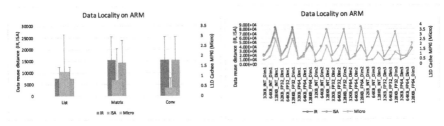

(a) The overview of data locality.   (b) Effects of different input data.

Fig. 3. Data locality of IoTBench on ARM platform.

Figure 4 depicts the correlation analysis of data locality across three layers. Several observations can be made: (i) The analysis results vary among the three layers. In Fig. 4a, it is evident that the change trends of IR and ISA layers are consistent, while the microarchitecture layer exhibits a different pattern. Specifically, for the list task, the data locality values are below average at the IR and ISA layers but above average at the microarchitecture layer. For the matrix task, the values consistently remain above average across all three layers. In the case of the convolution task, the values are above average at the IR and ISA layers but below average at the microarchitecture layer. (ii) There is a strong linear relationship (Pearson correlation coefficient of 0.99) between the IR and ISA layers. Additionally, there is a moderate linear relationship (Pearson correlation coefficient of 0.45) between the ISA and microarchitecture layers.

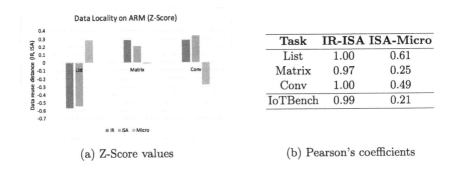

Task	IR-ISA	ISA-Micro
List	1.00	0.61
Matrix	0.97	0.25
Conv	1.00	0.49
IoTBench	0.99	0.21

(a) Z-Score values   (b) Pearson's coefficients

Fig. 4. Correlation analysis of data locality among three layers.

4.1.3 Branch Locality

Figure 5a illustrates the branch locality of three tasks from IoTBench on ARM across three layers. Several observations can be made: The microarchitecture layer exhibits significantly higher branch locality values for the convolution task compared to the other tasks. Specifically, the branch locality for the convolution task is 21 times larger than that of the list task and 107 times larger than that of the matrix task at the microarchitecture layer. One of the reasons for this significant difference is the presence of deep nesting loops within the convolution task, which poses challenges for branch prediction. The complex loop structures make it difficult for the processor to accurately predict the outcome of conditional branches, resulting in a higher branch locality. Figure 5b presents the variation of branch locality for the convolution task with different input data configurations. The following observations can be made: (i) At the IR and ISA layers, branch locality shows a slight increase with data dimension. The coefficient of variation (CoV) is 7% at the IR layer and 3% at the ISA layer. (ii) However, at the microarchitecture layer, the change in branch locality is drastic. The CoV is 46%, and the maximum value is three thousand times larger than the minimum value. The minimum value occurs when the data is one-dimensional and consists of integers.

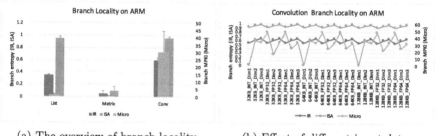

(a) The overview of branch locality.   (b) Effect of different input data.

Fig. 5. Branch locality of IoTBench and convolution task on ARM platform.

Further experiments conducted in our study have revealed that the significant increase in branch locality at the microarchitecture layer is primarily attributed to G++ compiler optimization. Figure 6a demonstrates the impact of different optimization levels (ranging from -O0 to -O3) on branch locality. The results indicate that at the IR layer, the branch locality remains consistent across different optimization levels. However, at the ISA and microarchitecture layers, the branch locality increases. Specifically, at the ISA layer, the branch locality experiences a moderate increase of approximately 1.4 times. In contrast, at the microarchitecture layer, the branch locality undergoes a dramatic increase of approximately 485.6 times. This observation suggests that the specific implementation of the branch predictor at the microarchitecture layer on the ARM platform does not perform well in conjunction with G++ compiler optimization. Actually, with the G++ optimization levels ranging from -O0 to -O3, the number of branch instructions decrease (Fig. 6b), but the performance is worse (Fig. 6c).

Figure 7 presents the correlation analysis of branch locality across three layers. Several observations can be made: (i) The analysis results differ among

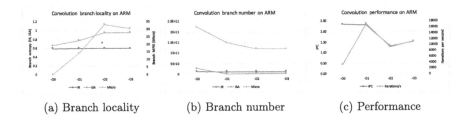

(a) Branch locality   (b) Branch number   (c) Performance

Fig. 6. The effect of G++ optimization.

the three layers. In Fig. 7a, the change trends of the IR and ISA layers exhibit consistency, whereas the microarchitecture layer displays a different pattern. Specifically: For the list task, the branch locality values are above average at the IR and ISA layers but below average at the microarchitecture layer. For the matrix task, the branch locality values consistently remain below average across all three layers. For the convolution task, the branch locality values consistently remain above average across all three layers. (ii) The linear correlations of the three tasks also differ. For the convolution task, there is a strong linear correlation between the IR and ISA layers (Pearson correlation coefficient of 0.99), indicating a close relationship. However, the ISA and microarchitecture layers are found to be linearly independent (Pearson correlation coefficient of 0.01). For the list and matrix tasks, there is a weak linear correlation between the IR and ISA layers (Pearson correlation coefficient of -0.2 for the list task, 0.49 for the matrix task). However, a stronger linear correlation is observed between the ISA and microarchitecture layers (Pearson correlation coefficient of 0.55 for the list task, 0.60 for the matrix task).

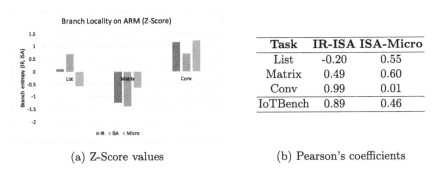

Task	IR-ISA	ISA-Micro
List	-0.20	0.55
Matrix	0.49	0.60
Conv	0.99	0.01
IoTBench	0.89	0.46

(a) Z-Score values   (b) Pearson's coefficients

Fig. 7. Correlation analysis of branch locality among three layers.

4.2   Comparative Experiment of ARM and X86

Figure 8 presents a comparison of locality results between ARM and x86 architectures. Generally, both ARM and x86 exhibit similar trends in terms of instruction

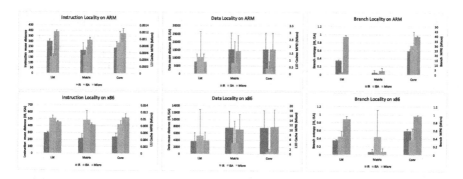

Fig. 8. Locality comparison between ARM and X86.

and data locality, but branch locality differs significantly. Specifically, the variance of instruction locality is relatively small, while the variance of data locality is relatively large. Notably, the most prominent characteristic of branch locality is the exceptionally high value observed for the convolution task on the ARM platform at the microarchitecture layer.

Instruction locality demonstrates minimal variation across different input data for both the ARM and x86 platforms. The coefficient of variation (CoV) remains below 14% for all three tasks at each of the three layers. Furthermore, the maximum value of instruction locality does not exceed 1.8 times the minimum value for any of the three tasks. Figure 9 illustrates that instruction locality is primarily influenced by data dimensions. Notably, at the IR and ISA layers, instruction locality shows a slight increase with the growth of data dimensions. However, at the microarchitecture layer, the relationship becomes more intricate and multifaceted.

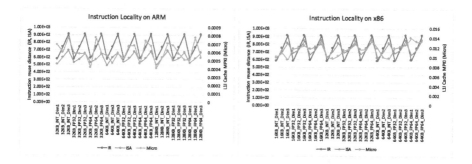

Fig. 9. Instruction locality comparison between ARM and X86.

Data locality changes drastically with different input data on both ARM and X86 platform. The variance in data locality is large and the CoV for different configurations is about 60% on both ARM and X86 at three layers. As discussed above in Sect. 4.1.2, this is because the size of the input data is different. The variation of instruction locality with data size is shown in Fig. 10. We can see that, at IR and ISA level, for every doubling of data size, data locality also doubles. At microarchitecture layer, when data size is larger than L1D, the L1 data MPKI will increase significantly.

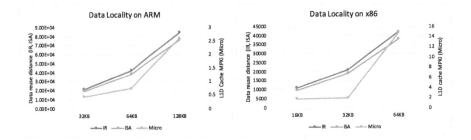

Fig. 10. Data locality comparison between ARM and X86.

As shown in Fig. 11, branch locality shows different trends on ARM and X86 platforms. At microarchitecture layer, the ARM's branch locality is much larger than that of X86. ARM's branch MPKI is 1.43, 0.28 and 30.52 for list, matrix and convolution task, while X86's branch MPKI is 0.45, 0.45 and 0.36 for those three tasks. We can see that, the branch MPKI of the convolution algorithm on the ARM is particularly large. As discussed above in Sect. 4.1.3, the intricate nature of the convolution algorithm, combined with limitations in G++ optimization techniques for ARM, leads to extremely high values of branch locality at the microarchitecture layer. Figure 11c illustrates that as the optimization level increases, the execution speed improves on x86 platforms. However, on ARM platforms, the execution speed initially increases but eventually decreases with higher optimization levels. The convolution task achieves optimal performance on the ARM platform with an optimization level of -O1. In this configuration, the branch locality is reduced by 0.45 times, and the execution speed is improved by 1.5 times compared to -O3 optimization level.

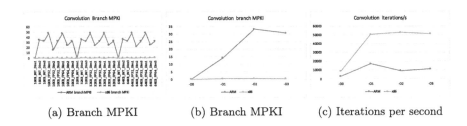

(a) Branch MPKI   (b) Branch MPKI   (c) Iterations per second

Fig. 11. G++ optimization comparison between ARM and X86.

4.3   Experiment Summary

We can summarize the key findings of the experiment as follows:

- The profiling revealed that different metrics are influenced by specific configuration parameters of the input data. Specifically, the instruction locality showed an increase with data dimensions, data locality increased with data size, and branch locality exhibited an increase with both data dimension and data type. These observations highlight the diverse impacts of input data configurations on various performance metrics.
- A strong linear correlation was observed between the IR and ISA layers, indicating that changes in the IR layer significantly affect the resulting ISA layer. However, a weak correlation was found between the ISA and microarchitecture layers, suggesting that factors beyond the ISA layer influence the microarchitecture layer's behavior.
- The ARM platform has a weakness in its branch predictor when dealing with deep nested for loops that are optimized by G++. This suggests that the ARM architecture and G++ optimization may not work well together when it comes to complex loop structures.

5   Conclusions

The paper introduces a novel cross-layer profiling approach to conduct a comprehensive analysis of IoTBench, considering the system stack divided into three distinct layers: IR, ISA, and microarchitecture layers. The study reveals several key findings: (1) The same metric exhibits diverse characteristics across different layers. Consequently, analyzing each layer in isolation may result in conflicting conclusions. This highlights the importance of considering multiple layers simultaneously for a holistic understanding of the workload. (2) A notable observation is that deep nesting of loops can lead to poor performance of the branch predictor on ARM when used in conjunction with G++ optimization. This finding emphasizes the impact of code structure and compiler optimizations on microarchitecture behavior.

Acknowledgments. This work is supported by the Strategic Priority Research Program of the Chinese Academy of Sciences, Grant No. XDA0320000 and XDA0320300.

References

1. Abdi, H., Williams, L.J., et al.: Normalizing data. Encyclopedia of research design **1** (2010)
2. IoT Analytics: State of IoT-Spring 2023 (2023). https://iot-analytics.com/number-connected-iot-devices/
3. Bienia, C., Kumar, S., Singh, J.P., Li, K.: The PARSEC benchmark suite: characterization and architectural implications. In: Proceedings of the 17th International Conference on Parallel Architectures and Compilation Techniques, pp. 72–81 (2008)

4. Bruening, D., Zhao, Q., Kleckner, R.: DynamoRIO: dynamic instrumentation tool platform (2020). http://www.dynamorio.org
5. Chen, S., Luo, C., Gao, W., Wang, L.: IoTBench: a data centrical and configurable IoT benchmark suite. BenchCouncil Trans. Benchmarks Stand. Eval. **2**(4), 100091 (2022)
6. (EEMBC) EMBC: CoreMark Benchmark (2021). https://www.eembc.org/coremark/
7. Ferdman, M., et al.: Clearing the clouds: a study of emerging scale-out workloads on modern hardware. ACM SIGPLAN Not. **47**(4), 37–48 (2012)
8. Guthaus, M.R., Ringenberg, J.S., Ernst, D., Austin, T.M., Mudge, T., Brown, R.B.: MiBench: a free, commercially representative embedded benchmark suite. In: Proceedings of the Fourth Annual IEEE International Workshop on Workload Characterization, WWC-4 (Cat. No. 01EX538), pp. 3–14. IEEE (2001)
9. Hoste, K., Eeckhout, L.: Microarchitecture-independent workload characterization. IEEE Micro **27**(3), 63–72 (2007)
10. Laghari, A.A., Wu, K., Laghari, R.A., Ali, M., Khan, A.A.: A review and state of art of Internet of Things (IoT). Arch. Comput. Methods Eng. 1–19 (2021)
11. Lattner, C., Adve, V.: LLVM: a compilation framework for lifelong program analysis & transformation. In: International Symposium on Code Generation and Optimization, CGO 2004, pp. 75–86. IEEE (2004)
12. Limaye, A., Adegbija, T.: A workload characterization of the SPEC CPU2017 benchmark suite. In: 2018 IEEE International Symposium on Performance Analysis of Systems and Software (ISPASS), pp. 149–158. IEEE (2018)
13. Panda, R., Song, S., Dean, J., John, L.K.: Wait of a decade: did SPEC CPU 2017 broaden the performance horizon? In: 2018 IEEE International Symposium on High Performance Computer Architecture (HPCA) (2018)
14. Pearson, K.: On the theory of contingency and its relation to association and normal correlation (1904)
15. Poovey, J.A., Conte, T.M., Levy, M., Gal-On, S.: A benchmark characterization of the EEMBC benchmark suite. IEEE Micro **29**(5), 18–29 (2009)
16. Shao, Y.S., Brooks, D.: ISA-independent workload characterization and its implications for specialized architectures. In: 2013 IEEE International Symposium on Performance Analysis of Systems and Software (ISPASS), pp. 245–255. IEEE (2013)
17. Wang, L., Ren, R., Zhan, J., Jia, Z.: Characterization and architectural implications of big data workloads. In: 2016 IEEE International Symposium on Performance Analysis of Systems and Software (ISPASS), pp. 145–146. IEEE (2016)
18. Wang, L., et al.: WPC: whole-picture workload characterization. arXiv preprint arXiv:2302.12954 (2023)
19. Weicker, R.P.: Dhrystone: a synthetic systems programming benchmark. Commun. ACM **27**(10), 1013–1030 (1984)
20. Yokota, T., Ootsu, K., Baba, T.: Introducing entropies for representing program behavior and branch predictor performance. In: Proceedings of the 2007 Workshop on Experimental Computer Science, pp. 17-es (2007)

MMDBench: A Benchmark for Hybrid Query in Multimodal Database

Along Mao[1,2], Chuan Hu[1,2], Chong Li[1], Huajin Wang[1], Junjian Rao[1,2], Kainan Wang[1,2], and Zhihong Shen[1(✉)]

[1] Computer Network Information Center, Chinese Academy of Sciences, Beijing, China
{almao,huchuan,lichong,wanghj,jjrao,knwang,bluejoe}@cnic.cn
[2] University of Chinese Academy of Sciences, Beijing, China

Abstract. Multimodal data, integrating various types of data like images, text, audio, and video, has become prevalent in the era of big data. However, there is a gap in benchmarking specifically designed for multimodal data, as existing benchmarks primarily focus on traditional and multimodel databases, lacking a comprehensive framework for evaluating systems handling multimodal data. In this paper, we present a novel benchmark program, named MMDBench, specifically designed to evaluate the performance of multimodal databases that accommodate various data modalities, including structured data, images, and text. The workload of MMDBench is composed of eleven tasks, inspired by real-world scenarios in social networks, where multiple data modalities are involved. Each task simulates a specific scenario that necessitates the integration of at least two distinct data modalities. To demonstrate the effectiveness of MMDBench, we have developed a hybrid database system to execute the workload and have uncovered diverse characteristics of multimodal databases in the execution of hybrid queries.

Keywords: Benchmark · Multimodal Database · Hybrid Query

1 Introduction

In the era of big data, the quantity and variety of data are growing at an unprecedented pace. Among these diverse data types, multimodal data has garnered significant attention. Multimodal data refers to the integration of multiple modes or types of data, such as images, text, audio, and video. This data often contains abundant and complementary information, enabling a more comprehensive understanding of underlying concepts and phenomena. Multimodal data has become increasingly prevalent in various domains, including social media analysis [4], healthcare [3], knowledge graph (Fig. 1) [15], and so on. Moreover,

Supported by National Key R&D Program of China(Grant No. 2022YFF0711600), National Key R&D Program of China(Grant No. 2021YFF0704200) and Informatization Plan of Chinese Academy of Sciences(Grant No. CAS-WX2022GC-02).

the emergence of artificial intelligence technologies has provided robust support and impetus for multimodal data analysis, enabling effective exploration and utilization of the latent information within multimodal data.

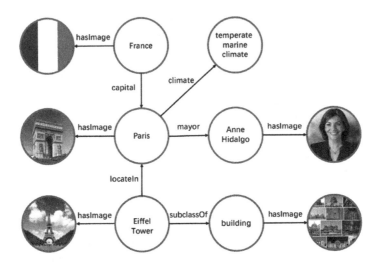

Fig. 1. An Example of Multimodal Data: Multimodal Knowledge Graph [21]

Despite significant advancements in benchmarking techniques for traditional databases and even multimodel databases, there still exists a gap when it comes to benchmarking specifically designed for multimodal data. Existing benchmarks primarily focus on relational databases [12], NoSQL databases [5], or evaluate the performance of multimodel data management systems [7,10,18,19]. In recent years, there has been an emergence of multimodal data management systems [16,20] that can handle both structured and unstructured data. However, there is a lack of comprehensive benchmarking frameworks specifically tailored for evaluating the performance of systems handling multimodal data.

In order to evaluate the performance advantages and bottlenecks of such systems in executing hybrid queries, enforce manufacturers to continuously improve the performance of the system, and promote the further development of new database technology, we put forward a benchmark which is called MMDBench. As shown in Fig. 2. It provides a multimodal data generator and a multimodal data analytic workload in social network scenario. The contributions of MMD-Bench are as follows:

- **Data Generator.** We have developed a generator capable of producing multimodal data in social network scenarios. It uses the property graph model as the foundation to associate unstructured data such as text, and images with the graph data. The generator supports the generation of data in various scales while adhering to the distribution patterns observed in real-world scenarios.

- **Query Workload.** We have designed a workload for hybrid queries that simulate typical operations of querying structured and unstructured data in social networks.
- **Benchmark Framework.** We have designed and implemented a unified framework that provides interfaces for system integration to facilitate the completion of benchmark testing. This framework serves as a standardized platform for evaluating different systems under consistent conditions, ensuring fairness and comparability in performance evaluations.
- **Experiment.** We selected several systems and databases for experimental validation and summarized the characteristics and applicable scenarios of hybrid queries based on the experimental results.

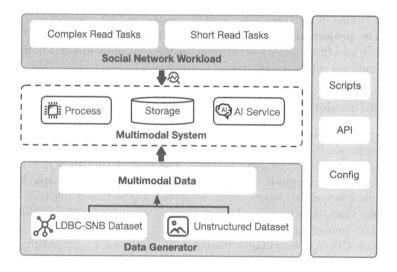

Fig. 2. Overview of MMDBench

This paper is organized as follows. In Sect. 2, we review related work in benchmark for multimodal data, highlighting the limitations of existing benchmarks. In Sect. 3, the modalities of different data are covered. In Sects. 4 and 5, details of the data generator and workload are introduced. The experimental results are shown in Sect. 6. Lastly, the conclusion is covered in Sect. 7.

2   Related Work

In the field of databases, conducting benchmark testing and performance evaluation for different types of data (structured, unstructured, and multi-model) is of great importance. Structured data refers to tabular data commonly found in traditional relational databases, while unstructured data includes data in formats such as text, images, and audio. On the other hand, multi-model data refers to database systems that can simultaneously handle multiple data models. This section provides an overview of the data models supported by these benchmark testing programs.

2.1 Single Model Benchmark Programs

Linkbench [1] is a benchmark tool developed for evaluating graph database systems. It provides a set of simple CRUD (Create, Read, Update, Delete) operations to replicate query patterns in Facebook's graph database TAO [2]. LDBC-SNB [6] is a comprehensive graph database benchmark. It evaluates systems across various social network workloads, including complex queries, updates, and data generation.

NOBENCH [5] is a benchmark testing tool developed for evaluating NoSQL database systems. It provides basic NoSQL queries for JSON documents, including selection, projection, and aggregation operations. By using NOBENCH, the performance and functionality of different NoSQL database systems in handling JSON documents can be evaluated.

2.2 Multi-model Benchmark Programs

Unibench [18,19] is a benchmark testing tool designed for evaluating multi-model database systems. It is designed to simulate various data operations and queries in multi-model data management systems. The goal of Unibench is to provide a repeatable and comparable way to assess the performance and capabilities of different multi-model database systems. Unibench supports multiple data models such as relational, document, and graph models, allowing for the simulation of complex data management and query tasks.

M2Bench [10] is a benchmark testing tool developed for evaluating multi-model database systems. It focuses on simulating multi-model queries and transaction processing in multi-model data management systems. M2Bench provides a set of complex queries and transaction scenarios, including cross-model queries, schema evolution, transaction consistency, and data consistency. By executing these queries and transactions and measuring their performance and resource consumption, the performance and scalability of multi-model database systems can be assessed.

3 Data Modalities

With the development of artificial intelligence, modern application analytics data is no longer limited to structured data, and the exploitation of unstructured data is becoming increasingly important. Many applications represent their data as a combination of multimodal data. Similarly, MMDBench represents a database in a combination of these modal data. This section will describe the data modality, focusing on the following two aspects:

Table 1. Key operations of MMDBench

Data type	Operation
Structured Graph Data	Join
	Selection
	Aggregation
	Pattern Matching
	Shortest Path
Unstructured Data	Unstructured Property Filtering
	Relationship Inference
	Similarity Matching

Data Representation. The property graph is one of the most suitable methods for describing social networks due to its convenience in implementation, and in MMDBench, graph data is chosen as the structured data representation. The property graph represents structured data using nodes and edges in a graph structure, which is formally expressed as G = (V, E, P), where G, V, E, and P represent the whole data, node collection, edge collection, and property collection, respectively. In this model, nodes represent entities or objects, and edges represent the relationships or connections between those entities. Each node and edge have properties associated with them. The graph is especially useful for representing and querying highly interconnected data, where relationships between entities are as important as the entities themselves. Nevertheless, alternative methods can also be employed to represent structured data.

On the other hand, unstructured data representation requires organizing and capturing semantic information that lacks a predefined data model. AI offers various approaches to achieve this, enabling the transformation of unstructured data into a meaningful and machine-readable format. For example, these data can be converted into vectors by AI models. Generally, the higher the dimension of the vector, the more information it can represent.

Data Manipulation. The key operations supported by MMDBench for multimodal data are summarized in Table 1. The structured graph data supports several typical operations, such as selection, join, aggregation, pattern matching, and advanced operations like finding the shortest path. Additionally, multimodal data can be treated as unstructured properties from which semantic information can be extracted and used as a filter condition for hybrid query. Moreover, these unstructured properties facilitate the exploration of latent relationships between nodes, which is called relationship inference. For instance, when we want to find topics of a post, we not only search for existing relationships but also extract semantic information from multimodal data to determine whether the post has a specific topic or not. Similarity matching in unstructured data is also a crucial operation. Generally, similarity algorithms are applied to vectors of unstructured data, including Cosine Distance, Euclidean Distance, Manhattan Distance, and others.

4   Data Generator

4.1   Constructing Data

MMDBench combines structured data with unstructured data to build multimodal datasets. For structured data, MMDBench utilizes public real-world datasets and some benchmark data generator tools. However, unstructured data is derived from realistic datasets. All the sources of the datasets are summarized in Table 2.

Table 2. Datasets of MMDBench

Data Name	Multimodal Data Type	Data Source
Social Network	Structured Graph	LDBC [6], News Category Dataset [11]
Person Faces	Image	LFW [9], IMDB-WIKI [13]
Comments	Short Text	Tweet Dataset [8]
Posts	Long Text	News Category Dataset

We employ the LDBC data generator to build linked data, which is one of the most popular data generators in the social network benchmark, and import this data into the property graph. The data generator has the capability to provide images and text, but the image file is an artificial filename rather than an existing URL or path. Moreover, the absence of sentiment tags in Messages makes it challenging to perform hybrid queries and validate the accuracy of the query results. To address these issues, we simplify the LDBC schema and replace its dictionary with some common unstructured data found in social platforms to align with our objectives. For instance, we incorporate face image files and sentiment texts, which are derived from publicly available datasets, including LFW, IMDB-WIKI, Tweet, and News Category.

As illustrated in Fig. 3, each Person node in the LDBC dataset is associated with a unique face image from either LFW or IMDB-WIKI. Each comment node contains a text and a corresponding sentiment label from the Tweet dataset. Additionally, each Post node contains a long news abstract text and a topic category from the News Category dataset. Each topic information extracted from the News Category dataset is treated as a node, facilitating relationship inference based on unstructured data. Specifically, when querying whether there is a relationship between two nodes, we not only search for existing relationships in the graph but also implicitly infer potential relationships between nodes by extracting semantic information from unstructured data.

4.2 Scaling Data from Different Modalities

MMDBench database is designed to be scalable with a specified scale factor. To accommodate different modalities of data, various expansion methods are employed. This section will provide a detailed explanation of the scaling-up methods.

Unstructured Data. When extending unstructured data, a process known as data augmentation in the field of Artificial Intelligence is employed. Several methods are used for image data enhancement, including geometric transformations, color space enhancement, kernel filters, mixed images, random erasure, feature space enhancement, generative adversarial networks, neural style transfer, and meta-learning [14]. To produce high-quality pictures, pre-trained models are a rational approach. However, generating large image datasets not only requires excellent hardware but also takes a significant amount of time, which will be addressed in our future work. Nonetheless, as for the public image dataset collected, it boasts a substantial scale, allowing us to employ the method of sampling from large-scale samples to scale up the image dataset.

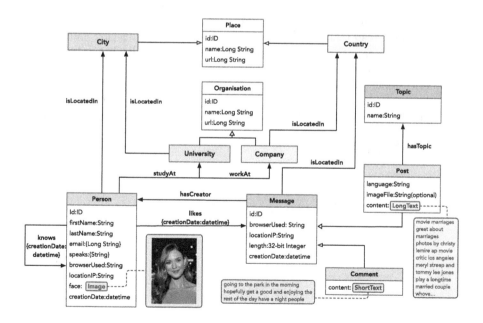

Fig. 3. The Multimodal Social Network Schema

For text data scaling up, as we did not find a text dataset of sufficient scale, we developed our data generator. EDA [17], a simple but powerful data augmentation method, consists of four important operations: synonym replacement, random insertion, random swap, and random deletion. We employ EDA in our data generator to achieve text data scaling up. The scale of expansion is limited by the scale of the original dataset. In the real world, text on social networks is often forwarded and rewritten, resulting in some similar data. This data augmentation method can partially simulate the generation of a substantial volume of data from emergency events, aligning with the characteristics of real-world data.

Structured Property Graph Data. MMDBench utilizes the extension method provided by LDBC's original data generator, enabling the generation of a social network of up to 36 million people, which sufficiently meets the requirements of MMDBench.

5   Workload

We have implemented our workload in the social network scenario, which is one of the most popular scenarios nowadays, covering a vast majority of typical operations. By default, our structured data representation is based on the property graph model. However, users have the flexibility to implement the interfaces provided by our framework to utilize other data models if needed. The tasks are divided into two parts: complex read and short read.

The complex read tasks involve multiple operations for querying multimodal data in a hybrid manner, including unstructured attribute filtering, relationship inference based on multimodal data, and more. On the other hand, the short read queries focus on the ability to process unstructured data using artificial intelligence and several simple structured data operations to fulfill typical query requirements. Each task involves data from at least two modalities, ensuring a comprehensive evaluation of the system's capabilities. A concise summary of the tasks can be found in Table 3.

Table 3. Tasks in MMDBench

	Task	Operation	Description
complex read	T1	Structured and unstructured property filtering	Given a starting person with an ID, the task is to find a friend within a 3-hop network who has specific facial features and first names. The objective is to return information about the friend's workplaces, residential cities, and study places.
	T2	Multiple unstructured property filtering	Given two individuals with their facial photos, the objective is to identify direct friendship relationships between them. If such a relationship exists, the task is to retrieve the ten most recent positive comments made by that friend.
	T3	Hybrid query with join	Search for a friend with a facial photo and geolocation information. When provided with a person's ID and a city's ID, the task is to return a friend of this person who resides in the specified city and resembles the given facial photo.
	T4	Hybrid query with aggregation	Given a person with an ID, the objective is to count the number of comments with a specific sentiment that are liked by the person's friends.
	T5	Hybrid query with Subgraph Matching	Given a person with a facial photo, the task is to query recent negative messages created by their friends or friends of friends.
	T6	Relationship inference	To find the topics of posts made by a given person with the ID, we can use both explicit and implicit relationships. Explicit relationships refer to direct connections and associations, such as topics explicitly assigned to the posts. Implicit relationships, on the other hand, involve analyzing patterns and context to identify related themes.
	T7	Hybrid query with unweighted shortest path	Given a person with an ID and a person with a facial photo, the aim is to find and return the shortest path connecting them.
short read	T8	Face recognition and pattern matching	Given a person's facial photo, the task is to retrieve their first name, last name, birthday, IP address, browser, and city of residence.
	T9	Face recognition and pattern matching	Given a person with a facial photo, the objective is to retrieve information about friends, including their ID, first name, last name, and the date they became friends
	T10	Sentiment analysis	Given a comment identified by its ID, the task is to determine its sentiment
	T11	Sentiment analysis and pattern matching	Given a person with id, the task is to retrieve the sentiment distribution of the last 10 messages they have sent

5.1 Framework of Benchmark Program

The most ideal situation would be to use a standardized query language to express tasks. However, currently, there is no unified and widely accepted multimodal data query language. To address this issue and improve the generality of benchmark programs, we have developed a framework to assist various databases in integrating with MMDBench. Specifically, we break down all the query tasks into individual atomic operations, and users can customize the implementation of these atomic operations and data models to use MMDBench. The framework consists of models and atomic operators:

– **Model**: Node, Relationship, and PathTriple represent components of the property model.
– **Read**: nodeAt(), nodes(), and relationships() are used for reading data.

We also offer to delete and update interfaces in MMDBench. Additionally, an AI service is provided for databases that do not have integrated AI capabilities to access MMDBench. Users can utilize our default AI operators, which may demonstrate moderate performance. If users aim for higher scores, they need to embed more powerful AI operators. We provide different AI capabilities for different types of data:

– **Text**: The ability of sentiment analysis and topic extraction is provided.
– **Image**: The ability of image information extraction is supported.

5.2 Multimodal Data Schema in Social Network

The multimodal social network schema of MMDBench is illustrated in Fig. 3. The structured data model comprises social network entities, including persons, topics, geographical locations, and organizations. Unstructured data is embedded within these nodes as unstructured properties, with each person having a facial image, each comment containing a short text, and each post containing a long news text. The social network graph is scalable, and while the unstructured data can also be expanded, its scale is limited by the cardinality of the public dataset. For example, the *Person* node contains 11,000 records, the *Comment* node contains 2,581,736 records, and the *Post* node contains 1,237,554 records when the scale factor is one (SF1).

5.3 Hybrid Query in Social Network

Hybrid query refers to the need to process multiple modalities of data simultaneously within a single system [16]. To demonstrate the technical challenges, we employ task one and task six as illustrative examples. Task one involves querying information about a person's friends, and the query process is depicted in Fig. 4. Traditionally, when querying friend nodes, methods rely on filtering based on the structured attributes of individuals. However, hybrid query harnesses the power of AI to extract information from unstructured data, enabling filtering of nodes

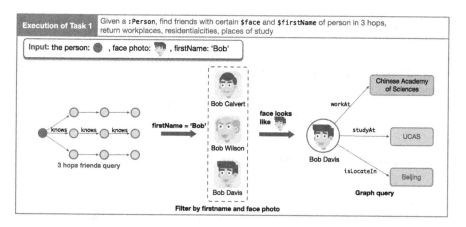

Fig. 4. Process of Hybrid Query in Task 1

based on their unstructured properties. Task 1 significantly tests the database's ability to correctly prioritize filtering conditions since processing unstructured data incurs much higher costs compared to structured data. By initially filtering $firstName$, the query process will be accelerated due to the extreme reduction of AI's search space. More complex tasks will process more multimodal data in one task, not only face photos. Task six, depicted in Fig. 5, demonstrates how to deduce relationships between nodes using unstructured data. Firstly, semantic information is extracted from news by AI operators to help uncover concealed topic types. Although the topic types inferred by AI operators might not precisely match the topic types in the schema, users can establish mapping relationships between them. Subsequently, the second sub-query conducts a direct search for $hasTopic$ relationships that may exist within the graph. Finally, the results from both queries are combined through a union operation. This task will test the ability to find all possible results using an AI-enhanced approach.

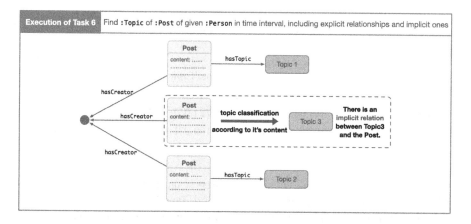

Fig. 5. Process of Hybrid Query in Task 6

6 Evaluation

To evaluate the effectiveness of MMDBench, a polyglot persistence system is developed to implement all tasks. The execution time of tasks is one of the important metrics for evaluating query performance. In the evaluation, we mainly focus on the end-to-end query time. The multimodal dataset is scaled up with the data generator to evaluate the scalability of the database systems.

6.1 Polyglot Persistence System for Evaluation

A Polyglot Persistence System refers to systems that employ multiple systems to achieve storage and query of multimodal data. In our benchmark, the polyglot persistence system provides storage ability for three types of data: structured data, images, and text. Graph data is stored in neo4j, unstructured data is stored in the file system, and AI capabilities are facilitated through the AI Web service.

To enable simultaneous access to data from multiple systems, a coordinating client is created on top of the subsystems. The client is responsible for collecting intermediate results from these subsystems and processing them to obtain the next intermediate result or the final result.

6.2 Data Generation

Experiment Setting. Our experiments are conducted on a high-performance computing cluster with 104 Intel(R) Xeon(R) Gold 6230R CPUs running at 2.10 GHz. The system has 256 GB of RAM, 4 TB of available disk space, and operated on CentOS Linux 7 (Core). The network bandwidth is 1000 Mb/s. The first five columns of Table 4 show the number of objects included in the dataset at different scales, and the last two columns show the time required for dataset generation and import.

Table 4. Characteristics of Datasets.

SF	Number					Import Time(ms)	Generator Time(ms)
	Person	Post	Comment	Likes	Has_Topic		
1	10,295	1,121,226	1,739,438	1,870,268	672,735	18,329	197,052
3	25,066	2,873,419	5,343,582	6,244,522	1,724,051	37,155	264,788
5	31,505	3,665,392	7,041,356	8,468,619	2,199,235	39,920	331,963

The data generation time consists of three stages: the time taken for generating structured data, unstructured data, and data integration. Furthermore, the dataset import time also includes the time required for index creation.

6.3   Baseline Evaluation

Figure 6 shows the execution time of all tasks on Polyglot Persistence System. Each bar represents the execution time of a task and is divided into two different colors to distinguish the time consumption of different modal data.

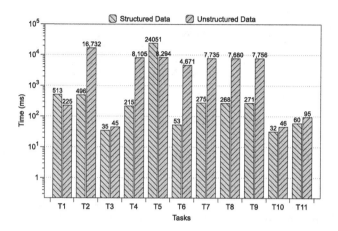

Fig. 6. Processing Time for Structured and Unstructured Data in Tasks

It is evident that the performance of structured data queries is significantly higher than that of unstructured data queries in most tasks because structured data is easier to index and filter while processing unstructured data may demand more computational resources and time. Task 5 is an exception, as it requires the execution of a highly complex subgraph matching operation.

As expected, utilizing the filtering criteria of structured data effectively reduces the search space of unstructured data, significantly reducing the query time. This has been evidenced by the results of Task 1 and Task 9. Task 1 involves querying 1 to 3 friend relationships, while Task 9 involves a much smaller number of friends. However, Task 1 smartly applies the filtering based on the structured attribute "firstName", which eliminates a substantial portion of the data. This relieves the burden on AI information extraction and greatly accelerates the entire query process.

6.4   Latency of Polyglot Persistence

In an ideal multimodal database, all storage engines and services are localized. Within the hybrid storage system discussed in this paper, latency primarily arises from interactions with AI services. If unstructured data is stored in an external object storage system, accessing this data also introduces significant network transmission latency, and frequent calls to external services incur additional overhead. Bulk submission of requests and deployment of AI services on the nodes where the data is stored were used to eliminate latency as much as possible(The scale of data transferred is out of our control). Figure 7 illustrates

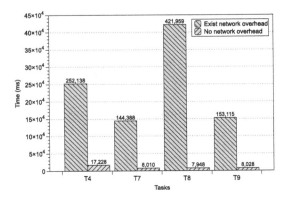

Fig. 7. Latency in Task 4, 7, 8, and 9

the execution times for tasks 4, 7, 8, and 9 after optimizing latency. It becomes evident that when transmitting substantial data volumes, the overhead from network transmission and external service calls far surpasses computational costs. Optimizing this aspect of latency can substantially enhance query acceleration. The Table 5 presents the performance improvements for all tasks after eliminating latency. In tasks 4,7,8,9, latency accounts for more than 90% of the execution time, and there is a lot of room for optimization of unstructured property filtering operation.

6.5   Scaling Data Evaluation

Figure 8 illustrates the performance of tasks on different dataset sizes. It is evident that as the dataset size increases, all task execution time exhibits a linear growth trend. Contrasting tasks 1 and 9, the advantage of prioritizing the execution of structured data filtering conditions becomes more pronounced as the dataset size increases. The elapsed time of task 2 and task 5 increases faster than the other tasks because the two tasks need to process more unstructured data as the size factor increases. The processing time for unstructured data accounts for the majority of the total runtime. Tasks 1 and 6 involve a small amount of unstructured data; thus, in comparison with other tasks, the overall runtime does not experience significant changes as the size factor increases.

6.6   Summary of Evaluation

Through the experiments above, several notable observations made in the evaluation are summarized below.

Table 5. Improvement after Eliminating Latency

T1	T2	T3	T4	T5	T6	T7	T8	T9	T10	T11
59%	53%	12%	93%	79%	30%	94%	98%	95%	7%	10%

Improvement Rate = (original time − improved time)/original time

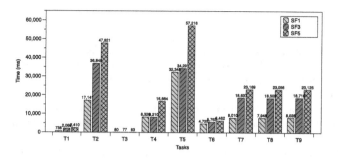

Fig. 8. Elapse time at Different Scales.

- In the Hybrid query of structured and unstructured data, executing filtering conditions on structured attributes first can effectively help accelerate the query process.
- A hybrid storage system is not an actual data management system, so communication between multiple systems and services can be optimized. Especially when dealing with large data volumes and frequent communication, the performance improvements after optimization are pretty significant.
- The query time of unstructured data is much higher than that of structured data. As the scale of data continues to increase, the more tasks touch unstructured data, the more obvious their elapse time increases.

7   Conclusion

The study presents a benchmarking program for multimodal databases in executing hybrid queries, aimed at assessing system performance when handling diverse data modalities, including structured data, and unstructured data like images and text. We propose a generator capable of producing multimodal data with different scales. To further simulate real-world demands, a multimodal social network workload is introduced to MMDBench, and some experiments are designed to demonstrate the effectiveness of the workload. We have also developed a framework that splits query into atomic operations to facilitate the integration of various types of databases into the benchmarking program. In the future, we plan to utilize AIGC to enable the generation of larger-scale datasets. Additionally, we intend to conduct experiments using real databases to obtain more precise performance evaluation reports.

References

1. Armstrong, T.G., Ponnekanti, V., Borthakur, D., Callaghan, M.: Linkbench: a database benchmark based on the Facebook social graph. In: Proceedings of the 2013 ACM SIGMOD International Conference on Management of Data, pp. 1185–1196 (2013)
2. Bronson, N., et al.: {TAO}:{Facebook's} distributed data store for the social graph. In: 2013 USENIX Annual Technical Conference (USENIX ATC 2013), pp. 49–60 (2013)
3. Cai, Q., Wang, H., Li, Z., Liu, X.: A survey on multimodal data-driven smart healthcare systems: approaches and applications. IEEE Access 7, 133583–133599 (2019)
4. Chandrasekaran, G., Nguyen, T.N., Hemanth D, J.: Multimodal sentimental analysis for social media applications: a comprehensive review. Wiley Interdisc. Rev.: Data Min. Knowl. Disc. 11(5), e1415 (2021)
5. Chasseur, C., Li, Y., Patel, J.M.: Enabling JSON document stores in relational systems. In: WebDB, vol. 13, pp. 14–15 (2013)
6. Erling, O., et al.: The LDBC social network benchmark: interactive workload. In: Proceedings of the 2015 ACM SIGMOD International Conference on Management of Data, pp. 619–630 (2015)
7. Ghazal, A., et al.: Bigbench v2: the new and improved bigbench. In: 2017 IEEE 33rd International Conference on Data Engineering (ICDE), pp. 1225–1236. IEEE (2017)
8. Go, A., Bhayani, R., Huang, L.: Twitter sentiment classification using distant supervision. CS224N Proj. Rep. Stanford 1(12), 2009 (2009)
9. Huang, G.B., Mattar, M., Berg, T., Learned-Miller, E.: Labeled faces in the wild: a database forstudying face recognition in unconstrained environments. In: Workshop on Faces in 'Real-Life' Images: Detection, Alignment, and Recognition (2008)
10. Kim, B., Koo, K., Enkhbat, U., Kim, S., Kim, J., Moon, B.: M2bench: a database benchmark for multi-model analytic workloads. Proc. VLDB Endowment 16(4), 747–759 (2022)
11. Misra, R.: News category dataset. arXiv preprint arXiv:2209.11429 (2022)
12. Nambiar, R.O., Poess, M.: The making of TPC-DS. In: VLDB, vol. 6, pp. 1049–1058 (2006)
13. Rothe, R., Timofte, R., Gool, L.V.: Deep expectation of real and apparent age from a single image without facial landmarks. Int. J. Comput. Vision 126(2–4), 144–157 (2018)
14. Shorten, C., Khoshgoftaar, T.M.: A survey on image data augmentation for deep learning. J. Big Data 6(1), 1–48 (2019)
15. Wang, Z., Li, L., Li, Q., Zeng, D.: Multimodal data enhanced representation learning for knowledge graphs. In: 2019 International Joint Conference on Neural Networks (IJCNN), pp. 1–8. IEEE (2019)
16. Wei, C., et al.: AnalyticDB-V: a hybrid analytical engine towards query fusion for structured and unstructured data. Proc. VLDB Endowment 13(12), 3152–3165 (2020)
17. Wei, J., Zou, K.: Eda: easy data augmentation techniques for boosting performance on text classification tasks. arXiv preprint arXiv:1901.11196 (2019)
18. Zhang, C., Lu, J.: Holistic evaluation in multi-model databases benchmarking. Distrib. Parallel Databases 39, 1–33 (2021)

19. Zhang, C., Lu, J., Xu, P., Chen, Y.: UniBench: a benchmark for multi-model database management systems. In: Nambiar, R., Poess, M. (eds.) TPCTC 2018. LNCS, vol. 11135, pp. 7–23. Springer, Cham (2019). https://doi.org/10.1007/978-3-030-11404-6_2

20. Zhao, Z., Shen, Z., Mao, A., Wang, H., Hu, C.: PandaDB: an AI-native graph database for unified managing structured and unstructured data. In: Wang, X., et al. (eds.) Database Systems for Advanced Applications, DASFAA 2023. LNCS, vol. 13946, pp. 669–673. Springer, Cham (2023). https://doi.org/10.1007/978-3-031-30678-5_53

21. Zhu, X., et al.: Multi-modal knowledge graph construction and application: a survey. IEEE Trans. Knowl. Data Eng. (2022)

Benchmarking Modern Databases
for Storing and Profiling Very Large Scale
HPC Communication Data

Pouya Kousha[✉][iD], Qinghua Zhou[iD], Hari Subramoni[iD],
and Dhableswar K. Panda[iD]

The Ohio State University, Columbus, OH 43210, USA
{kousha.2,zhou.2595}@osu.edu, {subramon,panda}@cse.ohio-state.edu

Abstract. Capturing cross-stack profiling of communication on HPC
systems at fine granularity is critical for gaining insights into the
detailed performance trade-offs and interplay among various components
of HPC ecosystem. To enable this, one needs to be able to collect, store,
and retrieve system-wide data at high fidelity. As modern HPC systems expand, ensuring high-fidelity, real-time communication profiling
becomes more challenging, especially with the growing number of users
employing profiling tools to monitor their workloads. We take on this
challenge in this paper and identify the key metrics of performance that
makes a database amenable to these needs. We then design benchmarks
to measure and understand the performance of multiple, popular, open-
source databases. Through rigorous experimental analysis, we demonstrate the performance and scalability trends of the selected databases
to perform different types of fundamental storage and retrieval operations
under various conditions. Through this work, we are able to achieve sub-
second complex data querying serving up to 64 users and demonstrate
a "9×" improvement in insertion latency through parallel data insertion,
achieving a latency of 55 ms and 50% less disk space for inserting 200,000
rows of profiling data collected from a potential system that is "4×" the
size of the state-of-the-art 19th-ranked Frontera supercomputing system
at TACC with 8,368 nodes.

Keywords: HPC · Storage · Database · Profiling · Communication

1 Introduction and Motivation

Advancements in High Performance Computing (HPC) have transformed our
ability to handle intricate phenomena and extensive datasets. As demand grows,
larger HPC systems, including exascale systems with thousands of nodes and
links, are emerging. In such systems, efficient communication is critical to overall

This research is supported in part by NSF grants #1818253, #1854828, #1931537,
#2018627, #2311830, #2312927, and XRAC grant #NCR-130002.

performance. Efficient data movement between nodes on the communication fabric is key for optimizing end-to-end solutions.

Communication profiling in HPC systems comes from hardware counters and communication libraries like the Message Passing Interface (MPI). Hardware counters offer metrics on performance, such as link utilization and different types of errors, while MPI profiling provides insights on software communication patterns and resource usage.

Overall, profiling at both the hardware and software levels is critical for in-depth analysing and achieving optimal performance on HPC systems and understanding the translation of communication library primitives to the hardware level communication. Several tools, such as TAU [6], Nvidia Nsight [8], XDMoD [11], OSU INAM [2], and Prometheus [1], periodically collect these counters, offering both low-level hardware performance as well as high-level view of communication patterns. The data schema for both MPI and InfiniBand counters in a HPC profiling tool is consistent, reflecting the standard InfiniBand hardware counters, errors, and MPI process data. For MPI processes, performance metrics include inter-/intra-node traffic characteristics, CPU and memory usage, one-sided communication traffic, and a breakdown of traffic in terms of collective or point-to-point operations.

The lack of real-time profiling, storing, and retrieving capabilities in HPC profiling tools typically results in their use for postmortem analysis, often leading to resource wastage. Considering the high power consumption of large-scale HPC systems, late detection of failures can be costly and impact system-level performance. Moreover, if a large-scale job causes issues, it can negatively impact system-level performance including other jobs. Therefore, a low-overhead, fine-grained profiling approach is needed for real-time identification and resolution of issues in production jobs to minimize resource wastage and ensure stable system performance.

1.1 Problem Statement

As HPC systems become larger, such as the Frontera [13] cluster with 8,368 compute nodes, 22,819 links, and 448,448 cores, and the state-of-the-art Frontier supercomputer [9] with 9,400 compute nodes and 8,730,112 cores, they introduce new challenges in ensuring real-time and scalable full system-level profiling. Due to the immense volume of fine-grained profiling data and the growth of HPC systems, achieving real-time, high-fidelity data collection, storage, and access for HPC is increasingly demanding and challenging.

State-of-the-art tools like INAM [7] leverages an efficient profiling methodology by running on single node within the cluster and then collecting and storing system-level metrics remotely at sub-second granularity for InfiniBand port counters/errors and MPI metrics for clusters of around 2,000 nodes [2]. However, upon in-depth analysis of the latest version of INAM on OSC cluster [10], we noticed some performance bottlenecks. Upon measuring the breakdown of system-wide InfiniBand port and error counters or the OSC cluster with 3,404 links and 1,544 nodes, we observe that the latency of the metric collection is significantly smaller compared to metric insertion into the database, requiring only 0.005 s for collection while taking 0.45 s for the insertion. This makes the overall performance of the HPC data processing to be bound by the database insertion performance. Despite our efforts to optimize MySQL (default option) for large data volumes, such as increasing cache size and database buffer pool size, performance limitations persist. This has prompted us to tackle the challenge of large-scale profiling data storage and retrieval, which helps the objective of developing more high-fidelity profiling tools that can provide fine-grained data with low overhead for exascale systems.

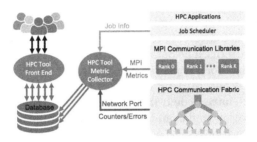

Fig. 1. High-level overview HPC profiling tool interaction with users and HPC layers - The database performance plays a vital role for tool's performance

Storing and accessing vast HPC communication profiling data from large systems requires thorough understanding and evaluation, as it forms a performance bottleneck in profiling capabilities for large-scale HPC systems, as shown in Fig. 1. Moreover, The nature of the data and the queries executed from various users, especially complex queries involving data filtration or aggregation, significantly impact database performance. For instance, a user might query to identify the MPI process ID within their own large-scale job that transmits the most data between two given timestamps.

To the best of our understanding, there's no current literature that assesses the performance of databases *for HPC data*. Given that database performance is influenced by the data's nature, this study is pivotal in determining the optimal database for HPC needs, considering factors like low-overhead requirement, performance, parallelism, and scalability. By designing various benchmarks to evaluate each database, our primary objective is to evaluate them holistically, not to probe their internal performance. We seek to shed light on the most suitable database choices for HPC profiling data, emphasizing the trade-offs that can enhance the performance of HPC profiling tools.

Database Selection: To effectively manage the fine-grained HPC communication profiling data from systems like Frontera and Frontier, we assessed open-source databases such as MySQL, InfluxDB [5], and ClickHouse [3]. This paper's goal is to evaluate the concurrent insertion and querying capabilities of these databases for extensive HPC communication data, using both single and multi-process methods. Each database represents a unique data storage strategy: MySQL (relational), InfluxDB (time-series), and ClickHouse (columnar). This diverse selection facilitates a thorough analysis across varied data management paradigms. These databases, being widely adopted, makes it easier to integrate them into database administration tools like DBeaver [4].

We initially assessed Cassandra [14], a NoSQL database, for our HPC data but found it under performing, particularly in read queries, due to its key-value structure. Such databases view values as opaque, hindering internal filtering or processing. Consequently, entire values are returned, leading to inefficient data filtering and handling, especially given the vast HPC data sizes. Updates necessitate overwriting entire values, even for minor changes. Despite the advantages of NoSQL databases, our research deemed them ill-suited for HPC profiling data storage and querying.

Dominant Data Schemas in HPC Profiling: Profiling tools typically collect a variety of schemas to analyze HPC communication and store them in tables. Upon measuring the size of the *in-production* gathered profiling tables during a week period wint 20 s collection interval in MySQL for the OSC cluster with 1,544 nodes, we observe that for the most the commonly collected schema include MPI, IB port counters, and IB port errors with other tables only consist of less than 1 GB in size. These schemas account for the largest amount of data collected by profiling tools since they are collected at each timestamp. Conversely, in other schemas, such as job information, links, and nodes, the tool updates existing rows and have a smaller impact on overall profiling tool performance due to smaller size and higher interval of collection.

The speed and efficiency of inserting and querying IB port counter, IB port errors, and MPI metrics are critical factors that significantly impact the overall performance of profiling tools to achieve higher granularity. To better clarify the problem and challenges we ask the following questions and seek to address them throughout the paper.

1. Is there a performance benefit between single and multiple writers when storing fixed volume of HPC data in databases?
2. Does batching the insertions help having faster insertion time? if so, what is the optimal batch size?
3. How do *concurrent users querying* data impact the performance across databases? How does it change when reading from multiple tables?
4. How does *concurrent insertions* into different tables influence the tool's storage performance across databases?
5. How does simultaneous read and write to different tables influence the tool's storage performance across databases? how does it vary by database?

1.2 Contributions

This study provides a systematic evaluation of three popular databases - MySQL, InfluxDB, and ClickHouse - for storing fine-grained HPC communication profiling data. To the best of our knowledge, there is no prior scientific literature that has evaluated these databases for this particular data. By analyzing the strengths and weaknesses of each database system, this study provides a deep understanding of database operation performance under various conditions, particularly for HPC profiling data schema. **To summarize, the key contributions of this paper are as follows:**

1. We evaluate and demonstrate the impact of parallelism for database insertion
2. We identify the impact of batched inserts on insertion performance while having users reading data across different databases.
3. We demonstrate how scaling the number of rows with optimized insertion batch size impacts the overall performance.
4. Through rigorous experiments, we evaluate the impact of scaling concurrent users reading data and increasing parallel insertions into different tables across the databases.
5. We examine the worst-case scenario with 64 concurrent users accessing profiling data and scaling parallel insertions up to 64 processes across multiple tables in various databases, exploring how this varies by database option.
6. Lastly, we integrated MySQL, InfluxDB, and ClickHouse with best-practices found as part of this study into an HPC monitoring tool, achieving a 30x speed-up in system-wide port counter/error collection.

2   Methodology for Realistic Benchmarking of Large-Scale HPC Profiling Data

This section outlines the methodology employed to develop benchmarks that simulate the insertion and querying of large communication profiling data. The primary objective of these benchmarks is to create worst-case scenarios that any HPC profiling tool might confront. To achieve this, we carefully crafted benchmarks that allow multiple insertions to overlap with one another, with the ability to write to different tables containing data, while concurrently querying the database. Additionally, we sought to synchronize the parallel querying of real-world queries across multiple users and overlap it with data insertion to evaluate the database performance when multiple users are using the tool simultaneously. Furthermore, we aimed to stress test the database by incorporating tens of millions of rows for each table. To ensure reliable performance and consistency, all of the benchmarks were designed in C++.

2.1   Data Schema and Table Design

We used a consistent data schema across all three database options - MySQL, InfluxDB, and ClickHouse - to maintain consistency and enable meaningful comparisons of their performance. The data schema included 3 tables that stored profiling data of InfiniBand (IB) port counters, IB port errors, and MPI profiling information per process. The schema for each table is shown in Tables 1, 2a, and 2b. For all the tables, we applied best practices like creating a secondary

Table 1. Fields and data types used for MPI profiling data

Field Name	Data Type	Field Name	Data Type	Field Name	Data Type
GUID	uint_64	Virtual Memory Size	uint_32	CPU User Time	int_32
Host Name	String	Peak Virtual Memory Size	uint_32	CPU System Time	int_32
Process Rank	int_16	Resident Set Size	uint_32	CPU Idle Time	int_32
Local ID (LID)	int_16	Peak Resident Set Size	uint_32	CPU ID	int_32
Job ID	int_16	I/O Read Bytes	uint_64	CPU Low Priority Time	int_32
Added_on	DateTime	I/O Write Bytes	uint_64	CPU I/O Wait Time	int_32
Bytes Sent	uint_64	Vbuf Allocated	uint_16	CPU IRQ Time	int_32
Bytes Received	uint_64	Vbuf Used	uint_16	CPU Soft IRQ Time	int_32
Packets Sent	uint_64	UD Vbuf Allocated	uint_16	CPU Steal Time	int_32
Packets Received	uint_64	UD Vbuf Used	uint_16	CPU Quest Time	int_32
Collective Bytes Sent	uint_64	SMP Bytes Received	uint_64	Lustre Read Times	uint_32
Collective Bytes Rcvd	uint_64	SMP Bytes Sent	uint_64	Lustre Read Min Time	uint_32
RMA Bytes Sent	uint_64	SMP Eager MaxSize Used	uint_32	Lustre Read Max Time	uint_32
Collective Packets Sent	uint_64	SMP Rendezvous Buff MS Used	uint_32	Lustre Read Total Time	uint_32
Collective Packets Rcvd	uint_64	SMP Eager Total Buffer Size	uint_32	Lustre Write Times	uint_32
RMA Packets Sent	uint_64	SMP Rendezvous Total Buffer Size	uint_32	Lustre Write Min Time	uint_32
		SMP Eager Buffer Used	uint_32	Lustre Write Max Time	uint_32
		SMP Rendezvous Buffer Used	uint_32	Lustre Write Total Time	uint_32

index on the "added_on" field for all databases to allow for efficient storage and querying of time-based data. The table creation also included creating an index on frequently queried columns like "GUID" and "port" for IB port counter/errors and "jobID", "process_rank", and "GUID" to optimize read performance. Moreover, the schema design ensured that the same type of data was inserted into all three databases to facilitate accurate comparisons of their performance. By utilizing a consistent data schema across all three databases, we were able to conduct a comprehensive evaluation of their performance and identify their respective strengths and weaknesses.

Table 2. InfiniBand port schemas

(b) InfiniBand port errors schema

Field Name	Data Type
GUID	uint_64
port	uint_32
SymbolErrors	uint_64
LinkRecovers	uint_64
LinkDowned	uint_64
RcvErrors	uint_64
RcvRemotePhysErrors	uint_64
RcvSwitchRelayErrors	uint_64
XmitDiscards	uint_64
XmitConstraintErrors	uint_64
RcvConstraintErrors	uint_64
LinkIntegrityErrors	uint_64
BufferOverrunErrors	uint_64
VL15Dropped	uint_64
addedOn	DateTime

(a) InfiniBand port counters schema

Field Name	Data Type
GUID	uint_64
port	uint_32
transmittedData	uint_64
receivedData	uint_64
transmittedPackets	uint_64
receivedPackets	uint_64
unicastXmitPackets	uint_64
unicastRcvdPackets	uint_64
multicastXmitPackets	uint_64
multicastRcvdPackets	uint_64
addedOn	DateTime

2.2 Data Querying Methodology

We developed our read benchmarks based on real queries used by profiling tools, such as obtaining all link errors and counters to update link utilization of a cluster, utilizing data from the previous 5 min. We also included queries that aggregate values of a table, filter multiple conditions through large volumes of high cardinality data, and find max/min values for a custom duration of time. The reader thread randomly selects one of these real-world queries to execute. Using the pthreads library in C++, we implemented this benchmark, simulating a realistic workload and evaluating database performance under these conditions. We synchronized our threads using barriers to ensure that all threads completed their setup before querying the database simultaneously. Each reader in our benchmark recorded the time taken to execute its query, providing us with the ability to measure the database's response time under various levels of concurrency.

2.3 Data Insertion Methodology

We utilized the pthreads library in C++ to design insertion benchmarks, allowing multiple writers to concurrently write uniformly random data to the database. Our implementation includes a barrier to ensure that all writers establish a database connection before executing insertion. This barrier spans all threads, including other writers to different tables and the reader processes, before querying the database starts. Each writer in our benchmark records the time taken to insert its data. With pthreads and synchronized barriers, we created realistic workloads and worst-case scenarios for insertion, enabling us to evaluate database performance under extreme conditions.

3   Performance Evaluation Methodology

We conducted a series of experiments to evaluate database performance for HPC profiling data, testing various parameters such as the number of rows, concurrent threads, write batch size, mode of operation, and the number and names of tables. We used three different tables (MPI, IB port counters, and IB port errors) as discussed in Sect. 1.1 and three databases (InfluxDB, MySQL, and ClickHouse), varying the number of concurrent reads, writes, and read and write from 1 to 64. The MPI process profiling data, IB counters, and IB errors tables take up significant space as they are updated every query time interval by adding new large-scale data.

We carried out six sets of experiments, evaluating optimal configurations for each table and database combination. For each database and table combination, we assessed the performance of a fixed number of row insertions, different write batch sizes evaluation, concurrent multi-process reads or/and writes, the impact of multi-process reads and/or writes to multiple tables, and finally the table storage size. Our goal was to determine the most effective configurations for handling large-scale data and optimizing database performance.

3.1   Evaluation Considerations

The purpose of this study is to provide a better understanding of the performance interplay between write batch size, multi-threading, and multi-table data access for HPC profiling data with a scale of exascale HPC systems. We assessed the performance of inserting 50,000 rows of IB port counters and errors per second using our benchmarks, chosen as it's twice the links and nodes of systems like Frontera with 8,368 nodes and 22,819 links.

In the evaluation of read queries, we utilized real-world HPC profiling queries to collect metrics from various tables. All queries monitor HPC system failures, send alerts to admins or users, and assess job performance at InfiniBand and MPI levels using aggregation and time/node/jobid filters. To evaluate worst-case performance scenarios from the tool's user perspective, we took the maximum latency among all readers if the read query involves reading from more than a single table (such as port counters and errors) with multiple readers scenarios. This approach emulates the behavior of loading a page and reading data from various tables. By simulating this real-world scenario, our evaluation provides a practical assessment of the performance of database options.

In the multi-table multi-process read/write evaluation, we stopped scaling the experiment if the latency of writing profiling data exceeded 90 s, as this is not a desirable database performance to deploy for the tool due to low fidelity profiling. Similarly, if the latency of both reading and writing exceeded 120 s, we also stopped the experiment from scaling as it is clear that the performance would be worse. This was done to ensure that the database performance remained within acceptable limits. Our results provide insights into the optimal configurations for handling large-scale data and optimizing database performance in HPC systems.

4   Database Performance Evaluation

4.1   Experimental Setup

We conduct our evaluation experiments on a single node of an HPC cluster with an Intel 28-core Broadwell CPU running at 2.40 GHz, a 35 MB L3 cache, and 125 GB of memory, including 18 GB of buffer memory and 3.7 GB of swap memory. We followed [12] instructions to optimize MySQL and InfluxDB. To ensure robustness and accuracy, we performed each experiment for a minimum of 20 iterations. To support concurrent read/write operations across three tables, we increased the maximum concurrent connections to 200 for all databases. The following terminologies are defined for the evaluation section:

Databases: CH (ClickHouse), MS (MySQL), FLX (InfluxDB)
Operations: R (Read query), W (Insert query)
Tables: PC (IB Port Counters), PE (IB Port Errors), MPI (MPI process info)

4.2   Impact of Parallelism on Data Insertion

This study addresses question #1 in Sect. 1.1 by investigating the performance variations between using multiple writers as opposed to a single writer for the insertion of communication profiling data into databases. The experiment is designed around a fixed dataset of 200,000 rows for PE and PC data, which is evenly distributed across writer threads ranging from 1 to 16 per table. To simulate a realistic scenario, 16 concurrent readers are added for each table.

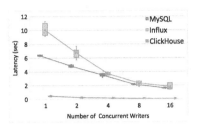

Fig. 2. Impact of scaling number of concurrent writes on the latency of inserting 200K rows for each PE and PC tables

The results of the experiment, as depicted in Fig. 2, indicate a substantial performance improvement when utilizing multiple writers. Specifically, employing 16 writers led to a speed-up factor of 9× for ClickHouse, 5× for MySQL, and 3× for InfluxDB. This enhancement was notable in ClickHouse, which exhibited a latency of only 55 ms.

Key Findings: These results show that the use of multiple writers can enhance the efficiency of inserting communication profiling data into databases.

4.3   Impact of Batching Rows on Data Insertion Performance

This experiment is designed to address question #2 in Sect. 1.1, investigating the impact of batched inserts on different table write performances across various databases and assessing the potential impact of concurrent read queries on this performance. The batch size is systematically varied from 200 to 30,000 rows for each MPI, PE, and PC table, to insert a total of 50,000 rows per table. The duration required to insert the complete dataset into the databases is measured for a single writer process, with the results presented in Figs. 3a, 3b, 3c. The findings suggest that an increase in batch size generally leads to a decrease in data insertion latency across the databases. However, an exception is observed in MySQL, which displays diminished performance for PE and MPI tables when the batch size exceeds 1,000 rows.

To further assess the influence of batch size, the experiment was replicated with the inclusion of a single reader process, as illustrated in Figs. 3d, 3e, 3f. The findings indicate that increasing the batch size continues to enhance performance for ClickHouse and InfluxDB. However, for MySQL, surpassing a batch size of 1,000 results in a decline in write performance. Although there is a slight increase in insertion latency when including a reader thread (by approximately 5%), the overall performance remains largely unaffected.

Key Findings: The experiment suggests that batched inserts can improve table write performance across various databases, with concurrent read queries having only a minor impact on this performance. Based on the experimental results, a

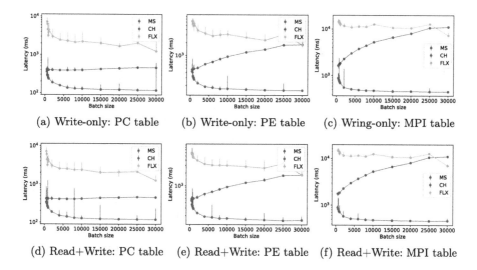

(a) Write-only: PC table   (b) Write-only: PE table   (c) Wring-only: MPI table

(d) Read+Write: PC table   (e) Read+Write: PE table   (f) Read+Write: MPI table

Fig. 3. Latency box plot: Impact of varying batch sizes (200–30,000 rows) on write performance in MySQL, ClickHouse, and InfluxDB for MPI, PE, and PC tables, in both single writer and concurrent reader-writer scenarios

batch size of 25,000 for ClickHouse, 1,000 for MySQL, and 30,000 for InfluxDB is recommended to optimize the performance of the data insertion. We used these batched sizes for the rest of the experiments in the paper.

4.4 Evaluation of Scaling Users Querying Data

Addressing question #3 in Sect. 1.1, this experiment delves into the impact of concurrent read queries on the overall performance of tools used for communication profiling data analysis across various database options. In a scenario where tool users are extracting data from single or multiple tables, the choice of the database becomes crucial to support the scaling of concurrent users reading data, which includes tasks such as aggregating values, filtering multiple fields, and accessing historical data. This scenario could be analogous to loading the jobs page of a tool where both MPI and IB level counters are read.

To evaluate the impact of different indexing methods used by each database, an experiment is conducted on a database loaded with 5 million rows of random values for each table. To guarantee a rigorous and worst-case scenario evaluation, we used a comprehensive read query that encompassed aggregation, filtering, timestamp searching, and max/min finding for all concurrent threads reading from the same table. A similar read query is applied to all tables. The maximum time among all threads for the read tests is measured to assess the worst-case performance of the database across single and multiple tables on large data. In other words, the operation is deemed complete once all the reads from the front end are finished. Figures 4 and 7a illustrate the impact of scaling both read operations and the number of tables read concurrently.

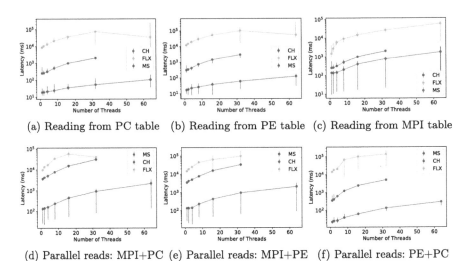

(a) Reading from PC table   (b) Reading from PE table   (c) Reading from MPI table

(d) Parallel reads: MPI+PC (e) Parallel reads: MPI+PE   (f) Parallel reads: PE+PC

Fig. 4. Latency box plot: Read-only performance scaling of MySQL, ClickHouse, and InfluxDB with increasing concurrent readers on PE, PC, MPI, MPI+PC, MPI+PE, and PC+PE tables, each thread reading 50K rows

Key Findings: Both MySQL and InfluxDB perform suboptimally when a large number of users are querying the database simultaneously. Some tests were curtailed as the total time exceeded the timing threshold of 120 s, as mentioned in Sect. 3.1. ClickHouse shows promising results for queries from a large number of users and even across all tables. We observe that for 64 users it takes a few seconds to read the data from all the tables. This experiment highlights how concurrent read queries from various users affect communication profiling data analysis tools' performance without concurrent insertions and emphasizes the need for an appropriate database in such situations.

4.5   Evaluation of Scaling Insertion Processes

Building on the previous section and addressing questions #4, this experiment evaluates the impact of concurrent writes when inserting 50,000 rows of non-zero random data into MPI, PE, and PC tables across different databases. The objective is to comprehend the implications of scaling up a tool's database to a larger cluster while preserving the same database threading configuration.

Figures 5a, 5b, and 5c illustrate the performance impact of scaling the number of writer threads for a single table. Figures 5d, 5e, 5f, and 7b further evaluate the same scenario but with scaling insertion to multiple tables.

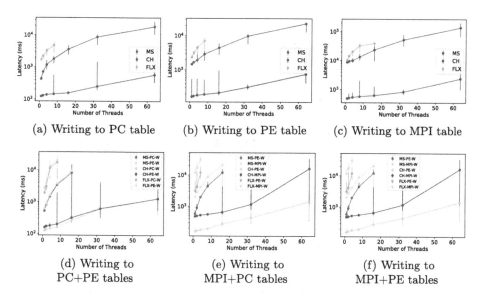

Fig. 5. Latency box plot: Write-only performance scaling of MySQL, ClickHouse, and InfluxDB with increasing concurrent writers on PE, PC, MPI, MPI+PC, MPI+PE, and PC+PE tables, each writer inserting 50K rows

Key Findings: We observe that InfluxDB performs the worst among all three database options, while ClickHouse achieves sub-second insertion for 64 writers for PE and PC tables but takes longer for the MPI table due to its larger number of columns and containing data. We observe more latency variation when writing to more than one table at the same time. When inserting to all tables with 64 users, the performance is impacted by MPI insertions. Overall, this experiment provides valuable insights into the impact of concurrent writes on the performance of tools used for gathering communication profiling data storage.

4.6   Scaling Simultaneous Insertion and Querying Processes

Regarding questions #5, we combine the last two experiments to explore the impact of concurrent multi-process read and write operations across our database options. We test the performance of combinations for three tables - MPI, PE, and PC - under a worst-case scenario where all threads of each table are simultaneously reading and inserting the same volume of data. We scale the number of simultaneous readers and writers, and we monitor the insertion latency for 50,000 rows per thread to each table while concurrently querying. This experiment includes the stress test shown in Fig. 1 where multiple users are leveraging the profiling tool at the same time of insertion across all tables.

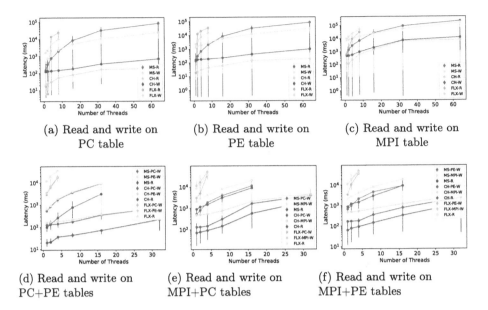

(a) Read and write on PC table

(b) Read and write on PE table

(c) Read and write on MPI table

(d) Read and write on PC+PE tables

(e) Read and write on MPI+PC tables

(f) Read and write on MPI+PE tables

Fig. 6. Latency box plot: Scaling performance comparison of database options: Increasing number of concurrent readers and writers for PE, PC, MPI, MPI+PC, MPI+PE, and PC+PE tables, Each thread handling 50K rows

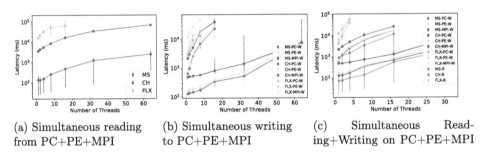

(a) Simultaneous reading from PC+PE+MPI

(b) Simultaneous writing to PC+PE+MPI

(c) Simultaneous Reading+Writing on PC+PE+MPI

Fig. 7. Latency box plots: Analyzing the impact of scaling the number of insertions or queries for 50k rows across PE, MPI, and PC tables in MySQL, ClickHouse, and InfluxDB databases

Our results, presented in Figs. 6 and 7c, show that ClickHouse outperforms all other database options. It demonstrates the ability to scale up to 64 users, inserting 50,000 data points with sub-second granularity. We observe that Clickhouse simultaneously enables 32 threads writing and reading to all the tables and achieves a latency of 2.3 s. As mentioned in Sect. 3.1, some experiments for InfluxDB and MySQL with 64 threads R/W for each table were not carried out due to poor performance, and the maximum value among all threads were used for read operations.

Key Findings: ClickHouse appears more suitable for exascale HPC profiling with sub-second granularity and concurrent read operations promoting support for more simultaneous users.

5   HPC Tool Integration and Evaluation

5.1   In-Production Performance Evaluation of Database Options

We have incorporated and deployed three database options into INAM, utilizing it on the OSC cluster to conduct high-fidelity profiling stress tests and validate our findings. The tests used a 1-second interval for profiling the InfiniBand network, a 5-second interval for profiling both MPI and jobs metrics with an 80% cluster load, and a background deletion of data older than 1 h. Consequently, this evaluation demonstrates a real-world deployment of INAM with varying database options. We also performed detailed timing measurements for each component.

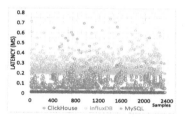

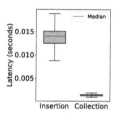

Fig. 8. Performance evaluation: assessing stability in PE+PC data collection and insertion across the entire OSC cluster - latency analysis of port inquiry sweep for 2,400 samples, using 8 threads at one-second query intervals

Fig. 9. Improved latency of system-wide PE and PC data collection and insertion using ClickHouse for our OSC cluster - using 8 threads, 1 s profiling intervals across 1,544 nodes - 30x times enhancement

Figure 8 presents a comparison of the total latency involved in gathering and storing PC and PE data from the network across various databases. Each point is reflecting the total latency across all threads for insertion and collection. Eight threads were employed for data insertion, and this experiment was repeated for 2,400 samples. Notably, ClickHouse consistently exhibited superior performance stability compared to the other databases. Figure 9 depicts the latency breakdown of each sweep when employing ClickHouse on OSC cluster. Compared to initial observation in Sect. 1, we observed a 30-fold improvement in data insertion speed from 0.45 s to 0.015 s. This optimization allowed for the collection and insertion of a complete OSC network sweep of counters and errors in a median time of just 15 ms.

5.2   Evaluation of Disk Space Usage for Each Table

We evaluated the disk usage of ClickHouse versus MySQL after having 26 Million rows of data in MPI, PE, and PC tables. We observed that ClickHouse uses 50% less disk space than MySQL due to its column-oriented storage structure, which eliminates redundant data storage. This makes ClickHouse a more storage-efficient option for large-scale data processing. The InfluxDB database was not evaluated due to the overall poor performance.

6   Conclusion and Future Work

The task of real-time storing and retrieving high-fidelity communication profiling data for large-scale HPC systems is challenging. It necessitates a database infrastructure that can efficiently manage extensive data volumes while facilitating intricate yet scalable user queries. Our research uniquely delves into the evaluation of HPC profiling data, a domain that remains underrepresented in the literature due to the inherent dependency of performance on the data.

We benchmarked MySQL, InfluxDB, and ClickHouse databases, each representing distinct data management paradigms, using standard benchmarks to gauge their performance and scalability. Our findings underscore the benefits of using multiple writers for enhanced data insertion latency and the advantages of batched inserts. Specifically, ClickHouse stood out, showcasing a 9x improvement in parallel insertion times compared to an optimized MySQL setup. It achieved a 2.3-second latency for inserting and reading 1.6 million rows of HPC data across multiple tables, even with 32 concurrent users executing complex queries. Moreover, for a system quadruple the size of the Frontera supercomputer at TACC, ClickHouse recorded a 55ms latency for profiling system-wide data insertion.

Further, we integrated the database options into INAM and perform evaluation on real HPC system, detailed in Sect. 2.1. On the OSC cluster, our tests with ClickHouse showed sub-second latencies for system-wide port counter/error collections, a 30x improvement in network monitoring, and halved disk space usage. This work offers practical insights for practitioners selecting databases for HPC data, emphasizing strategies seldom discussed in literature, as highlighted in Sects. 4.2 (benefits of multiple writers) and 4.3 (optimized batch sizes for insertion), and validating our findings with real HPC workloads.

As a part of future work, we plan on releasing INAM with ClickHouse support and collaborating with HPC administrators to deploy the enhanced monitoring tool to larger-scale clusters.

References

1. Prometheus exporter. https://github.com/prometheus/node_exporter
2. Kousha, P., et al.: Accelerated real-time network monitoring and profiling at scale using OSU INAM. In: Practice and Experience in Advanced Research Computing (PEARC 2020) (2020)

3. ClickHouse: Clickhouse official website. https://clickhouse.tech/
4. DBeaver Corp: Dbeaver - universal database tool. https://dbeaver.io/. Accessed 27 Dec 2023
5. InfluxData: Influxdb. https://www.influxdata.com/products/influxdb/
6. Malony, A.D., Shende, S.: Performance technology for complex parallel and distributed systems. In: Kotsis, G., Kacsuk, P. (eds.) Proceedings of the DAPSYS 2000, pp. 37–46 (2000)
7. Network based computing team: OSU INAM (2019). http://mvapich.cse.ohio-state.edu/tools/osu-inam/
8. NVIDIA Nsight Systems. https://developer.nvidia.com/nsight-systems
9. Oak Ridge National Laboratory: Frontier (2023). https://www.olcf.ornl.gov/frontier/. Accessed 27 Dec 2023
10. OSC: Ohio Supercomputer Center. https://www.osc.edu/
11. Palmer, J.T., et al.: Open XDMoD: a tool for the comprehensive management of high-performance computing resources. Comput. Sci. Eng. **17**(4), 52–62 (2015). https://doi.org/10.1109/MCSE.2015.68
12. Pouya Kousha: Best Practices with OSU INAM. http://mvapich.cse.ohio-state.edu/userguide/osu-inam/#_best_practices_with_osu_inam
13. Stanzione, D., West, J., Evans, R.T., Minyard, T., Ghattas, O., Panda, D.: Frontera: the evolution of leadership computing at the national science foundation. In: Practice and Experience in Advanced Research Computing, pp. 106–111. PEARC'20, ACM, New York, NY, USA (2020). https://doi.org/10.1145/3311790.3396656
14. The Apache Software Foundation: Apache cassandra. https://cassandra.apache.org/. Accessed 27 Dec 2023

A Linear Combination-Based Method to Construct Proxy Benchmarks for Big Data Workloads

Yikang Yang[1,2], Lei Wang[1,2(✉)], and Jianfeng Zhan[1,2]

[1] Institute of Computing Technology, Chinese Academy of Sciences, Beijing, China
{yangyikang23s,wanglei_2011,zhanjianfeng}@ict.ac.cn
[2] University of Chinese Academy of Sciences, Beijing, China

Abstract. During the early stages of CPU design, benchmarks can only run on simulators to evaluate CPU performance. However, most big data component benchmarks are unable to finish running on simulators at an acceptable time cost, as simulators are slower 100X–1000X times than physical platform. Moreover, big data benchmarks usually need the support of complex software stacks, which is hard to be ported on the simulators. Proxy benchmarks have the same micro-architectural characteristics as real benchmarks and do not require long running time or complex software stacks. Therefore, proxy benchmarks can replace real benchmarks to run on simulators.

The biggest challenge of proxy benchmark generation is how to guarantee that the proxy benchmarks have exactly the same micro-architectural metrics as real benchmarks when the number of micro-architectural metrics is very large. To deal with this challenge, we propose a linear combination-based proxy benchmark generation methodology that transforms this problem into solving a system of linear equations. We also design the corresponding algorithms to ensure the system of linear equations is astringency.

We generate fifteen proxy benchmarks and evaluate their running time and accuracy in comparison to the corresponding real benchmarks for MySQL and RockDB. On the typical Intel Xeon platform, the average running time is 1.62 s, and the average accuracy of every micro-architectural metric is over 92%, while the longest running time of real benchmarks is nearly 4 h. We also conduct two case studies that demonstrate that our proxy benchmarks are consistent with real benchmarks both before and after prefetch or Hyper-Threading is turned on.

Keywords: Micro-architectural metrics · Proxy benchmark · Linear combination

1 Introduction

In recent years, big data systems, including traditional relational databases, non-relational databases, and distributed data management systems, have been making an increasingly significant contribution to the development of economy [1–4].

© The Author(s), under exclusive license to Springer Nature Singapore Pte Ltd. 2024
S. Hunold et al. (Eds.): Bench 2023, LNCS 14521, pp. 120–136, 2024.
https://doi.org/10.1007/978-981-97-0316-6_8

The CPU requires more advanced designs to enhance performance, while benchmarks are important tools for evaluating CPU performance. Compared to traditional benchmarks like SPECCPU [5] and PARSEC [6], big data benchmarks like CloudSuite [7] and BigDataBench [8–10] can provide a more accurate evaluation of the CPU performance in processing big data tasks.

During the early stages of CPU design, the validity and effectiveness of many designs have to be verified on simulators due to the heavy cost of designing and implementing a CPU system. However, big data benchmarks can not run on simulators because of prohibitively heavy time costs and the lack of supporting complex software stacks on the CPU simulators.

Proxy benchmarks are workloads used to replace real benchmarks for evaluating CPU performance. Compared to real big data benchmarks, proxy benchmarks have a short running time and don't need to port complex software stacks on simulators. Moreover, they have the same micro-architectural metrics as real big data benchmarks, which means they can represent real benchmarks' micro-architectural characteristics. Han et al. propose Cloudmix [11] to construct proxy benchmarks for cloud systems, but these proxy benchmarks don't have similar metrics in cache behavior, branch prediction, and instruction mix. Panda et al. propose PerfProx [12] methodology to construct proxy benchmarks for database applications, but these proxy benchmarks don't align real benchmarks' micro-architectural metrics directly, which means there are gaps with real benchmarks in terms of micro-architectural metrics. Gao et al. propose a data motif-based proxy benchmark generation methodology [13,14], but this methodology requires the source codes of real benchmarks, which are sometimes not available.

The biggest challenge for constructing proxy benchmarks is how to guarantee the proxy benchmarks have exactly the same micro-architectural metrics as real benchmarks when the number of micro-architectural metrics is very large. Traditionally, CPI, branch misprediction rate, cache miss rate and instruction ratio are the metrics receiving most attention. Previous work primarily focused on small-scale metrics, which means they can just align part of above metrics and will meet great difficulties when aligned metrics increase. Because there are correlations between the metrics, they can mutually influence each other, making it difficult to align them simultaneously. We propose a linear combination-based proxy benchmark generation methodology to deal with the challenge. In this paper, we use big data benchmarks as samples to illustrate the validity of our methodology. This methodology can be applied for generating any other proxy benchmarks as long as their micro-architectural metrics can be measured.

Our contributions are three-fold as follows:

- We propose a linear combination-based proxy benchmarks generation methodology that transforms the problem of constructing a proxy benchmark into solving a system of linear equations by a non-negative least square method. This methodology can easily be expanded by just adding some equations into the system to deal with large-scale metrics.

- We generate fifteen proxy benchmarks for real big data benchmarks. The evaluation results demonstrate that the average accuracy of each micro-architectural metric is over 92% while the average running time is 1.62 s.
- We use the fifteen proxy benchmarks to conduct two case studies, which demonstrate that our proxy benchmarks are consistent with real benchmarks both before and after prefetch or Hyper-Threading is turned on.

The rest of this paper is organized as follows. Section 2 provides the proxy benchmark generation methodology. Section 3 conducts evaluations for proxy benchmarks. Section 4 presents two case studies for micro-architectural configuration settings. Section 5 discusses the related work. Section 6 draws conclusions.

2   Proxy Benchmark Generation Methodology

2.1   Problem Description

Proxy benchmarks constructed must have the same micro-architectural metrics as real benchmarks, while the metrics are listed in Table 1. The metrics can be divided into five categories, including processor performance, branch prediction, cache behavior, TLB behavior, and instruction mix. Perf [15,16], a hardware event counter, is used by us to collect these metrics. Because there are strong correlations between these metrics and their number is high, they can mutually influence each other, making it difficult to align them simultaneously. Except for the requirement of micro-architectural metrics, proxy benchmarks must have short running time and don't need complex software stacks.

Table 1. Micro-architectural Metrics

Category	Metric Name	Description
Processor Performance	CPI	cycles per instruction
Branch Prediction	Branch Miss	Branch misprediction rate
Cache Behavior	L1 DCache Miss	L1 data cache miss rate
	L1 ICache Miss	L1 instruction cache miss rate
	L2 Cache Miss	L2 cache miss rate
	L3 Cache Miss	L3 cache miss rate
TLB Behavior	DTLB Miss	data TLB miss rate
	ITLB Miss	instruction TLB miss rate
Instruction Mix	Instruction ratios	Ratios of load, store, branch, floating point, integer and vector instructions

We propose a linear combination-based proxy benchmark generation methodology illustrated in Fig. 1. Firstly, we measure the micro-architectural metrics of each real big data benchmark. These metrics will serve as the target metrics for our proxy benchmarks. Next, we select appropriate program fragments—basic

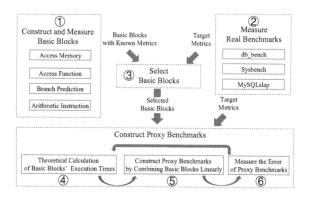

Fig. 1. Proxy Benchmark Generation Methodology.

blocks from the basic block set based on the target metrics. Finally, we combine these selected basic blocks linearly to construct proxy benchmarks. To reduce the gap between the real benchmarks and the proxy benchmarks, we adjust the execution times of each basic block in multiple rounds of iteration. This process ensures that the proxy benchmark closely resembles the real benchmark in terms of micro-architectural metrics.

2.2 Basic Block

We define a basic block as a program fragment consisting of a specific series of assembly instructions, while their structures can be divided into interior and exterior. In this paper, we use x86 assembly instructions to build basic blocks. The exterior structure is a loop, which can control the execution times of the basic block by changing the number of iterations. The interior structure is composed of a series of specific instructions, which determines the micro-architectural metrics of the basic block. Figure 2 presents an example of a basic block, in which the interior comprises several add instructions, and the exterior structure controls it to execute 300,000 times. Based on the differences in the interior instruction series, we have constructed a total of four distinct types of basic blocks.

Access Memory Basic Block. This kind of basic block primarily focuses on accessing memory at a fixed distance. The fixed distance between two adjacent memory accesses is denoted as STRIDE. An increase in STRIDE can result in a decrease in spatial locality, leading to higher miss rates in L1 DCache and DTLB. Furthermore, the increased miss rates in L1 DCache can potentially impact the miss rates of L2 Cache and L3 Cache. Therefore, by adjusting the STRIDE value, we can construct a set of access memory basic blocks with various miss rates in L1 DCache, L2 Cache, L3 Cache, and DTLB.

Access Function Basic Block. This kind of basic block focuses on accessing functions at a fixed distance. These functions all just have one return instruction

```
 1      movl    $3000000, %r13d
 2   .L0_B:
 3      addl    $0, %eax
 4      addl    $0, %ebx
 5      addl    $0, %ecx
 6      addl    $0, %edx
 7   ...
 8      subl    $1, %r13d
 9      je .L0_E
10      jmp .L0_B
11   .L0_E:
```

Fig. 2. An Example of Basic Block.

and are arranged sequentially in memory. The fixed distance between two adjacent function accesses is denoted as STRIDE. A larger STRIDE value decreases the temporal locality, resulting in increased miss rates in L1 ICache and ITLB. The increased miss rate in L1 ICache can potentially impact the miss rates of L2 Cache and L3 Cache. Therefore, by adjusting the STRIDE value, we can construct a set of access function basic blocks with various miss rates in L1 ICache, L2 Cache, L3 Cache, and ITLB.

Branch Prediction Basic Block. This kind of basic block utilizes a random number and a threshold value for branch prediction. It will generate a random number R between 0 and 1024 and compares R with a pre-set THRESHOLD. If R is bigger than THRESHOLD, a branch jump will happen; otherwise, it will not. As THRESHOLD approaches 512 (half of 1024), the branch jump becomes more random, making branch prediction more difficult and increasing the branch misprediction rate. By adjusting THRESHOLD, we can create a set of branch prediction basic blocks with a wide distribution of branch misprediction rates.

Arithmetic Instruction Basic Block. The interiors of these basic blocks primarily consist of various arithmetic instructions. These basic blocks are designed to show the differences in execution speeds among different arithmetic instructions. Specifically, add and sub instructions are typically faster, mul instructions are slower, and div instructions are the slowest. By designing a set of basic arithmetic instruction blocks with different combinations and sequences of these instructions, we can create basic blocks with various Cycles Per Instruction (CPI) values.

2.3 Linear Combination Method

We generate proxy benchmarks by linearly combining basic blocks. The linear combination involves both connection and scaling, with their definitions stated as Definition 1 and Definition 2.

Definition 1. *Connection refers to the act of linking two program fragments in a specific order. If we denote the higher-order program fragment as P_1 and another P_2, we will represent the connected program fragment as $P_1 + P_2$.*

Definition 2. *Scaling refers to altering the execution times of a basic block. If a basic block P is scaled by k times to create a modified basic block P', we will use $k \cdot P$ to represent P'.*

The basic blocks do not require any input data. The execution logic of basic blocks is fixed and does not depend on input data. Therefore, these basic blocks can be combined linearly without considering input data.

During the execution of every program, various hardware events will occur on the microprocessor, including the misses and accesses of Cache at all levels, the misses and accesses of DTLB and ITLB, the branch predictions and the branch mispredictions, etc. If we use $f(P)$ to represent the number of times a hardware event f occurs during the execution of program P, then Eq. 1 and Eq. 2 will hold true under ideal conditions.

$$f(P_1 + P_2) = f(P_1) + f(P_2) \tag{1}$$

$$f(k \cdot P) = k \cdot f(P) \tag{2}$$

Therefore, as Fig. 3 describes, when two basic blocks are connected together, the occurrence times of each hardware event will equal the original sum, and when a basic block is scaled by 2 times, the occurrence times of each hardware event will double.

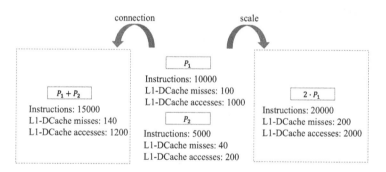

Fig. 3. Explanation of Linear Combination.

We run all basic blocks $N_0(N_0 = 10^7)$ times and use Perf to measure the occurrence times of all hardware events. For a proxy benchmark, we construct it with basic blocks $P_1, P_2, .., P_m$ and denote the execution times of the k-th basic block as N_k. During the execution of the proxy benchmark, for a hardware event f, it will occur $\sum_{j=1}^{m} f(P_j) \cdot \frac{N_j}{N_0}$ times. Additionally, every micro-architectural metric can be calculated as the quotient of two hardware events. For example, the miss rate of L1 DCache can be calculated through dividing the L1 DCache misses by the L1 DCache accesses. Similarly, CPI can be calculated through dividing the total cycles by the total number of instructions. That means we can predict our proxy benchmark's micro-architectural metrics if we know the execution times of each basic block.

In order to make the proxy benchmark's micro-architectural metrics closely align those of the real benchmark and also ensure that the proxy benchmark's running time stays less than specified limit, we need to determine appropriate values for $N_1, ..., N_m$ that satisfy the constraints of Eq. 3. Within Eq. 3, the first equation represents multiple terms. In this equation, $metric^i$ refers to the i-th target micro-architectural metric, which can be calculated as the quotient of f_A^i and f_B^i. If we hope proxy and real benchmarks align more micro-architectural metrics, we just need to add more equations into Eq. 3, which is very simple. Just by adding equations, our method can deal with the problem that the micro-architectural metric set is large.

$$\frac{\sum_{j=1}^m f_A^i(P_j) \cdot \dfrac{N_j}{N_0}}{\sum_{j=1}^m f_B^i(P_j) \cdot \dfrac{N_j}{N_0}} = metric^i, i = 1, 2, ..., q$$

$$\sum_{j=1}^m instructions(P_j) \cdot \frac{N_j}{N_0} = ins_1 \tag{3}$$

The last equation in Eq. 3 is used to limit the total number of instructions ins_1 in the proxy benchmark. Equations 3 can be easily transformed into a system of linear equations. Although sometimes this system of linear equations doesn't have a unique solution, we can always find the best solution by a non-negative least square method. After that, we can construct a proxy benchmark that meets micro-architectural metrics and time limit requirements in theory.

2.4 Algorithm Flow

In the process of constructing a proxy benchmark, many basic blocks are redundant. With the number of basic blocks increasing, the mutual influences between them become more complex. Therefore, it's necessary to select a subset of basic blocks before formally constructing a proxy benchmark. For a proxy benchmark, we initially consider using all basic blocks to construct and solve Eq. 3. As a result, some of the basic blocks will have zero execution times, while others will not. We will select the latter basic blocks.

The linear combination method described in Sect. 2.3 allows us to theoretically construct a proxy benchmark that meets the micro-architectural metrics and time limit requirements. However, in practice, the proxy benchmark may not meet the metric requirements when it actually runs. This can be attributed to several factors, including the mutual influences between the basic blocks, the error of measuring tools, the instability of the system environment, etc.

To solve the above problem, we conduct multiple rounds of iteration on the proxy benchmark. During each round, we run the proxy benchmark, measure micro-architectural metrics, and increase the execution times of each basic block based on the measurement results. The algorithm used for this process is provided in Algorithm 1. In Eq. 4, f_A^i and f_B^i represent the occurrence times of hardware events of the previous round's proxy benchmark, while $f_A^i(P_j)$ and $f_B^i(P_j)$

remain the same meaning as Eq. 3. Additionally, we utilize ΔN_k to denote the increase in execution times of the k-th basic block in the present round. Δins represents the total increase of instructions in this round, and the rest of variables remain the same meaning as Eq. 3. Equation 4 can be easily transformed into a linear system, and we can also find its best solution by the non-negative least square method and ensure the linear equation is astringent.

Algorithm 1. Align

Require: Picked basic block subset B, target metrics, the number of instructions of the first round's proxy benchmark ins_1, iteration rounds n
Ensure: The proxy benchmark PB
$(N_1, N_2, ..., N_p) \leftarrow$ solve Equations 3
$PB \leftarrow$ construct a proxy benchmark according to $(N_1, N_2, ..., N_p)$
run PB and measure its hardware events' occurrence times
for $epoch \leftarrow 2$ to n **do**
  $\Delta ins \leftarrow instructions \times 0.2$ // instructions is the number of instructions of the last round's proxy benchmark
  $(\Delta N_1, \Delta N_2, ..., \Delta N_p) \leftarrow$ solve Equations 4
  $(N_1, N_2, ..., N_p) \leftarrow (N_1 + \Delta N_1, N_2 + \Delta N_2, ..., N_p + \Delta N_p)$
  $PB \leftarrow$ construct the proxy benchmark according to $(N_1, N_2, ..., N_p)$
  run PB and measure its hardware events' occurrence times
end for
return PB

$$\frac{f_A^i + \sum_{j=1}^m f_A^i(P_j) \cdot \frac{\Delta N_j}{N_0}}{f_B^i + \sum_{j=1}^m f_B^i(P_j) \cdot \frac{\Delta N_j}{N_0}} = metric^i, i = 1, 2, 3..., q$$

$$\sum_{j=1}^m instructions(P_j) \cdot \frac{\Delta N_k}{N_0} = \Delta ins$$

(4)

3 Evaluation

In this section, we evaluate the effectiveness of our proxy benchmark generation methodology. Many database systems are equipped with stress testing tools, such as db_bench [17] in RocksDB, SysBench [18], and MySQLslap in MySQL. We use these tools to obtain 15 real benchmarks as listed in Table 2. Details of db_bench and SysBench can be found in [17] and [18]. There are two items in MySQLslap benchmarks, normal and partition. Their main performance are both inserting random data into table. The difference is that partition use horizontal partition table and normal does not. The names of these benchmarks are too long so we use letters and numbers to denote them in the rest of our paper (e.g., fillrandom is denoted as D1). By using our methodology, we generate 15 proxy benchmarks. Finally, we measure the accuracy of their micro-architectural metrics and their running time.

Table 2. Real Benchmarks

Benchmark Tool	Workloads
db_bench	fillrandom(D1), compact(D2), readrandom(D3)
SysBench	oltp_delete(S1), oltp_insert(S2), oltp_point_select(S3), oltp_read_only(S4), oltp_read_write(S5), oltp_write_only(S6), oltp_update_non_index(S7), oltp_update_index(S8), select_random_points(S9), select_random_ranges(S10)
MySQLslap	normal(M1), partition(M2)

3.1   Experiment Setups

We use a Linux server to conduct our experiments. This server is equipped with two Intel Xeon E5645 processors, each having six physical cores. The operation system is CentOS 6.10 with the Linux kernel version 3.11.10. The server has a total memory of 32GB. The total bandwidth is 72 bps, while the data bandwidth is 64 bps. We use GCC 5.4.0 to compile our proxy benchmarks, and all GCC configurations are set to default.

3.2   Accuracy

Equation 5 is used to compute the accuracy for each metric in Table 1. $Metric_R$ represents the metric value of the real benchmark, and $Metric_P$ represents the metric value of the proxy benchmark. The overall accuracy for a category of metrics is represented by the lowest accuracy among them.

$$Accuracy(Metric_R, Metric_P) = 1 - |\frac{Metric_R - Metric_P}{Metric_R}| \qquad (5)$$

To construct the proxy benchmark for each real benchmark, we follow the method described in Sect. 2.3, which involves a 10-round iteration. In the first round, we create a proxy benchmark containing 0.5 billion instructions. In each subsequent round, the number of instructions is increased by 20% to correct any metric errors. After 10 rounds of iteration, we obtain the proxy benchmark we require. Figure 4 shows the process of constructing the proxy benchmark of a real benchmark (M1). Each curve represents the change of one metric in every round. In the 10th round, the accuracy of every metric is over 95%.

Processor Performance Accuracy. Figure 5 displays the processor performance accuracy of our proxy benchmarks compared to real benchmarks. The lowest accuracy is 92.6%, while the average accuracy is 98.4%. These results

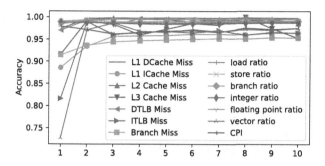

Fig. 4. A Sample of Constructing M1 Proxy Benchmark.

prove that our proxy benchmarks closely resemble the corresponding real benchmarks in terms of processor performance.

Branch Prediction. Figure 5 shows the branch prediction accuracy of our proxy benchmarks. The minimal accuracy is 92.7% belonging to D3 real benchmark. The average accuracy is 97.3%.

Cache Behavior. Our proxy benchmarks' cache behavior accuracy can be observed from Fig. 5. The lowest accuracy is 85.9%, and the average accuracy is 92.7%. It's worth noting that more than half of the proxy benchmarks exhibit an accuracy over 90%.

TLB Behavior. According to Fig. 5, the minimal accuracy observed in TLB behavior is 92.5%, and the average accuracy is 96.5%. It is important to note that the majority of the proxy benchmarks demonstrate an accuracy of over 95%.

Instruction Mix. In terms of instruction mix, according to Fig. 5, the minimal accuracy observed is 90.6%, and the average accuracy is 97.0%. Most of them have a higher instruction mix accuracy than 95%. Our proxy benchmarks have similar instruction structures to corresponding real benchmarks.

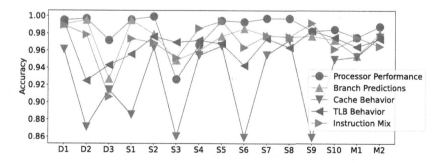

Fig. 5. Accuracy of All Proxy Benchmarks.

From the perspectives of metrics, we can conclude that our proxy benchmarks exhibit similar characteristics to the corresponding real benchmarks.

3.3 Running Time

We measure the running time of fifteen proxy benchmarks, and the results are displayed in Fig. 6. It can be observed that the running time of each db_bench proxy benchmark is below 1 s, and the running time of each proxy benchmark is below 3 s. The average running time of these proxy benchmarks is just 1.62 s.

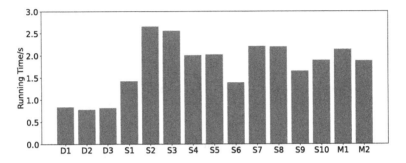

Fig. 6. Running Time of Proxy benchmarks.

3.4 Summary

The average accuracy of every micro-architectural metric between the proxy benchmark and the real benchmark is over 92%, which proves that our proxy benchmarks have almost the same micro-architectural characteristics as real benchmarks. Moreover, the average running time of the proxy benchmarks is just 1.62 s. Therefore, our proxy benchmark methodology is valid and effective for the micro-architectural metrics.

4 Case Studies

In this section, we conduct two use case studies to evaluate the consistency between real and proxy benchmarks in terms of micro-architectural metrics across different configurations. We will evaluate them from the following perspectives: 1) can proxy and real benchmarks keep consistent when prefetch is enabled? 2) can proxy and real benchmarks keep consistent when Hyper-Threading is enabled?

To perform these evaluations, we will modify the configurations of our machine. We will rerun both our real benchmarks and proxy benchmarks and measure their respectively micro-architectural metrics. The correlation coefficient will be calculated using Eq. 6, while the average error will be calculated using Eq. 7. Here, x represents the micro-architectural metric of the real benchmarks, while y represents the metric of corresponding proxy benchmarks.

$$\rho(x,y) = \frac{\sqrt{\sum_{i=1}^{n}(x_i - \overline{x})(y_i - \overline{y})}}{\sqrt{\sum_{i=1}^{n}(x_i - \overline{x})^2 \sum_{i=1}^{n}(y_i - \overline{y})^2}} \tag{6}$$

$$\overline{error(x,y)} = \frac{\sum_{i=1}^{n}|\frac{y_i - x_i}{x_i}|}{n} \tag{7}$$

4.1 Prefetch Strategy Setting

Prefetch is a strategy employed by the CPU to fetch data from memory into the cache in advance. The decision to use prefetch can impact the cache behavior and, ultimately, the processor performance. We will focus on cache behavior and processor performance in this part. Figure 7 and Fig. 8 present the micro-architectural metrics of real and proxy benchmarks when prefetch enabled.

Figure 7a presents the CPI of real benchmarks and corresponding proxy benchmarks. We observe that most of them exhibit similar CPI. Although the largest error can achieve 36%, the average error remains acceptable, just 7.5%. Moreover, the real benchmarks and proxy benchmarks display a high correlation ($\rho = 0.980$). These results illustrate that the proxy benchmarks can retain the processor performance characteristic of the real benchmarks, even when prefetch is enabled.

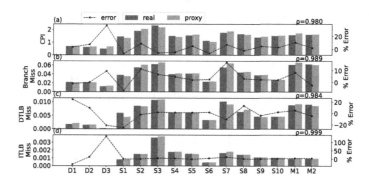

Fig. 7. CPI, Branch Miss, DTLB Miss, ITLB Miss When Prefetch is enabled.

Figure 8a, Fig. 8b, Fig. 8c and Fig. 8d present the cache behavior of real and proxy benchmarks. The average errors are respectively 4.8%, 7.0%, 10.8%, 43.4%, and the correlation coefficients are respectively 0.986, 0.993, 0.820, 0.846. We can find that L1 DCache and ICache Miss both have small errors and strong correlations. The average errors of L2 and L3 Cache Miss are bigger, but they still keep correlation at a high level. We can conclude that our proxy benchmarks can retain the cache behavior characteristic of real benchmarks. For Branch Miss, DTLB Miss, and ITLB Miss, their average errors are respectively 5.26%, 8.5%, 14.4%, and their correlation coefficients are respectively 0.983, 0.984, 0.999.

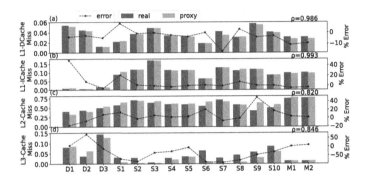

Fig. 8. Miss of L1 DCache, L1 ICache, L2 Cache, L3 Cache When Prefetch is enabled.

4.2   Hyper-Threading Technology

Hyper-Threading (HT) is Intel's parallel computation technology. HT enhances the parallel computation performance of a CPU by offering two logical threads on one core. Figure 9 and Fig. 10 present the metrics of real benchmarks and proxy benchmarks when running with HT enabled on the server.

Figure 9a compares the CPI between real benchmarks and proxy benchmarks. A strong correlation ($\rho = 0.876$) is observed between the CPI of real and proxy benchmarks. However, there are significant gaps in some cases, such as S10, which has an error of 31.4%. It can be observed that the CPI is quite close for the first three real benchmarks and proxy benchmarks but not for the others. This can be explained by the fact that only the first three real benchmarks are single-thread programs, while all proxy benchmarks are single-thread programs. Therefore, our proxy benchmarks can retain single-thread real benchmarks' properties better. In addition to CPI, as shown in Fig. 9b, similar patterns can be observed in the results of Branch Miss. Branch Miss between the first three real benchmarks and proxy benchmarks are quite close. This may be due to the impact of frequent thread switches on branch prediction.

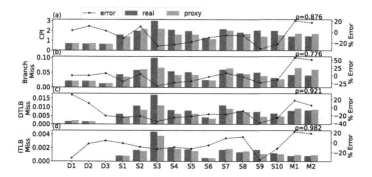

Fig. 9. CPI, Branch Miss, DTLB Miss, ITLB Miss When HT is enabled.

Figure 10a, Fig. 10b, Fig. 9a and Fig. 9b prove proxy benchmarks retain real benchmarks' properties well in L1 DCache, L1 ICache, DTLB and ITLB. The correlation coefficients are respectively 0.950, 0.982, 0.921, and 0.982. The average errors are respectively 10.2%, 7.4%, 21.8%, and 13.2%. The results of L2 Cache and L3 Cache are worse, while the average errors are 16.2% and 25.5%, and the correlation coefficients are 0.800 and 0.991.

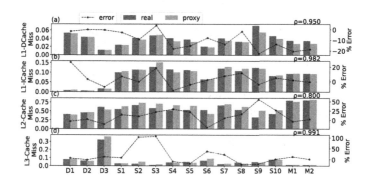

Fig. 10. Miss of L1 DCache, L1 ICache, L2 Cache, L3 Cache When HT is enabled.

When HT is enabled, the correlation coefficients of most micro-architectural metrics keep at a high level, which demonstrates that our proxy benchmarks can keep consistent with real benchmarks. For CPI and Branch Miss, the decrease in correlation can be attributed to our methodology's shortcoming that the proxy benchmark can't retain the real benchmark's multi-thread characteristic well.

4.3   Summary

When prefetch or HT is enabled, most micro-architectural metrics' correlation coefficients are high. Therefore, the micro-architectural metrics of real and proxy benchmarks can keep consistent before and after prefetch or HT is enabled. This implies that our proxy benchmark methodology could be used for micro-architectural design evaluations.

5   Related Work

Many big data benchmarks have been proposed to evaluate big data system performance. Such as BigBench [19], TPC-DS [20], BigDataBench [8–10], Cloud-Suite [7], and YCSB [21]. However, it's difficult for these benchmarks to run on simulators because of their complex software stacks and long running time.

Reducing data size is an effective way to reduce running time for workloads. Keeton et al. successfully reduce running time by replacing complex queries with simple ones, thus reducing data size [22]. Shao et al. achieve similar goals by modifying queries, reducing the number of concurrent clients, and overall data size for DSS and OLTP workloads [23]. Barroso et al. and Ertvelde et al. opt for using partial datasets instead of the entire dataset [24,25], which also proved to be a feasible method for reducing running time. Although these methods effectively reduce running time, they still depend on complex software stacks.

Extracting workload segments is another popular way. [26–28] sample the instruction stream and fuse the sampled segments into new programs. Kernel benchmarks, consisting of a set of kernels extracted from real application [29], such as [30], are widely used in high-performance computing. SimPoint [31] method uses BBV [32] to select some basic blocks to represent the overall program. However, when these methods are applied in big data field, they must need the support of complex software stacks. For example, applying SimPoint method on a MySQL benchmark must depend on its storage engine(e.g., InnoDB).

The last way is to construct proxy benchmarks [11–14]. This method involves using small program segments to construct proxy benchmarks, which can then be used to replace the real benchmarks while can both reduce running time and get rid of complex software stacks.

6   Conclusion

In this paper, based on simple program fragments called basic blocks, we propose a novel proxy benchmark generation methodology. This methodology involves linearly combining basic blocks and adjusting their execution times through iteration to mimic real benchmarks. Our case studies also demonstrate that our proxy benchmarks are consistent with real benchmarks before and after prefetch or Hyper-Threading is turned on.

References

1. Indrawan-Santiago, M.: Database research: are we at a crossroad? Reflection on NoSQL. In: 2012 15th International Conference on Network-Based Information Systems, pp. 45–51. IEEE Computer Society (2012)

2. Boicea, A., Radulescu, F., Agapin, L.I.: MongoDB vs Oracle - database comparison. In: 2012 Third International Conference on Emerging Intelligent Data and Web Technologies, pp. 330–335. IEEE Computer Society (2012)
3. Pavlo, A., et al.: A comparison of approaches to large-scale data analysis. In: Proceedings of the 2009 ACM SIGMOD International Conference on Management of Data, pp. 165–178. ACM (2009)
4. Li, Y., Manoharan, S.: A performance comparison of SQL and NoSQL databases. In: 2013 IEEE Pacific Rim Conference on Communications, Computers and Signal Processing (PACRIM), pp. 15–19. IEEE (2013)
5. SPECCPU2017. https://www.spec.org/cpu2017/
6. Bienia, C.: Benchmarking modern multiprocessors. Princeton University (2011)
7. Ferdman, M., et al.: Clearing the clouds: a study of emerging scale-out workloads on modern hardware. In: Proceedings of the 17th International Conference on Architectural Support for Programming Languages and Operating Systems (ASPLOS), pp. 37–48. ACM (2012)
8. Gao, W., et al.: BigDataBench: a scalable and unified big data and AI benchmark suite. arXiv preprint arXiv:1802.08254 (2018)
9. Gao, W., et al.: BigDataBench: a big data benchmark suite from web search engines. arXiv preprint arXiv:1307.0320 (2013)
10. Wang, L., et al.: BigDataBench: a big data benchmark suite from internet services. In: 2014 IEEE 20th International Symposium on High Performance Computer Architecture (HPCA), pp. 488–499. IEEE Computer Society (2014)
11. Han, R., Zong, Z., Zhang, F., Vázquez-Poletti, J.L., Jia, Z., Wang, L.: Cloudmix: generating diverse and reducible workloads for cloud systems. In: 2017 IEEE 10th International Conference on Cloud Computing (CLOUD), pp. 496–503. IEEE Computer Society (2017)
12. Panda, R., John, L.K.: Proxy benchmarks for emerging big-data workloads. In: Proceedings of the 26th International Conference on Parallel Architectures and Compilation Techniques (PACT), pp. 105–116. IEEE Computer Society (2017)
13. Gao, W., et al.: Data motifs: a lens towards fully understanding big data and AI workloads. In: Proceedings of the 27th International Conference on Parallel Architectures and Compilation Techniques (PACT). ACM (2018)
14. Gao, W., et al.: Data motif-based proxy benchmarks for big data and AI workloads. In: Proceedings of the 2018 IEEE International Symposium on Workload Characterization (IISWC), pp. 48–58. IEEE Computer Society (2018)
15. Intel. https://perfmon-events.intel.com/
16. Perf. https://perf.wiki.kernel.org/index.php/Main_Page
17. db_bench. https://github.com/EighteenZi/rocksdb_wiki/blob/master/Benchmarking-tools.md
18. SysBench. https://github.com/akopytov/sysbench
19. Ghazal, A., et al.: BigBench: towards an industry standard benchmark for big data analytics. In: Proceedings of the 2013 ACM SIGMOD International Conference on Management of Data, pp. 1197–1208. ACM (2013)
20. Pöss, M., Smith, B., Kollár, L., Larson, P.: TPC-DS, taking decision support benchmarking to the next level. In: Proceedings of the 2002 ACM SIGMOD International Conference on Management of Data, pp. 582–587. ACM (2002)
21. Dey, A., Fekete, A.D., Nambiar, R., Röhm, U.: YCSB+T: benchmarking web-scale transactional databases. In: 2014 IEEE 30th International Conference on Data Engineering Workshops (ICDE), pp. 223–230. IEEE Computer Society (2014)

22. Keeton, K., Patterson, D.A.: Towards a simplified database workload for computer architecture evaluations. In: Workload Characterization for Computer System Design, pp. 49–71 (2000)

23. Shao, M., Ailamaki, A., Falsafi, B.: DBmbench: fast and accurate database workload representation on modern microarchitecture. In: Proceedings of the 2005 Conference of the Centre for Advanced Studies on Collaborative Research, pp. 254–267. IBM (2005)

24. Barroso, L.A., Gharachorloo, K., Bugnion, E.: Memory system characterization of commercial workloads. In: Proceedings of the 25th Annual International Symposium on Computer Architecture, pp. 3–14. IEEE Computer Society (1998)

25. Ertvelde, L.V., Eeckhout, L.: Benchmark synthesis for architecture and compiler exploration. In: Proceedings of the 2010 IEEE International Symposium on Workload Characterization (IISWC), pp. 1–11. IEEE Computer Society (2010)

26. Conte, T.M., Hirsch, M.A., Menezes, K.N.: Reducing state loss for effective trace sampling of superscalar processors. In: 1996 International Conference on Computer Design (ICCD 1996), VLSI in Computers and Processors, pp. 468–477. IEEE Computer Society (1996)

27. Wunderlich, R.E., Wenisch, T.F., Falsafi, B., Hoe, J.C.: SMARTS: accelerating microarchitecture simulation via rigorous statistical sampling. In: 30th International Symposium on Computer Architecture (ISCA), pp. 84–95. IEEE Computer Society (2003)

28. Lu, F., Joseph, R., Trajcevski, G., Liu, S.: Efficient parameter variation sampling for architecture simulations. In: Design, Automation and Test in Europe (DATE), pp. 1578–1583. IEEE (2011)

29. Hennessy, J.L., Patterson, D.A.: Computer Architecture - A Quantitative Approach, 5th edn. Morgan Kaufmann, Burlington (2012)

30. Bailey, D.H., et al.: The NAS parallel benchmarks. Int. J. High Perform. Comput. Appl. **5**(3), 63–73 (1991)

31. Sherwood, T., Perelman, E., Hamerly, G., Calder, B.: Automatically characterizing large scale program behavior. In: Proceedings of the 10th International Conference on Architectural Support for Programming Languages and Operating Systems (ASPLOS-X), pp. 45–57. ACM Press (2002)

32. Sherwood, T., Perelman, E., Calder, B.: Basic block distribution analysis to find periodic behavior and simulation points in applications. In: Proceedings of the 10th International Conference on Parallel Architectures and Compilation Techniques (PACT), pp. 3–14. IEEE Computer Society (2001)

AGIBench: A Multi-granularity, Multimodal, Human-Referenced, Auto-Scoring Benchmark for Large Language Models

Fei Tang[1,2], Wanling Gao[1], LuZhou Peng[3], and Jianfeng Zhan[1(✉)]

[1] Research Center for Advanced Computer Systems, State Key Lab of Processors, Institute of Computing Technology, Chinese Academy of Sciences, Beijing, China
{tangfei,gaowanling,zhanjianfeng}@ict.ac.cn
[2] University of Chinese Academy of Sciences, Beijing, China
[3] Department of Finance and Public Administration, Shanghai Lixin University of Accounting and Finance, Shanghai, China

Abstract. Large language models (LLMs) like ChatGPT have revealed amazing intelligence. How to evaluate the question-solving abilities of LLMs and their degrees of intelligence is a hot-spot but challenging issue. First, the question-solving abilities are interlaced with different ability branches like understanding and massive knowledge categories like mathematics. Second, the inputs of questions are multimodal that may involve text and images. In addition, they may have varying levels of difficulty while lacking a unified standard to judge which one is more difficult. Third, the response format of LLMs is diverse and thus poses great challenges for result extraction and evaluation. Several benchmarks have been proposed to evaluate LLMs, yet they still exhibit significant shortcomings.

In this paper, to tackle the above challenges, we propose AGIBench—a multi-granularity, multimodal, human-referenced, and auto-scoring benchmarking methodology for LLMs. Instead of a collection of blended questions, AGIBench focuses on three typical ability branches and adopts a four-tuple <ability branch, knowledge, difficulty, modal> to label the attributes of each question. First, it supports multi-granularity benchmarking. Second, it contains multimodal input, including text and images. Third, it classifies all the questions into five degrees of difficulty according to the average accuracy rate of abundant educated humans (human-referenced). Fourth, it adopts zero-shot learning to avoid introducing additional unpredictability and provides an auto-scoring method to extract and judge the result. Finally, it defines multi-dimensional metrics. Our experiments on twelve state-of-the-art LLMs show the effectiveness of our benchmark. AGIBench is publicly available from https://www.benchcouncil.org/agibench.

Keywords: LLMs · Benchmark · Intelligence

S. Hunold et al. (Eds.): Bench 2023, LNCS 14521, pp. 137–152, 2024.
https://doi.org/10.1007/978-981-97-0316-6_9

1   Introduction

Intelligence is an abstract concept and has no unified definition yet [8]. Research about human intelligence has been conducted for decades and formed a series of theories, e.g., triarchic theory of intelligence [13], fluid and crystallized intelligence [2], theory of multiple intelligences [5], etc., while having no unified standard about how to evaluate human intelligence. In this condition, the difficulties aggravate evaluating artificial intelligence (AI), which has shown powerful abilities to solve problems or questions and reflects the tremendous potential to approach human intelligence, especially the emerging large language models (LLMs) like ChatGPT. Different from the previous AI applications that mainly target a single task or a specific domain, LLMs anticipate achieving general intelligence. Hence, the previous benchmarking methodologies that focus on specific tasks or application domains are not applicable anymore. A new benchmarking methodology is a necessity but no easy feat.

On the one hand, how to construct a benchmark with diverse, typical, and difficulty-differentiated input questions is challenging. Similar to human intelligence, the intelligence of LLMs has no unified benchmarking standard since the input questions or problems to be solved are massive and interlaced. First, the input questions or problems may not only involve multiple ability branches like understanding and reasoning but also involve numerous knowledge categories with varying levels of difficulties like mathematics and geography. Second, the input questions or problems are multimodal with a combination of text and images, for example, geometry problems in mathematics, talking about pictures in linguistics, etc.

On the other hand, how to evaluate the benchmarking results and choose comprehensive and important metrics is challenging. From the perspective of analyzing the results, the response formats of LLMs are diverse. For example, the response may (1) answer the choice from four choices marked A, B, C, and D, with an explanation and analysis of the above four choices one by one; (2) only answer the choice without an explanation; (3) answer the choice with a partial explanation. In addition, the orders of choices and explanations vary, and the text words are discrepant. Even though a human being can distinguish the result easily, however, it is extremely hard for a computer program. From the perspective of the evaluation metrics, the performance of LLMs is multidimensional and not merely average accuracy. For example, the LLMs may be adept in specific ability branches, knowledge categories, or difficulty levels; the response results may change during multiple runs, etc.

Many efforts have been proposed to benchmark the LLMs [7,9,12,18–20]; however, they fail to solve the above challenges. First, almost all adopt one or more open-source datasets with a collection of blended text questions at a per-dataset or per-ability branch granularity. However, these blended questions may cover different knowledge categories and different difficulty levels. We may hardly distinguish the performance on each ability branch, knowledge, or difficulty level, except for a total score on a dataset. Furthermore, even some of those benchmarks [20] provide different difficulty levels; however, these difficulty levels are applied to a per-dataset granularity, which means the overall difficulty of the entire question dataset while not a specific question. Second, to solve the challenges of analyzing the response results, most of them [7,9,20] adopt prompt engineering like few-shot and chain-of-thought (CoT) to increase the accuracy or normalize the response format. However, our experiments and the related work show that no matter few-shot or CoT would introduce unpredictable performance impacts. Our experiments especially show that with few-shot, the accuracy variance achieves 5% when using different random seeds. C-Eval [7] shows that with CoT, the accuracy increases on some models (e.g., ChatGLM-6B, +3%) while decreases on other models (e.g., Chinese-LLaMA-13B, -11.9%). Some of the efforts [18] adopt a zero-shot approach to avoid the unpredictable impact, however, they have to analyze the response result manually, which results in unacceptable evaluation costs. Third, most of those efforts only report average accuracy and lack a comprehensive and multidimensional evaluation. While HELM [9] incorporates multiple metrics, it omits human-referenced evaluation and does not include a multimodal dataset.

Table 1. Observations and Implications for LLMs using AGIBench.

Observations	Implications
Multi-granularity: (1) ChatGLM v2-6B outperforms ChatGLM-130B even with less parameters; (2) LLMs reflect good common sense (e.g., GPT-4 outperforms humans by 15.84%) and understanding ability (e.g., GPT-4 is comparable with humans) while poor reasoning ability (e.g., GPT-4 underperforms humans by 25.94%). (3) GPT-4 has the highest performance on most ability branches and knowledge categories.	(1) Architecture improvement and high-quality training data are more pivotal than large model size; (2) Reasoning ability is a direction of optimization
Multimodal: (1) The image understanding and reasoning abilities are poor for the four LLMs that support open image access. (2) For LLMs that have no image processing ability, a majority of the responses cannot admit the limitation and output hallucinational and nonsense responses.	(1) The multimodal abilities need optimizations
Human-referenced Difficulty: (1) Humans perform better than LLMs on simple questions (i.e., Level 1 to 3) while worse on difficult questions (i.e., Level 4 and 5). (2) The accuracy of GPT-4 is higher than humans for common sense, comparable for understanding, and worse for reasoning.	(1) The solving abilities of simple questions and reasoning need optimizations
Multi-dimensional metrics: (1) The worst-case accuracy of LLMs is significantly below the corresponding average one, which means the model does not always give a correct answer during three times evaluations, indicating a poor reliability of LLMs. (2) The best-case accuracy of LLMs is much higher than the other cases, which means the model has a high probability to give a correct answer during three evaluations. (3) The majority voting accuracy is similar to the average one, which means most of the time, the model can give a correct answer.	(1) The reliability of LLMs needs optimization

This paper proposes AGIBench—a multi-granularity, multimodal, human-referenced, and auto-scoring benchmarking methodology and benchmark for LLMs. Instead of a collection of blended questions, AGIBench focuses on fundamental ability branches and adopts a four-tuple <ability branch, knowledge, difficulty, modal> to label the attributes of each question. In total, AGIBench provides 927 questions, covering three kinds of ability branches, i.e., common sense, reasoning, and understanding, covering 20 knowledge categories and 68 knowledge subclasses. First, it supports multi-granularity benchmarking, e.g., per-question, per-ability branch, per-knowledge, per-difficulty level, per-dataset, and per-modal granularities. Second, it contains multimodal input, including various contexts like text-only, image-only, text with images, text with tables, and a combination of text, images, and tables. Third, it classifies all the questions into five degrees of difficulty according to the average accuracy rate of abundant educated humans (human-referenced). Fourth, it adopts zero-shot learning to avoid additional unpredictability and provides an auto-scoring method to extract and judge the result. Finally, it defines multi-dimensional metrics, including accuracy under the average, worst, best, and majority voting cases, and repeatability. Our experiments on twelve state-of-the-art LLMs show the effectiveness of our benchmark. Table 1 presents the main observations and implications of LLMs using AGIBench.

2   Related Work

Many efforts have been proposed to evaluate traditional natural language processing (NLP) algorithms and LLMs. GLUE [15] and SuperGLUE [14] are benchmarks for traditional NLP tasks, primarily evaluating understanding capabilities. However, the questions are limited in scope and mainly focus on sentence classification, which cannot comprehensively reflect the complexities of human language [11]. Thus, these benchmarks cannot meet the need for evaluating LLMs.

For evaluating LLMs, from the perspective of the question dataset, most of the related work uses closed-ended questions since the answer is definitive without subjectivity. BIG-Bench [12] and HELM [9] use a combination of multiple datasets like MATH [6] and GSM8K [3]. On the one hand, such an approach may incur question redundancy and result in limited coverage. On the other hand, they only support the benchmarking at the per-dataset or per-ability branch granularity and thus cannot reveal the abilities from different perspectives. For example, they only output a score on a specific dataset with blended questions that involve different difficulty levels. Hence, we can hardly know the ability for a specific knowledge category or a specific difficulty level. ScienceQA [11] collects questions from elementary and high school science curricula. However, these questions are too easy for humans. AGI-Eval [20], C-Eval [7], and GAOKAO [18] focus on the LLMs benchmarking using the Chinese language. They utilize exams like national civil service and college entrance exams as question datasets. However, these benchmarks only use average accuracy as the evaluation metric, which is overly simplistic. Several efforts attempt to use open-ended questions for LLMs benchmarking. Chandrasekaran et al. [1] collect a series of open-ended and multimodal questions to evaluate GPT-4; however, evaluating and scoring the results is extremely hard. In addition, the evaluation results are hard to reproduce, considering the subjectivity of different persons.

From the perspective of evaluation and scoring method, a majority of the existing efforts adopt prompt engineering for evaluation, such as few-shot learning [16] and Chain-of-Thought (CoT) [17]. Although these methods have been proven to have the potential to standardize the format of the response result or increase model accuracy, however, C-Eval [7] and our experiments show that they may not always be effective and would introduce unpredictable performance impacts. In this condition, we cannot evaluate the abilities of LLMs accurately since the response results may be impacted by prompt engineering. Additionally, using these methods requires case-by-case tuning, which exacerbates the benchmarking costs and cannot assure the fairness of benchmarking. MT-Bench [19] explores the use of GPT-4 as an approach to judge the correctness of the response results of LLMs and compare it with human judgment. They find that the decisions from GPT-4 and humans have an 80% similarity. However, MT-Bench only selects 80 questions and thus has limited representativeness. Additionally, using GPT-4 directly for scoring would incur huge labor costs since we still need to check the judgment for every question.

3   The Design and Implementation

This section illustrates the design and implementation of AGIBench. Section 3.1 describes the benchmarking methodology. Section 3.2 presents an AGIBench overview.

3.1   Methodology

To evaluate the different question-solving abilities of LLMs and their degrees of intelligence, we adopt a multi-granularity, multimodal, human-referenced, and auto-scoring benchmarking methodology, covering the question dataset construction, evaluation methodology, and evaluation metrics.

First, to support multi-granularity benchmarking instead of only per-dataset or per-ability branch benchmarking adopted in the related work, we use a four-tuple <ability branch, knowledge, difficulty, modal> to label the attributes of each question. The ability branch focuses on the most fundamental and essential abilities like understanding. Knowledge includes a broad spectrum of knowledge categories within each ability branch, e.g., passage reading within understanding ability. Difficulty indicates a question's difficulty level, i.e., Levels 1 to 5, from easy to difficult. Modal indicates the modal of a question like text or image.

Second, to construct a representative and typical question dataset, we aim to cover many questions with diverse and varied attributes. Specifically, we choose the three most fundamental ability branches: common sense, understanding, and reasoning. We single out twenty comprehensive and representative knowledge categories for these three ability branches in total. Knowledge for common sense covers six categories: humanities, technology, law, geography, politics, and economy; Knowledge for understanding includes passage reading, sentence grammar, fill-in-the-blank, and long text reading; Knowledge for reasoning includes graphical reasoning, definition judgment, comprehensive materials, tabular materials, textual materials, graphical materials, analogical reasoning, logical judgment, mathematical calculation, and numerical reasoning. For the difficulty attribute of each question, we adopt a human-referenced methodology based on big data statistics, which uses the accuracy rate answered by millions of well-educated humans to label the question's difficulty level. For example, Level 1 is the easiest one with an 80% to 100% accuracy rate, which means 80% to 100% of millions of humans can give a correct answer. Level 2 has a 60% to 80% accuracy rate. Level 3 has a 40% to 60% accuracy rate. Level 4 has a 20% to 40% accuracy rate. Level 5 is the most difficult and has a 0% to 20% accuracy rate. We cover multimodal input that encompasses various contexts, including text-only, text with tables, text with images, image-only, and a combination of text, images, and tables.

Third, to cope with the diversity of the response format and avoid the unpredictable performance impacts of prompt engineering, we do not use prompt engineering and attempt to find a series of regex patterns to extract the answers and perform judgment.

Fourth, we define multi-dimensional metrics for LLMs benchmarking: accuracy under different cases and repeatability.

3.2 AGIBench Design and Implementation

We design and implement the AGIBench based on the methodology, including the question dataset construction, evaluation and scoring, and metrics.

Question Dataset. AGIBench selects questions related to human life, especially for the Chinese. We mainly choose the questions from national civil service examinations since they satisfy the diversity and fundamentality requirements. We use a four-tuple <ability branch, knowledge, difficulty, modal> to label the attributes of each question. The ability branch covers common sense, understanding, and reasoning abilities. The knowledge contains 20 categories and 68 subclasses covering humanities, physics, chemistry, economics, law, politics, culture, geography, history, engineering, mathematics, etc. Table 2 shows the ability branch and knowledge attributes of the AGIBench dataset. Regarding difficulty, our dataset uses human accuracy as the reference, and the accuracy is based on the highly educated human. We carefully select the difficulty of questions and classify five levels from Levels 1 to Level 5. A higher number means a more challenging degree. From Level 1 to Level 5, the responding human accuracy is [80%, 100%], [60%, 80%), [40%, 60%), [20%, 40%), and [0%, 20%). Figure 1 shows the distribution of difficulty levels of AGIBench. As for the modal, we include multimodal input covering various contexts, i.e., text-only, image-only, text with images, text with tables, and a combination of text, images, and tables. The corresponding number of questions for these contexts are 863, 5, 38, 10, and 11, respectively. In total, we provide 927 questions. Note that the image is processed as a URL in the questions. Additionally, the text dataset contains plain text,

Table 2. Ability Branch and Knowledge Attributes of Question Dataset in AGIBench.

Ability Branch	Knowledge	Knowledge Subclass (Percentage)
Common Sense	Economics	Economics (1.08%)
	Geography	Environmental (0.76%), National and Social Conditions (1.08%), Natural (1.08%)
	Humanities	Chinese History (1.08%), Cultural (1.08%), Literary (1.08%), World History (1.08%)
	Law	Administrative Law (1.08%), Civil Law (1.08%), Commercial and Economic Law (1.08%), Constitutional Law (1.08%), Criminal Law (0.97%), Jurisprudence (1.08%), Procedural Law (2.16%)
	Politics	Politics (1.08%)
	Technology	Biology Fundamentals (1.08%), Chemistry Fundamentals (1.08%), Everyday Knowledge (1.08%), Physics Fundamentals (1.08%), Technology Theories and Achievements (1.08%)
Reasoning	Analogical Reasoning	Grammatical Relations (0.86%), Logical Relations (5.07%), Semantic Relations (3.02%)
	Comprehensive Materials	Comprehensive Materials (1.08%)
	Definition Judgment	Multiple Definitions (1.08%), Single Definition (1.08%)
	Graphic Materials	Graphic Materials (1.08%)
	Graphic Reasoning	Attribute Principles (0.86%), Pattern Principles (1.83%), Positional Principles (1.94%), Quantity Principles (1.4%), Spatial Reconstruction (0.22%), Special Principles (0.86%)
	Logical Judgment	Combinations and Arrangements (1.08%), Daily Conclusions (1.08%), Reason Explanations (0.97%), Strengthened Types (1.08%), Translation Reasoning (1.08%), True-False Reasoning (0.97%), Weakened Types (1.08%)
	Mathematical Calculation	Core Methods (5.18%), Economic Profit and Comprehensive Planning (2.91%), Engineering (1.08%), Inclusion-Exclusion Principle (12.51%), Journey (1.08%), Permutation, Combination, and Probability (2.16%), Solution Problems (0.97%)
	Numerical Reasoning	Basic Sequences (0.76%), Exponential Sequences (0.97%), Fractional Sequences (1.08%), Mechanical Split Sequences (1.94%), Multi-level Sequences (1.08%), Multiple Sequences (0.54%), Recursive Sequences (1.08%)
	Tabular Materials	Tabular Materials (1.08%)
	Textual Materials	Textual Materials (1.08%)
Understanding	Fill-in-the-blank	Content Word Fill-in-the-blank (1.08%), Idiom Fill-in-the-blank (1.08%), Mixed Fill-in-the-blank (1.08%)
	Long Text Reading	Long Text Reading (1.08%)
	Passage Reading	Central Understanding (1.62%), Detail Judgment (1.08%), Sentence Understanding (1.08%), Title Insertion (1.08%)
	Sentence Grammar	Flawed and Ambiguous (1.08%), Following Sentence Choice (1.08%), Sentence Fill-in-the-blank (1.08%), Sentence Ordering (1.08%)

complex mathematical formulas, and table data. We adopt the latex format for mathematical formulas, and for table data, we use the markdown format.

We further consider the length of questions. Figure 2 shows the length distribution of questions, and our dataset covers a broad spectrum. The size of most questions is more significant than 100 while many others are less than ten words [10]. Our dataset contains several long-length questions whose length exceeds 1000, which also shows the difficulty and variety of our dataset.

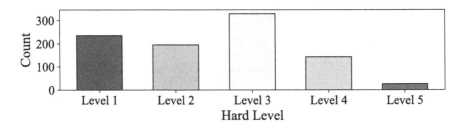

Fig. 1. The Distribution of Five Difficulty Levels. Using the accuracy rate answered by millions of well-educated humans as references.

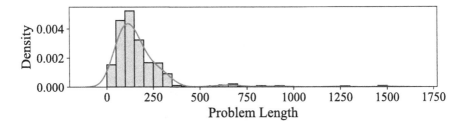

Fig. 2. The Length Distribution of the Question Dataset in AGIBench.

Evaluation and Scoring. To avoid the impact of prompt engineering and meanwhile essentially reduce labor costs, we adopt an auto-scoring methodology that combines a heuristic regular expression searching algorithm (HRE for short) and GPT-4. On the one hand, we use an HRE algorithm to search the regex patterns, as shown in Algorithm 1. We repeat N iterations and randomly select M responses from the total responses during each iteration. For the M responses of each iteration, we set a threshold "minimum_limit", indicating the minimum number of occurrences that a response format can be added as a new regex pattern. After that, we obtain a set that contains frequently occurring regex patterns. Our evaluation statistics in Sect. 4.2 verify the effectiveness of the HRE algorithm. Among hundreds of thousands of responses from LLMs, about 67% of the response results can be adequately extracted using HRE. On the other hand, in terms of the remaining small fraction that cannot be extracted by HRE, we use GPT-4 to extract the results. Note that we do not use GPT-4 directly because its accuracy cannot achieve 100%, and we still need to verify the judgments artificially. By adopting HRE, we reduce about seventy percent labor costs.

Metrics. We collect many metrics to evaluate LLMs comprehensively, not merely average accuracy, which is the only metric for most related work. We widely include the average accuracy, the worst-case accuracy, the best-case accuracy, the majority voting accuracy, and the repeatability to indicate the performance of LLMs under different cases. We detail these metrics as follows. Note that we evaluate each LLM using a question three times to ensure the fairness

---

Algorithm 1. Heuristic regular expression searching (HRE)

1: pattern_sets ← []
2: **for** $i \leftarrow 1$ **to** N **do**
3:     sampled_responses ← sample(total_responses, M)
4:     **while** max_number_of_common_patterns(sampled_responses) > minimum_limit **do**
5:         temp_pattern ← propose_pattern(sampled_responses)
6:         patched_to_pattern_sets ← False
7:         **for** pattern ∈ pattern_sets **do**
8:             **if** can_patch(pattern, temp_pattern) **then**
9:                 pattern ← patch(pattern, temp_pattern)
10:                patched_to_pattern_sets ← True
11:                **break**
12:            **end if**
13:        **end for**
14:        **if** not patched_to_pattern_sets **then**
15:            pattern_sets.append(temp_pattern)
16:        **end if**
17:        sampled_responses ← sampled_responses − match(sampled_responses, temp_pattern)
18:     **end while**
19: **end for**

---

and the reliability of benchmarking. For each time, if the answer is correct, the score is 1, otherwise 0.

(1) Average accuracy. For the three times' evaluations on an LLM using the same question, we use the average score as the score of the LLM for that question. Then we calculate the average score for all questions as the final average accuracy.

(2) The worst-case accuracy. Different from the average accuracy, if all three times' evaluations give the correct answer, the score is 1, otherwise 0. Then the average value on all questions is reported as the final worst-case accuracy.

(3) The best-case accuracy. More relaxed compared to the worst-case one, if greater than or equal to one answer gives the correct answer, the score is 1, otherwise 0.

(4) The majority voting accuracy. If at least two answers are correct, the score is 1, otherwise 0.

(5) Repeatability. The similarity of the responses during three different runs. A high similarity indicates good repeatability.

4   Evaluation

This section presents the evaluation, including the evaluation methodology (Sect. 4.1), experiment setup Sect. 4.2, and evaluation results Sect. 4.3.

4.1   Evaluation Methodology

LLMs Overview. We choose representative LLMs with different underlying technology, differentiated model sizes, and state-of-the-art performance. We also consider additional training data, architectures, target purposes, and whether open-sourced. Specifically, we choose 12 models from OpenAI, Anthropic, Meta, Tsinghua, Baidu, Alibaba, and iFlytek, including GPT-3.5, ChatGPT, and GPT-4 from OpenAI, Claude from Anthropic, LLaMA-13B and Vicuna-13B (LLaMA based) from Meta, ChatGLM-6B, ChatGLM v2-6B, and ChatGLM-13B from Tsinghua, Ernie from Baidu, Qianwen from Alibaba, and Spark from iFlytek. The model size ranges from 6 billion to 175 billion. The detailed information is listed in Table. 3.

Table 3. The Overview of Evaluated LLMs.

Model	Model Size	Training Data Composition	Temperature	Developer	Open Source	Access
ChatGLM-6B	6 billion	Chinese and English	0.5/1	Tsinghua	Yes	Local
ChatGLM v2-6B	6 billion	Chinese and English	0.5/1	Tsinghua	YES	Local
ChatGLM-130B	130 billion	Chinese and English	Not support	Tsinghua	No	Web
GPT-3.5	175 billion	Primarily English	1.0/2	OpenAI	No	API
ChatGPT	175 billion	Primarily English	1.0/2	OpenAI	No	API
GPT-4	Unknown	Primarily English	1.0/2	OpenAI	No	API
Claude	Unknown	Primarily English	Not support	Anthropic	No	Web
LLaMA-13B	13 billion	Primarily English	0.5/1	Meta	Yes	Local
Vicuna-13B	13 billion	Primarily English	0.5/1	UC Berkeley et al	Yes	Local
Ernie	175 billion	Chinese and English	Not support	Baidu	No	Web
Qianwen	Unknown	Chinese and English	Not support	Alibaba	No	Web
Spark	Unknown	Chinese and English	Not support	iFlytek	No	Web

Evaluation Method. We do not use prompt engineering like few-shot learning and chain-of-thought (CoT) to avoid unpredicted impacts, verified by related work [7]. They find the CoT performs better on some models (e.g., ChatGLM-6B, +3%) and worse on others (e.g., Chinese-LLaMA-13B, -11.9%). We also conduct an experiment to evaluate the impact of few-shot learning. On ChatGLM v2-6B, we randomly select several question-and-answer pairs as examples to evaluate the impact. Then we use different random seeds and run them three times for each seed. Table. 4 shows the result. The bold text shows the best results (about 37.54%), and the underlined text shows the worst results (about 32.69%). The accuracy gap using different random seeds is large, achieving about 5%.

Table 4. Few-shot experiment on ChatGLM v2-6B using different random seeds and run three times for each seed. Bold text represents the best results, and underlined test represents the worst results.

Seed	Run #1	Run #2	Run #3
0	**37.54%**	**37.54%**	**37.32%**
1	33.44%	33.33%	34.52%
2	32.15%	34.84%	32.69%
3	35.28%	35.49%	34.41%
4	33.23%	33.01%	33.33%

4.2 Experiment Setup

We locally deploy ChatGLM-6B and ChatGLM v2-6B on a single NVIDIA V100 GPU and deploy LLaMA-13B and Vicuna-13B on four NVIDIA 1080 Ti GPUs. For close-sourced models that provide API access, we perform evaluations using their APIs, including GPT-3.5, ChatGPT, and GPT-4. For other close-sourced models that do not offer API access but provide web-based products, we perform evaluations by simulating user input in the browser, including Claude, ChatGLM-130B, Ernie, Qianwen, and Spark. To ensure fairness, we set the temperature parameter as half of the maximum value of the model for all twelve models, except for the web-based products, which do not provide the interface to set the temperature parameter.

Regex	Number	Ratio
Not Matching	32875	33%
【?答案】?(?:和原因)?(?:为|(?:应该)?是|选择)?[:：ׁ]?\s?(?:选项)?([A-Z])[^A-Z]*?(?:ׁ |$)	29508	29%
^(?:选项\s?)?([A-Z])[\.。，\s][^A-Z]*?$	20038	20%
选择?: ?\s?([A-Z])(?:选项)?[^A-Z]*?(?:ׁ |$)	6179	6%
(?:[Aa]nswer|statement|[Ss]olution)\s?(?:to (?:your|this) question)? is:? (?: option)?\"?([A-Z])\"?(?:\.|ׁ |:|$)	3706	4%
作为一个人工智能语言模型，我还没学习如何回答这个问题，您可以向我问一些其它的问题，我会尽力帮您解决的。	2299	2%
^(?:答案[: :]\s?)?([A-Z])(?:\.|ׁ |\s)?$	2173	2%
^(?:选项\s?)?([A-Z])[\.。，\s](?:[^A-Z]|(\1))*?$	1765	2%
(?:选项)?\s?([A-Z])\s?[是|为]正确答案	683	1%
^(?:答案[: :]\s?)?((?:[A-Z]\s?[、\s\.-]?\s?)+)ׁ ?$	458	0%
^\s*$	432	0%

Fig. 3. Regex Patterns Identified by HRE Algorithm.

For the response extraction and judgment, we use the HRE algorithm illustrated in Algorithm 1 and GPT-4 to avoid the unpredictable performance impacts of prompt engineering. We set N as 10, M as 100, and minimum_limit as 2, which means repeating 10 iterations and randomly selecting 100 responses during each iteration. If a response format occurs at least two times, we will add this pattern. We collect 100,116 responses from LLMs, and the regex patterns identified by the HRE algorithm are shown in Fig. 3. These patterns support extracting and judging 67% answers of the total responses, demonstrating the effectiveness of our algorithm. The remaining 33% responses that have no unified regex pattern are processed by GPT-4, and the judgments are manually checked. We use the chain-of-thought (CoT) prompt shown in Fig. 4 to fix the judgment output of GPT-4 when extracting the answers. Note that this prompt is used to judge the correctness of the remaining responses without impacting the model evaluation process.

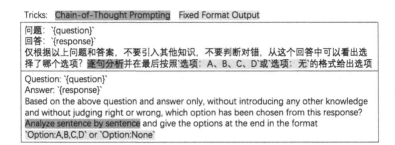

Fig. 4. The Prompt Used to Extract and Judge Answers.

4.3   Evaluation Results

We report the evaluation results including multi-granularity, multimodal, and human-referenced difficulty level, and response repeatability benchmarking. Further, using comprehensive metrics, we evaluate the accuracy of LLMs under different cases.

Multi-granularity Benchmarking. Table 5 shows the multi-granularity benchmarking results at a per-dataset, per-ability branch, and per-knowledge granularities. Note that the "Human" column indicates human accuracy as a reference. The average accuracy on the whole dataset is 60.91%. GPT-4 outperforms others largely on many ability branches and knowledge categories. Most LLMs have better understanding abilities than common sense and reasoning abilities, and the reasoning ability performs the worst. Compared to the human accuracy, GPT-4 outperforms humans by 15.84% for the common sense branch and has similar accuracy to humans (73.16% vs. 74.82%) for the understanding branch, while performing worse than humans for the reasoning branch with a gap of 25.94%.

Table 5. Multi-granularity Benchmarking Results.

Ability	Knowledge	ChatGLM	ChatGLM v2-6B	ChatGLM-130B	GPT-3.5	ChatGPT	GPT-4	Claude	LLaMA-13B	Vicuna-13B	Ernie	Qianwen	Spark	Human
Common Sense	Avg	32.15%	46.30%	36.99%	34.88%	40.28%	**65.84%**	36.47%	23.25%	23.97%	31.28%	17.23%	19.65%	50.00%
	Humanities	31.67%	41.67%	28.06%	19.17%	36.94%	**56.11%**	34.44%	18.33%	18.89%	25.56%	17.22%	9.72%	48.54%
	Technology	33.78%	47.11%	46.00%	36.89%	48.00%	**75.78%**	36.22%	28.44%	26.22%	35.56%	22.22%	37.78%	51.10%
	Law	29.25%	44.16%	31.50%	35.30%	33.61%	**57.81%**	33.47%	22.22%	25.74%	30.52%	13.50%	8.72%	49.00%
	Geography	36.63%	52.67%	44.03%	32.10%	43.21%	**79.42%**	34.98%	21.40%	20.99%	31.28%	23.87%	35.39%	49.43%
	Politics	26.67%	65.56%	41.11%	82.22%	54.44%	**68.89%**	56.67%	22.22%	18.89%	35.56%	6.67%	14.44%	60.70%
	Economics	42.22%	41.11%	47.78%	44.44%	45.56%	**78.89%**	53.33%	31.11%	32.22%	34.44%	14.44%	17.78%	49.10%
Reasoning	Avg	27.95%	29.29%	29.29%	25.82%	32.95%	**36.03%**	27.87%	18.85%	21.75%	24.91%	23.91%	30.75%	61.97%
	Graphic Reasoning	**26.60%**	24.41%	21.89%	12.96%	21.21%	9.43%	27.27%	21.21%	18.35%	20.37%	20.37%	20.20%	71.76%
	Definition Judgment	32.22%	34.44%	57.78%	40.56%	63.33%	**72.22%**	36.11%	31.11%	24.44%	33.89%	20.00%	41.11%	76.20%
	Analogical Reasoning	26.10%	31.86%	37.88%	12.72%	**38.02%**	29.72%	22.09%	12.32%	17.67%	25.84%	14.59%	34.94%	67.08%
	Logical Judgment	34.48%	38.89%	44.12%	37.58%	45.92%	**61.27%**	42.65%	21.90%	32.03%	35.46%	31.21%	38.07%	70.73%
	Mathematical Calculation	27.04%	26.99%	24.77%	28.61%	30.00%	**36.11%**	25.42%	20.28%	20.32%	25.28%	27.27%	34.81%	49.53%
	Numerical Reasoning	22.22%	25.93%	27.05%	26.57%	32.37%	**34.62%**	28.34%	15.46%	23.03%	17.71%	21.74%	24.15%	67.08%
	Text Analysis	**38.89%**	52.22%	0.00%	36.67%	**38.89%**	34.44%	22.22%	11.11%	21.11%	28.89%	18.89%	0.00%	72.10%
	Table Analysis	**53.33%**	25.56%	22.22%	25.56%	17.78%	46.67%	23.33%	21.11%	27.78%	6.67%	30.00%	12.22%	76.36%
	Graphic Analysis	20.00%	22.22%	20.00%	20.00%	13.33%	16.67%	20.00%	13.33%	14.44%	27.78%	**30.00%**	10.00%	78.50%
	Comprehensive Analysis	32.22%	31.11%	18.89%	23.33%	**37.78%**	36.67%	22.09%	12.22%	30.00%	10.00%	10.00%	13.33%	59.00%
Understanding	Avg	44.53%	57.42%	46.22%	44.89%	62.58%	**73.16%**	42.84%	26.40%	33.78%	39.82%	22.04%	40.27%	74.82%
	Passage Reading	51.11%	68.40%	60.25%	55.80%	73.83%	**79.51%**	48.40%	29.88%	43.70%	43.70%	51.85%		74.66%
	Sentence Grammar	41.94%	45.56%	43.33%	35.00%	56.67%	**66.11%**	38.33%	26.30%	28.33%	40.28%	22.78%	41.39%	74.43%
	Fill-in-the-blank	34.44%	51.48%	42.22%	33.33%	44.44%	**67.41%**	41.85%	25.93%	27.04%	39.63%	24.81%	32.22%	78.38%
	Long Text Reading	55.56%	73.33%	6.67%	70.00%	**90.00%**	**90.00%**	38.89%	12.22%	31.11%	21.11%	0.00%	7.78%	66.40%

Multimodal Benchmarking. We mainly perform the multimodal benchmarking on Ernie, ChatGLM-130B, Qianwen, and Spark models, since they provide Internet connectivity and can access images. For the other eight models that do not provide Internet connectivity including GPT-3.5, ChatGPT, GPT-4, Claude, LLaMA-13B, Vicuna-13B, ChatGLM-6B, and ChatGLM v2-6B, we also input the image URL to them.

For the eight models that have no image processing ability, the ideal response is to admit they have no such ability and cannot comprehend images. However, our evaluations find that only slight responses of GPT-3.5, ChatGPT, and GPT-4 can admit the image processing limitations. The other models just generate hallucinational and nonsense responses.

For the four models that have image processing ability, through comprehensive multimodal benchmarking, we discover that none of the evaluated LLMs accurately comprehend image content. When facing a multimodal question that contains both text and image, their responses are either text or text with images. However, we find that the output response has a low correlation with the input image. Even though Ernie has a certain probability to accurately comprehend the conventional images like ImageNet [4], however, the accuracy decreases largely (nearly zero) when facing geometric images.

Difficulty Benchmarking Using Human-Referenced Accuracy. We evaluate the ability to solve questions with different difficulty levels, using human accuracy as references, as shown in Fig. 5. Note that Level 1 to Level 5 is from simple to complex, with the easiest Level 1 and the most difficult Level 5. The human label indicates the human accuracy on that level, and humans can achieve 89.92%, 69.20%, 51.11%, 32.64%, and 14.98% average accuracy from Level 1 to 5, respectively.

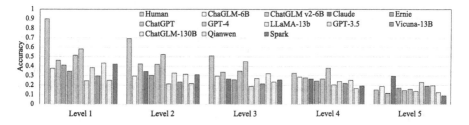

Fig. 5. The Average Accuracy on Five Difficulty Levels. Level 1 is the easiest, and Level 5 is the most difficult. The human label means the human accuracy on that level.

From Level 1 to 4, GPT-4 performs best among all twelve LLMs. For Level 5, Claude performs the best. Another exciting and counterintuitive phenomenon is that humans usually perform better than LLMs for simple difficulty levels like Levels 1 to 3. In contrast, humans perform worse than some LLMs for challenging levels like Levels 4 and 5. For example, GPT-4 has a higher average accuracy than

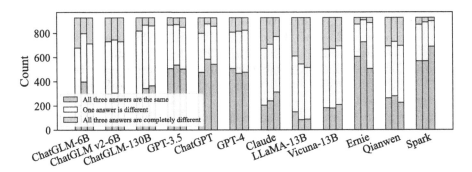

Fig. 6. Sensibility to Prompts and Response Repeatability of LLMs.

humans on Level 4. On Level 5, many LLMs have similar or even higher average accuracy than humans, including ChaGLM, Claude, Ernie, ChatGPT, GPT-4, GPT-3.5, Vicuna-13b, and ChatGLM-130b. The gap between the human and the best LLM on each level is 31.67%, 16.68%, 6.09%, -5.23%, -14.51%, respectively.

Response Repeatability. We further evaluate the repeatability of the responses. For each question, we ask LLMs using three different prompt types each of which repeats three times. The three prompt types are (i) only question without any prompt; add (ii) "The answer is:" and (iii) "The answer and the reason are:" at the end of the question, respectively. Figure 6 shows the results. We classify the responses into three categories: (1) all three answers are the same, like choosing A three times, (2) one answer is different, like A, A, and B for three answers. And (3) all three answers are entirely different, like A, B, and C for three answers. Note that the (1) category means the best repeatability while (3) means the worst repeatability. We find that Spark and Ernie have the best response repeatability, while LLaMA-13B is the worst.

The Average, Worst-Case, Best-Case, Majority Voting Accuracy. Figure 7 presents the accuracy results under the average, worst, best, and majority voting cases. We also use three kinds of prompt types, which use the same prompt setting with the above response repeatability evaluation. We find the following observations. (1) GPT-4 achieves the highest accuracy under four cases. (2) ChatGLM v2-6B performs better than ChatGLM-130B, which means the model architecture and the quality of training data are more important than merely increasing the model size. (3) The worst-case accuracy of LLMs is significantly below the corresponding average one, which means the model does not always give a correct answer during three times evaluation, indicating a poor reliability of LLMs. (4) The best-case accuracy of LLMs is much higher than the other cases, which means the model has a high probability to give a correct answer during three times evaluations. (5) The majority voting accuracy is similar to the average one, which means most of the time, the model can give a correct answer.

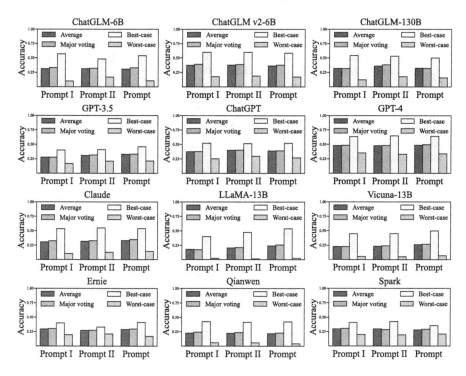

Fig. 7. The Average, Worst-case, Best-case, Majority Voting Accuracy of LLMs.

5   Conclusion

This paper provides a multi-granularity, multimodal, human-referenced, and auto-scoring benchmark for evaluating large language models—AGIBench, including a question dataset, auto-scoring evaluation, and comprehensive metrics. Through labeling each question with four attributes, including ability branch, knowledge, difficulty, modal, AGIBench supporting multi-granularity benchmarking at per-dataset, per-ability branch, per-knowledge, per-difficulty level, per-modal, and per-question granularities. We use the accuracy rate answered by millions of well-educated humans to label each question's difficulty level and include text and image modals. Instead of only using average accuracy as a metric, we define multi-dimensional metrics to evaluate the LLMs comprehensively. Our experiments on twelve LLMs show the effectiveness of AGIBench.

References

1. Bubeck, S., et al.: Sparks of artificial general intelligence: early experiments with GPT-4 (2023)
2. Cattell, R.B.: Theory of fluid and crystallized intelligence: a critical experiment. J. Educ. Psychol. **54**(1), 1 (1963)

3. Cobbe, K., et al.: Training verifiers to solve math word problems (2021)
4. Deng, J., Dong, W., Socher, R., Li, L.J., Li, K., Fei-Fei, L.: ImageNet: a large-scale hierarchical image database. In: 2009 IEEE Conference on Computer Vision and Pattern Recognition, pp. 248–255. IEEE (2009)
5. Gardner, H.: The theory of multiple intelligences. Ann. Dyslexia 19–35 (1987)
6. Hendrycks, D., et al.: Measuring mathematical problem solving with the math dataset. In: Thirty-Fifth Conference on Neural Information Processing Systems Datasets and Benchmarks Track (Round 2) (2021)
7. Huang, Y., et al.: C-Eval: a multi-level multi-discipline Chinese evaluation suite for foundation models (2023)
8. Legg, S., Hutter, M., et al.: A collection of definitions of intelligence. Front. Artif. Intell. Appl. **157**, 17 (2007)
9. Liang, P., et al.: Holistic evaluation of language models (2022)
10. Lu, P., et al.: Learn to explain: Multimodal reasoning via thought chains for science question answering. In: Advances in Neural Information Processing Systems, vol. 35, pp. 2507–2521 (2022)
11. Raji, I.D., Bender, E.M., Paullada, A., Denton, E., Hanna, A.: AI and the everything in the whole wide world benchmark. arXiv preprint arXiv:2111.15366 (2021)
12. Srivastava, A., et al.: Beyond the imitation game: quantifying and extrapolating the capabilities of language models. Trans. Mach. Learn. Res. (2023)
13. Sternberg, R.J.: The triarchic theory of intelligence (1997)
14. Wang, A., et al.: SuperGLUE: a stickier benchmark for general-purpose language understanding systems. In: Advances in Neural Information Processing Systems, vol. 32 (2019)
15. Wang, A., Singh, A., Michael, J., Hill, F., Levy, O., Bowman, S.R.: GLUE: a multi-task benchmark and analysis platform for natural language understanding. In: International Conference on Learning Representations (2019)
16. Wang, Y., Yao, Q., Kwok, J.T., Ni, L.M.: Generalizing from a few examples: a survey on few-shot learning. ACM Comput. Surv. (CSUR) **53**(3), 1–34 (2020)
17. Wei, J., et al.: Chain-of-thought prompting elicits reasoning in large language models. In: Advances in Neural Information Processing Systems, vol. 35, pp. 24824–24837 (2022)
18. Zhang, X., Li, C., Zong, Y., Ying, Z., He, L., Qiu, X.: Evaluating the performance of large language models on Gaokao benchmark (2023)
19. Zheng, L., et al.: Judging LLM-as-a-judge with MT-bench and chatbot arena (2023)
20. Zhong, W., et al.: AGIEval: a human-centric benchmark for evaluating foundation models (2023)

Automated HPC Workload Generation Combining Statistical Modeling and Autoregressive Analysis

Zechun Zhou⊙, Jingwei Sun$^{(\boxtimes)}$⊙, and Guangzhong Sun⊙

School of Computer Science and Technology, University of Science and Technology of China, Hefei, China
zhouzechun@mail.ustc.edu.cn, {sunjw,gzsun}@ustc.edu.cn

Abstract. Understanding the characteristics of workloads is essential to improving the management of a High Performance Computing (HPC) cluster. However, due to the restrictions of privacy and confidentiality, real HPC workloads are rarely open for studying. Generating synthetic workloads that mimic real workloads can facilitate related research, such as cluster planning and scheduling. Thus automated HPC workload generation has long been an active research topic. In this paper, we introduce a workload modeling approach that combines statistical modeling and autoregressive analysis. The model we built can generate complex, realistic HPC workloads with features that clearly describe the scheduling process, including job arrival time and other job attributes that affect scheduling such as job run time and job requested resources. Job arrivals in HPC clusters are generally represented by stochastic processes. In our proposed approach, job arrivals will be generated by a statistical model that consists of multiple Poisson processes with constraints provided by Gamma distribution. Then, we perform autoregressive analysis on the changing trends of job attributes to extract sequence information from historical workload trends that reflect user habits and scheduling habits in the cluster. Our approach generates job attributes based on the extracted sequence information for each job in the generated job arrival sequence. We evaluate the performance of the proposed approach using multiple metrics as well as a real-world use case. Experiments on real workloads from four supercomputing centers validate the effectiveness of the proposed method.

Keywords: Workload generation · Workload characterization · Cluster scheduling · Statistical modeling · Autoregressive analysis

1 Introduction

Understanding the characteristics of workloads is essential to promoting the management of an HPC cluster. These known workload characteristics enable better services that have data dependence on workload status, such as cluster

© The Author(s), under exclusive license to Springer Nature Singapore Pte Ltd. 2024
S. Hunold et al. (Eds.): Bench 2023, LNCS 14521, pp. 153–170, 2024.
https://doi.org/10.1007/978-981-97-0316-6_10

planning and scheduling [4,34]. However, real HPC workloads are rarely open for studying because of the restrictions of privacy and confidentiality. Due to the lack of publicly available real HPC workloads, synthetic workloads are widely used in HPC research. For example, with synthetic workloads, portable I/O analysis of commercially sensitive HPC applications can be conducted [11]. The evaluation of scheduling algorithms also relies on the large number of synthetic workloads available [24,30]. In particular, learning-based schedulers can be more fully trained on a large number of available synthetic workloads [12,13]. Therefore, automated HPC workload generation has long been an active research topic among HPC providers and researchers [4,23].

To accurately synthesize HPC workloads, characterizing workload patterns is essential. Some of these characteristics are intuitive and straightforward, such as the natural fluctuations in workloads throughout the week. Weekday workloads tend to be heavier than weekend workloads. Besides, there are implicit characteristics, such as workload fluctuations due to user habits [9]. Therefore, it is crucial to construct a detailed model and incorporate a broad set of factors to facilitate the extraction of all workload characteristics. With a comprehensive understanding of these workload characteristics, synthetic workloads can then be generated reasonably.

The classic approach to workload generation is statistical modeling [8,25,35]. Statistical modeling is a type of modeling method based on the regression of a large number of independent data to obtain the statistical distribution of the objective. For example, Poisson regression is a conventional method to simulate job arrivals [4]. It assumes that a large number of randomly arriving jobs usually follow a Poisson distribution. Then based on the time-dependent features, the regression model will fit a Poisson distribution for the job arrivals in each time interval. Other job attributes such as job run time are also typically generated by statistical modeling. The distribution of job run time is usually obtained by the empirical counting of the run time of all jobs in a period [8].

However, relying solely on statistical modeling frequently falls short of accurate workload generation. The primary focus of statistical modeling is on the distribution of workloads, neglecting potential correlations between various workload sequences. In this paper, we combine statistical modeling and autoregressive analysis for automatic HPC workload generation. At first, the job arrivals are obtained by modeling and simulation. Then other job attributes are further generated for the generated job arrival sequence.

In our workload generation approach, a statistical model combining Poisson regression and Poisson-Gamma regression is used to generate job arrivals. The commonly used Poisson regression works well in clusters with large amounts of job arrivals [9]. But in clusters with sparse workloads, the Poisson distribution assumption of job arrival distribution is difficult to be satisfied. Overdispersion of job arrivals occurs in these cases [32], which we deal with by introducing a Poisson-Gamma distribution. The hybrid model of Poisson regression and Poisson-Gamma regression can handle more job arrival distributions than Poisson regression alone.

Other job attributes, such as job requested resource and job run time, are generated by the autoregressive model in our approach. These job attributes are organized as time series in the historical job arrival sequences. In our approach, we perform attentive sequential generation for these job attributes based on autoregressive analysis of serial autocorrelation. Compared with statistical modeling, our model can better reproduce the data correlation in the series [4]. Based on the seasonal scheduling behavior derived from historical workloads, coupled with simulated job sequences provided by the job arrival model, job attributes of each job can be reasonably generated in our approach.

We evaluate the proposed workload generation approach on real HPC workload traces from four different real-world supercomputing centers. Our results show that our model can reveal the characteristics of real workload accurately. The synthetic workload generated by the proposed model reproduces scheduling information in the real workloads. In the evaluation, we use multiple metrics to measure the effectiveness of existing methods as baselines and show the superiority of our model.

The main contributions of this study are summarized as follows:

- We simulate job arrivals based on statistical modeling combining Poisson regression and Poisson-Gamma regression, with which more diverse arrival situations can be accurately represented.
- We conduct an autoregressive analysis to better model serialized workload information so that we can perform attentive sequential generation for job attributes realistically. So that the job attributes can be realistically generated for the simulated job sequence.
- We evaluate the proposed method on real workload traces from four supercomputing centers. All evaluations demonstrate the superiority of using our model to generate synthetic workloads.

Table 1. Specifications of workload traces from four platforms.

	#nodes	#cores/node	#jobs	Time span
Platform A	450	24/28	288K	364 days
Platform B	100	64	248K	364 days
Platform C	416	12	264K	364 days
Platform D	114	28	23K	364 days

2   Preliminary

We conduct our experiments on real traces from four different supercomputing centers. They are Supercomputing Center of University of Science and Technology of China [3], Center for High Performance Computing in Shanghai Jiao Tong

University [1], Shanghai Supercomputing Center [2], and Gansu Supercomputing Center respectively, and are subsequently referred to as platforms A, B, C, and D. The workload trace data from platform A is a typical dataset to conduct our experiments, and the inspiration for building our workload generation model is mainly based on our exploration of it. The workload trace data from the other three platforms are used as supplementary datasets in our evaluation experiments to verify the generalization of our approach. The specifications of traces from these four platforms are shown in Table 1. Among them, the traces of the first three platforms have similar specifications, while the data size of platform D is smaller.

These workload traces are recorded in the Standard Workload Format (SWF) proposed by David Talby and refined through discussions by Dror Feitelson, James Patton Jones, and others [6]. For each job, we mainly pay attention to its user ID, submit time, run time, and requested resources. A complete job sequence plus these job attributes can describe a complete scheduling process. For evaluation of workload generation, the last 10 weeks of each trace will be used as a test window, while all the data will be used to train the workload generation model.

The above platforms used for evaluation experiments mainly carry scientific computing workloads for researchers in various fields [1–3]. They are dominated by these tightly coupled MPI jobs. Common scientific computing software, such as VASP (Vienna Ab initio Simulation Package) [18] and Gaussian [10], often submits a large-scale parallel computing job to the cluster. For reasons such as adaptation or price, users' main choice for computing resources is the CPU rather than other acceleration devices such as GPU. The computing power of the computing nodes of the above platforms is indeed mainly provided by the CPU. So in this paper, job requested resources refer to the number of requested computing nodes, most of which are computing nodes with multiple CPU cores. Moreover, as the computing model expands, the run time of scientific computing tasks will increase beyond linear corresponding increases [19]. Therefore, the run times of jobs in these workloads vary greatly, with the longest scientific computing jobs running for weeks and the shortest test jobs running for just seconds.

3   Modeling Methodology

The workload generation model proposed in this paper consists of two major components, the job arrival model and the job attribute model. The overview of the modeling framework is shown in Fig. 1.

First, the arrival of jobs within each hour will be described by stochastic processes. The job arrival model employs two regression tasks to model job arrivals. Then, for each generated job with unknown attributes, the job attribute model autoregressively generates job attributes that conform to user habits at the user granularity, including requested resources, run time, job queue, etc.

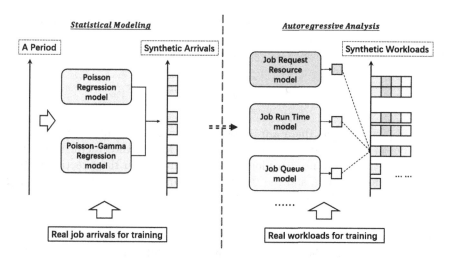

Fig. 1. Overview of modeling framework.

3.1   Job Arrival Model

The job arrival model employs two regression tasks, Poisson regression and Poisson-Gamma regression to model the stochastic process of job arrivals. We treat job arrivals at one-hour intervals within the trace range as random arrivals. The feature vector of each interval is determined by the following three features:

- *HoD*: One-hot code, to indicate this interval belongs to which hour of the day. Its dimension is 24.
- *DoW*: One-hot code, to indicate this interval belongs to which day of the week. Its dimension is 7.
- *WoY*: One-hot code, to indicate this interval belongs to which week of the year. Its dimension is 52.

HoD and *DoW* determine the feature vector of this interval in the regression task. They describe the temporal characteristics of job arrivals on day and week scales, respectively. *WoY* does not participate in the regression task. We use it to calculate a trend correction term for job arrivals that changes with the No. of weeks to make the regression model more generalizable. *WoY* is also used as the basis for us to assign user IDs to jobs within a week.

Poisson Model. Poisson regression is widely used in the simulation of job arrivals [4,13,16]. The probability distribution of a single Poisson distribution is: $f(y = k; \lambda_i) = \frac{\lambda_i^k}{k!} e^{-\lambda_i}, k = 0, 1, \dots$, and Poisson process assumes that in interval i, it contains y_i events arrive randomly. For interval i, we use feature vector $\boldsymbol{x}_i$ to describe its temporal features. *HoD* and *DoW* determine a 168×168 one-hot code feature matrix $\boldsymbol{X}$. For any feature vector, it can be matched to a row in the feature matrix. Then, the distribution parameters can be expressed as $\lambda = e^{X\beta}$, where X is the feature matrix composed of independent feature vectors, and β is the parameter matrix that needs to be regressed. The log-likelihood function of Poisson regression can be calculated by:

$$l(\beta) = \sum_{i=1}^{n}(y_i x_i \beta - e^{x_i \beta}), \tag{1}$$

where n represents that there are n observations in the training set, and y_i is the number of event arrivals when the corresponding feature vector is x_i. The partial derivative of the negative log-likelihood function in the direction of β is used as *Loss* for training, and the β parameter can be optimized by minimizing the negative log-likelihood estimation.

Poisson-Gamma Model. In real data, due to problems such as overdispersion and zero-inflation [32], the naive Poisson process is difficult to fully describe the arrivals in the real world. For such data, Its probability distribution can be better represented by a negative binomial distribution, or a Poisson-Gamma mixture distribution: $f(y = k; r, p) = \frac{\Gamma(k+r)}{\Gamma(k+1)\Gamma(r)}p^r(1-p)^k, k = 0, 1, \ldots$. For the overdispersed part, negative binomial regression can be chosen instead of naive Poisson regression, by replacing the parameters as follows: $\alpha_i = \frac{1}{r}$, $\mu_i = \frac{1-p}{\alpha p}$. Then the log-likelihood function of negative binomial regression can be calculated by:

$$l(\alpha, \mu) = \sum_{i=1}^{n}\{y_i ln\frac{\alpha x_i \mu x_i}{1 + \alpha x_i \mu x_i} + ln\Gamma(y_i + \frac{1}{\alpha x_i})$$
$$-\frac{1}{\alpha x_i}ln(1 + \alpha x_i \mu x_i) - ln\Gamma(y_i + 1) - ln\Gamma(\frac{1}{\alpha x_i})\}. \tag{2}$$

Hybrid Model. The above two regression models will be trained to convergence taking into account zero inflation of the data. At this point, we have two different models describing job arrivals during each one-hour interval. The Poisson model is more suitable for describing data with sufficient statistics and less interference. The Poisson-Gamma model can describe overdispersed data more accurately. We fuse these two models into a unified hybrid model based on Bayesian generalized additive models [21].

This hybrid model serves as our final job arrival model to simulate job arrivals within each one-hour interval. These job arrivals will be modified based on the correction of the weekly job arrival trend according to the interval's WoY. Then a sequence of jobs with just arrival time is generated, $J = \{j_1, j_2, j_3, \cdots\}$. Also based on WoY, we count the proportion of job arrivals for each user every week and randomly assign user IDs to all jobs within a week according to the generalized Bernoulli processes, which is based on the multinomial distribution of job arrivals over the user set. Let the user set be $U = \{u_1, u_2, u_3, \cdots\}$, and the entire job sequence J can be divided into multiple subsequences based on user IDs: $J^{u_1} = \{j_1^{u_1}, j_2^{u_1}, j_3^{u_1}, \cdots\}, J^{u_2} = \{j_1^{u_2}, j_2^{u_2}, j_3^{u_2}, \cdots\}, \cdots$.

3.2   Job Attribute Model

The function of the job attribute model is to generate reasonable job attributes for each job in the simulated job arrival sequence $\{j_1, j_2, j_3, \cdots\}$. Then we describe the attribute embedding, the autoregressive analysis process, and the attentive sequential workload generation in our job attribute model.

Attribute Embedding. The job attributes recorded in HPC cluster trace include many items, such as requested resources, run time, job queue, job status, etc. The job attributes that are the targets of our modeling generation can be specific to the following two items: (1) Job Requested Resource, indicates the number of computing resources requested by this job, for example, 5 Computing node cores; (2) Job Run Time, indicates the time that this job occupies computing resources while running; Based on these two items, the job scheduling process within an HPC cluster can be clearly constructed. Other miscellaneous items that have a minor impact on the scheduling process are not our modeling generation targets due to the inconsistency in trace record attribute types across platforms. But all items will contribute features to our attribute embedding, let the number of items be k. In order to facilitate attribute generation, we quantize the job attributes, in which the values of these items will be mapped to k discrete sets by clustering. In this way, the job attributes can be uniquely represented by one-hot codes $\in \mathbb{R}^{k \times D}$, where D is the dimension of discrete sets. We encode these items together into an embedding vector to represent the attributes of the job:

$$A(j) = Embed[R(j), T(j), O(j)], \qquad (3)$$

where $R(j)$, $T(j)$, and $O(j)$ respectively represent the requested resources, run time, and other miscellaneous items of job j. $A(j) \in \mathbb{R}^d$ is an embedding vector representing the attributes of job j. From this, job attributes can be generated based on a multinomial distribution over k discrete sets. Our job attribute model is built based on autoregressive analysis.

Autoregressive Analysis. For a user's sequence of jobs sorted by arrival time, job attributes are autocorrelated over time scales [4]. This temporal correlation contains the user's habit of submitting jobs in the cluster. We autoregressively analyze this temporal correlation between jobs to obtain the possible job attribute distribution. Assume a specific user u, we need to generate job attributes $\{A(j_1^u), A(j_2^u), \cdots\}$ for each job in u's simulated job sequence $\{j_1^u, j_2^u, \cdots\}$. The basis of this generation process is an autoregressive analysis on u's historical job attribute sequence, $\{A(j_{h1}^u), A(j_{h2}^u), A(j_{h3}^u), \cdots\}$.

Generally, for the attribute generation of user u's i-th job, we have to extract information from the previous part of the historical sequence to obtain its attribute distribution:

$$M(j_i^u) = softmax[extrac\{A(j_{h(i-n)}^u), \cdots, A(j_{h(i-2)}^u), A(j_{h(i-1)}^u)\}], \quad (4)$$

where $M(j_i^u)$ represents the multinomial distribution of attribute values of user u's i-th job. In the following section, we will introduce how the approach proposed in this paper autoregressively extracts historical sequence information to perform workload generation.

Attentive Sequential Generation. The proposed approach mainly uses the attention layer to extract historical sequence information. Compared with RNNs (Recurrent neural networks) and statistical time series models such as ARIMA (Autoregressive Integrated Moving Average Model), Transformer networks based on the attention mechanism are superior in extracting long-term dependencies in sequence information [31]. The attention mechanism can be defined as:

$$Attention(\boldsymbol{Q}, \boldsymbol{K}, \boldsymbol{V}) = softmax(\frac{\boldsymbol{Q}\boldsymbol{K}^T}{\sqrt{d}})\boldsymbol{V}, \quad (5)$$

where $\boldsymbol{Q}$ represents the queries, $\boldsymbol{K}$ the keys and $\boldsymbol{V}$ the values. The attention block calculates a weighted sum of all values, where the weight between query i and value j relates to the interaction between query i and key j. The scale factor $\sqrt{d}$ is to avoid overly large values of the inner product. In our method, the attention layer is used to extract historical sequence information:

$$\begin{aligned} \boldsymbol{A}_i^u &= \{A(j_{h(i-n)}^u), \cdots, A(j_{h(i-2)}^u), A(j_{h(i-1)}^u)\}, \\ \boldsymbol{E}_i^u &= Attention(\boldsymbol{A}_i^u \boldsymbol{W}^Q, \boldsymbol{A}_i^u \boldsymbol{W}^K, \boldsymbol{A}_i^u \boldsymbol{W}^V), \end{aligned} \quad (6)$$

where $\boldsymbol{W}^Q, \boldsymbol{W}^K, \boldsymbol{W}^V \in \mathbb{R}^{d \times d}$ is the linear projection matrices. The intermediate representation $\boldsymbol{E}_i^u$ is then transformed through the feed-forward layer and softmax layer, and finally the multinomial distribution $M(j_i^u)$ of the attributes of job j_i^u is obtained. $M(j_i^u) \in \mathbb{R}^{k \times D}$ is the probability distribution of job attributes based on the user's long-term habits obtained by autoregressively analyzing the user u's historical job sequence. $A(j_{h(i)}^u) \in \mathbb{R}^{k \times D}$ before embedding is the one-hot code of the job attributes actually submitted by the user in this order, which reflects the short-term considerations of user u. Generally, we randomly generate job attributes for all jobs in the simulated job sequence according to the probability distribution $[M(j_i^u) + A(j_{h(i)}^u)]/2$. At this point, the workload generation that mimics the cluster scheduling behavior but is not restricted to historical workload patterns is completed.

4   Evaluation

In this section, we evaluate whether synthetic workloads can mimic the scheduling behavior exhibited by real workloads from multiple perspectives. We first evaluate the generated job arrivals and then evaluate the overall workload generation results. Also, we evaluate our workload generation model on a use case.

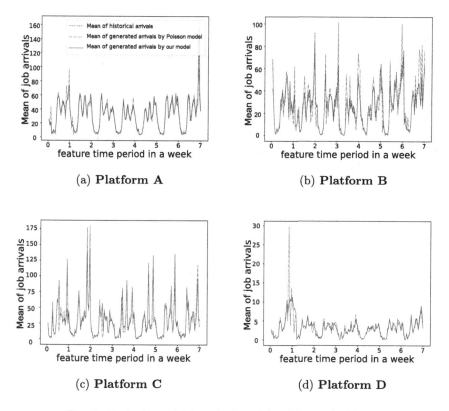

Fig. 2. Evaluation of job arrival models with metric *Mean*.

4.1   Evaluation of Job Arrival Generation

We evaluate our job arrival generation model by comparing its outputs with the outputs of Poisson regression model as the baseline. We use the following evaluation metrics:

- *Mean*, is the average number of job arrivals in each feature interval.
- *Devi*, is the regression deviance that is twice the difference between the maximum achievable log-likelihood and the log-likelihood of the fitted model: $Devi = 2[l(\boldsymbol{y}) - l(\boldsymbol{\alpha}, \boldsymbol{\mu})]$.

As described in Sect. 3.1, the feature vector of each interval in the job arrival model, which is a 168-dimensional one-hot code (7 days a week, multiplied by 24 h a day), represents the one-hour interval in one hour of the day of the week.

We evaluate job arrival generation results over time intervals represented by all 168 different one-hot feature vectors. The evaluation will compare whether the distribution of simulated job arrivals at each feature interval can approach the distribution of real job arrivals from the above metrics.

For the metric, *Mean*, it is intended to judge whether the arrival model can generate a reasonable number of job arrivals. The evaluation results for this metric are shown in Fig. 2. It can be seen that our model and the Poisson regression model both can generate a reasonable number of job arrivals in each feature interval. In each feature interval, the average number of generated job arrivals is very close to the statistical results in the real trace.

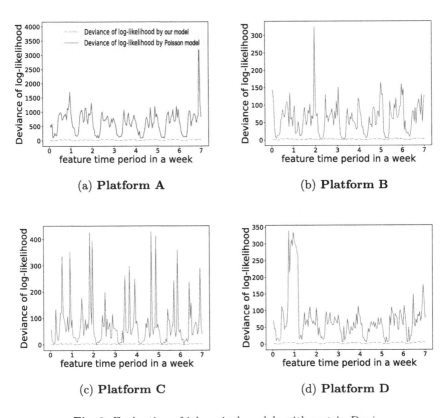

(a) **Platform A**

(b) **Platform B**

(c) **Platform C**

(d) **Platform D**

Fig. 3. Evaluation of job arrival models with metric *Devi*.

The metric, *Devi*, is intended to judge whether the regressions in arrival models converge well or not. The distribution obtained by Poisson regression will be approximated for calculation of deviance as a negative binomial distribution of $\mu = \lambda$ and $\alpha = 10^{-5}$. The evaluation results for this metric are shown in Fig. 3. Taking platform A as an example, it can be seen that naive Poisson regression is difficult to converge on the trace of platform A, while our model converges perfectly. This result shows that although the Poisson regression model can generate a reasonable number of job arrivals, it cannot restore the overdispersion in the original data distribution. Notably, the periodic variation of deviance in Poisson regression is strongly correlated with the periodic variation of the mean of job arrivals in all features. The periodic variation in the mean of job arrivals is due to the change in the amount of user job submissions caused by the alternation of day and night. Similar periodic variation in regression deviance of job arrivals indicates that there is a strong positive correlation between the degree of overdispersion of job arrivals and the number of job arrivals in the evaluated HPC cluster.

4.2 Evaluation of Workload Generation

We evaluate our overall workload generation results by comparing them with the results of existing methods as baselines:

- **Multinomial**: This type of method directly generates workloads based on the multinomial distribution of user job attributes based on statistics on all historical traces. Many classic HPC workload modeling methods are of this type [8,25,35].
- **RepeatFlav**: This method generates duplicate job attributes for all user jobs in a period based on the most frequently occurring user job attributes in this period. It was used as the main baseline in the work of Bergsma et al. [4].
- **Bergsma**: The work of Bergsma et al. serves as our main baseline [4]. Their method can represent the state-of-the-art deep learning-based workload generation methods. They used LSTM combined with survival prediction as the backbone network to conduct autoregressive analysis of historical sequence information and gradually job attribute distribution step by step.

We use the following evaluation metrics:

- **Coverage Accuracy**, indicates how accurately the distribution used for job attribute generation covers the real job attributes. For a job, if the probability of generating real job attribute values in its generation distribution exceeds 80%, then this step of generation is counted as an accurate generation.
- **Cosine Similarity**, represents the cosine similarity between synthetic workload sequences and real workload sequences, **Cosine Similarity**$(W, \hat{W}) = W \cdot \hat{W}/(||W||\ ||\hat{W}||)$

These two metrics measure the correlation between model output and real workloads from different perspectives.

Table 2 shows the metrics comparison on all platform traces of job requested resource sequence generated by our model and baselines. It can be seen that

Table 2. Evaluation of job requested resource generation.

Platform A		
	Coverage Accuracy	Cosine Similarity
Multinomial	67.15%	0.5018
RepeatFlav	72.17%	0.5183
Bergsma	80.28%	0.6672
Our model	**82.93%**	**0.7042**

Platform B		
	Coverage Accuracy	Cosine Similarity
Multinomial	77.93%	0.6512
RepeatFlav	80.82%	0.6791
Bergsma	88.21%	0.7117
Our model	**89.14%**	**0.7291**

Platform C		
	Coverage Accuracy	Cosine Similarity
Multinomial	69.41%	0.5293
RepeatFlav	78.96%	0.6174
Bergsma	83.22%	0.6713
Our model	**83.58%**	**0.7132**

Platform D		
	Coverage Accuracy	Cosine Similarity
Multinomial	77.37%	0.6884
RepeatFlav	79.51%	0.7375
Bergsma	85.16%	0.7927
Our model	**90.84%**	**0.9015**

our model has higher coverage accuracy and can better reflect the job requested resource correlation in real workloads, compared to all baselines. In all platforms on the dataset, the variation of job requested resources is not large, so even Multinomial model can effectively generate the job requested resource for all jobs.

Table 3 is the metrics comparison on all platform traces of job run time generated by our model and baselines. Unlike the evaluation of the job requested resource model, the performance of Multinomial model and RepeatFlav model are poor, due to the variation of run time being too large in all platform traces. In contrast, Bergsma model and our model achieve much better results on the generation of job run time. Compared with the Bergsma model, our job running time generation method also has advantages in both metrics.

Table 3. Evaluation of job run time generation.

Platform A

	Coverage Accuracy	Cosine Similarity
Multinomial	27.31%	0.2018
RepeatFlav	37.26%	0.1475
Bergsma	51.40%	0.6034
Our model	**57.32%**	**0.6437**

Platform B

	Coverage Accuracy	Cosine Similarity
Multinomial	34.76%	0.2910
RepeatFlav	45.81%	0.3049
Bergsma	60.84%	0.6826
Our model	**60.43%**	**0.6728**

Platform C

	Coverage Accuracy	Cosine Similarity
Multinomial	33.19%	0.2941
RepeatFlav	44.29%	0.3121
Bergsma	59.11%	0.6186
Our model	**59.41%**	**0.6472**

Platform D

	Coverage Accuracy	Cosine Similarity
Multinomial	43.72%	0.3219
RepeatFlav	50.14%	0.4112
Bergsma	69.11%	0.7236
Our model	**69.17%**	**0.7311**

4.3   Use Case of Workload Generation

We evaluate our workload generation model on a real-world use case: cluster planning [4]. Cluster planning is when the workload in the cluster is overloaded/underloaded, we need to plan the appropriate number of nodes to add/reduce. For this problem, synthetic workloads are necessary to more fully simulate and verify whether the cluster is load balanced after adding or reducing the corresponding number of nodes. Figure 4 shows our evaluation results on the trace of platform A of whether the synthetic workloads reflect cluster load levels. In this experiment, we assume that the cluster has no limit on the number of computing resources, and then count the number of computing node cores occupied by the workloads in each time period to represent the cluster load level. It can be seen that our synthetic workloads can well reflect the real load level, where we treat the attribute distribution of each job as a discretization of the

Gaussian distribution to calculate the 90% confidence interval of the synthetic load level. Our synthetic workloads can be generated in large numbers based on random patterns while simulating real load levels, making cluster planning simulations more sufficient and credible.

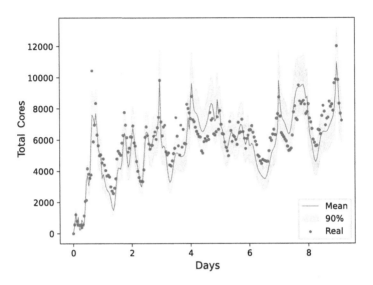

Fig. 4. Evaluation of whether the synthetic workloads reflect cluster load levels.

5   Related Work

5.1   Workload Modeling in HPC

Workload modeling has long been an active topic in the HPC community. Many existing works [8,25,35] were devoted to using statistical multinomial distribution to fit the workload modeling of supercomputing systems, which is a classic HPC modeling method. Rodrigo et al. further characterized the workloads in their HPC systems based on the system life cycle and evolution trends [29] and proposed a modeling method for heterogeneous workloads based on this portrayal [28]. Our approach is inspired by these existing state-of-the-art methods and further proposes a more comprehensive workload modeling for workload generation.

5.2   Workload Modeling in Cloud Computing

For cloud computing, although the main workload service types are different, their workload scheduling forms are similar to those in classic supercomputing systems. The mainstream method of workload modeling in cloud computing is to describe workloads' changing stochastic processes. Calheiros et al. introduced a workload prediction model based on ARIMA [5]. Gao et al. conducted a detailed study on the prediction of cloud resource allocation [15]. Cortez et al. constructed a time series model of the complete workload trend from the historical characteristics of virtual resource workload sequences [9]. Bergsma et al. established workload modeling also based on historical sequence characteristics, which can effectively generate complex and realistic workloads [4]. Our approach also draws from stochastic considerations and generation techniques in modeling workloads in cloud computing.

5.3   Resource Management in HPC

Workload modeling is beneficial for managing resources to improve utilization of HPC clusters. Many resource management services are based on workload profiling. The foundation of performance modeling and optimization of existing scheduling systems such as Slurm is workload modeling [26,34]. Cluster planning also relies on workload models for more adequate simulation [4]. Workload modeling and generation is more widely used in the evaluation of scheduling algorithms [24,30], ranging from classic schedulers [17], heuristic-based schedulers [7,20,22], prediction-based schedulers [14], deep reinforcement learning-based schedulers [12,13,27,33,36,37]. Motivated by these existing works, we plan to design a novel cluster scheduler based on our workload modeling in future work.

6   Conclusion

In this paper, we proposed a method to model the workload in HPC clusters and generate synthetic workloads for HPC clusters. We combined statistical modeling and autoregressive analysis in our model to better characterize the workload scheduling behavior exhibited by real workloads. Using the proposed model, we can generate a synthetic workload at any time involved in modeling, which can reflect the most consistent workload distribution based on accurate historical characteristics extraction of real workloads. The proposed method greatly improved the quality of automatically generated workloads and made the workload generation model more reliable for resource management services, such as cluster planning and scheduling.

In the future, we plan to further evaluate how the synthetic workload reflects real scheduling behavior and determine whether it can play a role in data augmentation. On this basis, we will design a more efficient data-driven learning-based cluster scheduler that can be further enhanced with synthetic workloads for training.

Acknowledgements. We thank the anonymous reviewers for their valuable comments. This study was supported by NSF of China (Grant No. 62202441). The experiments of this study were supported by Supercomputing Center of University of Science and Technology of China.

References

1. Center for High Performance Computing in Shanghai Jiao Tong University. https://hpc.sjtu.edu.cn/
2. Shanghai Supercomputing Center. https://www.ssc.net.cn/
3. Supercomputing Center of University of Science and Technology of China. https://scc.ustc.edu.cn/
4. Bergsma, S., Zeyl, T., Senderovich, A., Beck, J.C.: Generating complex, realistic cloud workloads using recurrent neural networks. In: Proceedings of the ACM SIGOPS 28th Symposium on Operating Systems Principles, pp. 376–391 (2021)
5. Calheiros, R.N., Masoumi, E., Ranjan, R., Buyya, R.: Workload prediction using ARIMA model and its impact on cloud applications' QoS. IEEE Trans. Cloud Comput. **3**(4), 449–458 (2014)
6. Chapin, S.J., et al.: Benchmarks and standards for the evaluation of parallel job schedulers. In: Feitelson, D.G., Rudolph, L. (eds.) JSSPP 1999. LNCS, vol. 1659, pp. 67–90. Springer, Heidelberg (1999). https://doi.org/10.1007/3-540-47954-6_4
7. Chen, X., et al.: A WOA-based optimization approach for task scheduling in cloud computing systems. IEEE Syst. J. **14**(3), 3117–3128 (2020)
8. Cirne, W., Berman, F.: A comprehensive model of the supercomputer workload. In: Proceedings of the Fourth Annual IEEE International Workshop on Workload Characterization, WWC-4 (Cat. No. 01EX538), pp. 140–148. IEEE (2001)
9. Cortez, E., Bonde, A., Muzio, A., Russinovich, M., Fontoura, M., Bianchini, R.: Resource central: understanding and predicting workloads for improved resource management in large cloud platforms. In: Proceedings of the 26th Symposium on Operating Systems Principles, pp. 153–167 (2017)
10. Curtiss, L.A., Redfern, P.C., Raghavachari, K.: Gaussian-4 theory. J. Chem. Phys. **126**(8), 084108 (2007)
11. Dickson, J., et al.: Enabling portable I/O analysis of commercially sensitive HPC applications through workload replication. In: Cray User Group 2017 Proceedings (CUG2017 Proceedings), pp. 1–14 (2017)
12. Fan, Y., Lan, Z.: DRAS-CQSim: a reinforcement learning based framework for HPC cluster scheduling. Softw. Impacts **8**, 100077 (2021)
13. Fan, Y., Lan, Z., Childers, T., Rich, P., Allcock, W., Papka, M.E.: Deep reinforcement agent for scheduling in HPC. In: 2021 IEEE International Parallel and Distributed Processing Symposium (IPDPS), pp. 807–816. IEEE (2021)
14. Gainaru, A., Aupy, G.P., Sun, H., Raghavan, P.: Speculative scheduling for stochastic HPC applications. In: Proceedings of the 48th International Conference on Parallel Processing, pp. 1–10 (2019)
15. Gao, J., Wang, H., Shen, H.: Machine learning based workload prediction in cloud computing. In: 2020 29th International Conference on Computer Communications and Networks (ICCCN), pp. 1–9. IEEE (2020)
16. Ghaderi, J.: Randomized algorithms for scheduling VMs in the cloud. In: IEEE INFOCOM 2016-The 35th Annual IEEE International Conference on Computer Communications, pp. 1–9. IEEE (2016)
17. Gómez-Martín, C., Vega-Rodríguez, M.A., González-Sánchez, J.L.: Fattened backfilling: an improved strategy for job scheduling in parallel systems. J. Parallel Distrib. Comput. **97**, 69–77 (2016)
18. Hafner, J.: *Ab-initio* simulations of materials using VASP: density-functional theory and beyond. J. Comput. Chem. **29**(13), 2044–2078 (2008)

19. Heath, M.T.: Scientific Computing: An Introductory Survey, Revised Second Edition. SIAM (2018)
20. Houssein, E.H., Gad, A.G., Wazery, Y.M., Suganthan, P.N.: Task scheduling in cloud computing based on meta-heuristics: review, taxonomy, open challenges, and future trends. Swarm Evol. Comput. **62**, 100841 (2021)
21. Klein, N., Kneib, T., Lang, S.: Bayesian generalized additive models for location, scale, and shape for zero-inflated and overdispersed count data. J. Am. Stat. Assoc. **110**(509), 405–419 (2015)
22. Kuchumov, R., Korkhov, V.: Analytical and numerical evaluation of co-scheduling strategies and their application. Computers **10**(10), 122 (2021)
23. Lin, W., Yao, K., Zeng, L., Liu, F., Shan, C., Hong, X.: A GAN-based method for time-dependent cloud workload generation. J. Parallel Distrib. Comput. **168**, 33–44 (2022)
24. Liu, Y., Wang, L., Wang, X.V., Xu, X., Zhang, L.: Scheduling in cloud manufacturing: state-of-the-art and research challenges. Int. J. Prod. Res. **57**(15–16), 4854–4879 (2019)
25. Lublin, U., Feitelson, D.G.: The workload on parallel supercomputers: modeling the characteristics of rigid jobs. J. Parallel Distrib. Comput. **63**(11), 1105–1122 (2003)
26. Reuther, A., et al.: Scalable system scheduling for HPC and big data. J. Parallel Distrib. Comput. **111**, 76–92 (2018)
27. Reza, M.F., Zhao, B.: Deep reinforcement learning with different rewards for scheduling in high-performance computing systems. In: 2021 IEEE International Midwest Symposium on Circuits and Systems (MWSCAS), pp. 183–186. IEEE (2021)
28. Rodrigo, G.P., Östberg, P.O., Elmroth, E., Antypas, K., Gerber, R., Ramakrishnan, L.: Towards understanding HPC users and systems: a NERSC case study. J. Parallel Distrib. Comput. **111**, 206–221 (2018)
29. Rodrigo Álvarez, G.P., Östberg, P.O., Elmroth, E., Antypas, K., Gerber, R., Ramakrishnan, L.: HPC system lifetime story: workload characterization and evolutionary analyses on NERSC systems. In: Proceedings of the 24th International Symposium on High-Performance Parallel and Distributed Computing, pp. 57–60 (2015)
30. Singh, S., Chana, I.: A survey on resource scheduling in cloud computing: issues and challenges. J. Grid Comput. **14**(2), 217–264 (2016). https://doi.org/10.1007/s10723-015-9359-2
31. Vaswani, A., et al.: Attention is all you need. In: Advances in Neural Information Processing Systems, vol. 30 (2017)
32. Ver Hoef, J.M., Boveng, P.L.: Quasi-Poisson vs. negative binomial regression: how should we model overdispersed count data? Ecology **88**(11), 2766–2772 (2007)
33. Wang, Q., Zhang, H., Qu, C., Shen, Y., Liu, X., Li, J.: RLSchert: an HPC job scheduler using deep reinforcement learning and remaining time prediction. Appl. Sci. **11**(20), 9448 (2021)
34. Yoo, A.B., Jette, M.A., Grondona, M.: SLURM: simple Linux utility for resource management. In: Feitelson, D., Rudolph, L., Schwiegelshohn, U. (eds.) JSSPP 2003. LNCS, vol. 2862, pp. 44–60. Springer, Heidelberg (2003). https://doi.org/10.1007/10968987_3
35. You, H., Zhang, H.: Comprehensive workload analysis and modeling of a petascale supercomputer. In: Cirne, W., Desai, N., Frachtenberg, E., Schwiegelshohn, U. (eds.) JSSPP 2012. LNCS, vol. 7698, pp. 253–271. Springer, Heidelberg (2013). https://doi.org/10.1007/978-3-642-35867-8_14

36. Zhang, D., Dai, D., He, Y., Bao, F.S., Xie, B.: RLScheduler: an automated HPC batch job scheduler using reinforcement learning. In: SC 2020: International Conference for High Performance Computing, Networking, Storage and Analysis, pp. 1–15. IEEE (2020)

37. Zhao, J., Rodríguez, M.A., Buyya, R.: A deep reinforcement learning approach to resource management in hybrid clouds harnessing renewable energy and task scheduling. In: 2021 IEEE 14th International Conference on Cloud Computing (CLOUD), pp. 240–249. IEEE (2021)

Hmem: A Holistic Memory Performance Metric for Cloud Computing

Yuyang Li[1], Ning Li[1], Yilei Zhang[1], Jianmei Guo[1(✉)], Bo Huang[1], Mengbang Xing[2], and Wenxin Huang[2]

[1] School of Data Science and Engineering, East China Normal University, Shanghai 200062, China
{yuyangli,ningli,ylzhang}@stu.ecnu.edu.cn,
{jmguo,bhuang}@dase.ecnu.edu.cn
[2] Tencent Cloud, Shenzhen 518000, China
{rockyxing,victorhuang}@tencent.com

Abstract. With the proliferation of cloud computing, cloud service providers offer users a variety of choices in terms of pricing and computing performance. A critical factor impacting computing performance is main memory, often evaluated using bandwidth and access latency metrics. For two evaluations with the same workload while under different system configurations, it is hard to determine which system delivers better memory performance for the particular workload if neither evaluation data achieves higher bandwidth and lower latency simultaneously. This dilemma is further exacerbated under different memory access patterns. We recognize that state-of-the-art memory performance metrics cannot well address the dilemma. To address this challenge, we define a holistic memory performance metric, named *Hmem*, which is calculated from a fusion of bandwidth and latency metrics across different access patterns. To reflect the overall performance of a given workload, we calculate the correlation between our proposed metric and the workload's throughput. Experimental results show that Hmem exhibits an average improvement of 70% on correlation coefficients compared to state-of-the-art memory performance metrics. A large cloud service provider has adopted Hmem to improve the efficiency of their memory performance evaluation and cloud server selection.

Keywords: Memory metric · Memory performance evaluation · Comprehensive evaluation · Cloud computing

1 Introduction

As cloud computing proliferates, many cloud service providers offer consumers a range of pricing and performance choices [1]. Memory directly impacts the speed at which computers can process data because it is a critical component of a computer. Evaluating main memory performance is essential to understanding and comparing overall computer performance. Typically, main memory performance

© The Author(s), under exclusive license to Springer Nature Singapore Pte Ltd. 2024
S. Hunold et al. (Eds.): Bench 2023, LNCS 14521, pp. 171–187, 2024.
https://doi.org/10.1007/978-981-97-0316-6_11

is evaluated using bandwidth and access latency (abbreviated as latency) metrics. However, holistic main memory performance evaluation and selection, which jointly evaluates bandwidth and latency metrics, are often faced with *comparing conflicts* between bandwidth and latency. For example, one computer system may have better bandwidth but worse latency. If neither metric achieves both higher bandwidth and lower latency, it is difficult to determine which system has better memory performance for the same workload.

Modern memory benchmarks [2,3] support the generation of a variety of test scenarios that are incorporated from memory access patterns, including read/write ratios, spatial-temporal locations, load intensity, etc. Different workloads have unique memory access patterns, and it is an important part of performance evaluation to assess how well a memory system performs under these varying conditions. For example, memory latency under different patterns would be affected by the hardware prefetching design of different systems. The variation in metric results under different test scenarios further exacerbates the dilemma of comparing conflicts, as no rational overall comparative conclusions can be drawn. The dilemma challenges us to apply bandwidth and latency metrics in cloud server selection, as conflicting comparison results cause us to be ineffective in reflecting the workload performance. Therefore, a critical research question is:

RQ: *How can we calculate a holistic metric that fuses bandwidth and latency to better represent the overall performance of main memory across multiple test scenarios?*

Some work focuses on which average methods are more appropriate to aggregate a single metric of a set of benchmark results [4,5] but holistic memory performance cannot be reflected by only one metric. Access per cycle (APC) derived from CPU evaluation metric instructions per cycle (IPC) is adopted to evaluate overall memory performance, while typically in a simulation environment [6]. In order to evaluate memory performance in a real-world environment, memory-level parallelism (MLP) and power metrics are identified as state-of-the-art holistic memory performance metrics. MLP metric [7] represents the level of concurrency within the computer system, calculated from the product of memory bandwidth and latency. Power metric [8] proposed to comprehensively evaluate system performance with throughput and latency metrics, calculated by dividing throughput and latency. MLP and Power metrics help to resolve the comparing conflicts in memory bandwidth and latency. However, we find that they are not effective in practice for evaluating overall memory performance, mainly due to their unclear physical meaning and insufficient reflection of the workload's performance.

To address these challenges, we propose the Hmem metric to represent holistic memory performance, defined as the average relative performance improvement of bandwidth and latency. It can also be applied to different test scenarios for a more comprehensive evaluation. We also conduct a comparative analysis of state-of-the-art of holistic memory performance metrics, including MLP and Power metrics. To validate the physical meaning of metrics, we use dimensional analysis to verify whether these metrics have clear physical meaning. Compared to other metrics, Power metric's unclear physical meaning may mislead evaluation conclusions. To reflect the overall performance of a given workload, we compute the correlation between our proposed metric and the workload's throughput, which is equivalent to the SPECspeed and SPECrate metrics of the SPEC CPU 2017 benchmark suites. We perform two non-parametric correlation tests: spearman rank correlation coefficient and the kendall rank correlation coefficient. The correlation coefficients of the statistical variables show that Hmem has spearman rank correlation coefficient of 0.85 and kendall rank correlation coefficient of 0.75, which shows an average improvement of 70% compared to other holistic metrics. This indicates that Hmem is a more appropriate metric for measuring overall memory performance. Our contributions are as follows:

- We reveal the comparing conflicts between bandwidth and latency metrics in overall memory performance evaluation. We illustrate the ineffectiveness of bandwidth and latency metrics in reflecting the overall performance of a given workload. We also present the cloud server selection framework to illustrate the application scenario of holistic memory performance metrics.
- We define the Hmem metric to represent holistic memory performance, comprehensively evaluating main memory performance through a meaningful fusion of bandwidth and latency metrics, which can also be applied in different test scenarios for a more comprehensive evaluation.
- We recognize and compare state-of-the-art holistic memory performance metrics with Hmem. Through dimensional analysis, we verify that the Power metric has an unclear physical meaning, which may mislead evaluation conclusions. To reflect the overall performance of a given workload, we calculate the correlation between our proposed metric and the workload's throughput. Experimental results indicated that Hmem has around 70% improvement in the correlation coefficient compared to other holistic metrics. It confirms that Hmem is more appropriate than state-of-the-art metrics for measuring overall memory performance.
- Hmem has been adopted in the cloud server evaluation platform of a large cloud service provider to help engineers effectively address the challenge of conflicting memory metrics.[1] The Hmem metric is automatically calculated on each execution of the evaluation pipeline, which is conducted hundreds of times daily. We also summarize three points of industrial experience in cloud server selection from the perspective of comprehensive memory performance evaluation.

2   Related Work

2.1   Cloud Memory Performance Evaluation

Memory performance evaluation is vital for cloud providers and consumers to make comparisons [2]. To meet performance requirements, cloud providers have

---

[1] https://jihulab.com/solecnu/hmem.

a wide range of DRAM options to choose from, including new additions to existing interfaces and architectures (DDR3, DDR4, DDR5) [9,10]. The performance impact of these memory systems on the overall computer system necessitates rigorous benchmarking for evaluation and comparison. Traditional memory metrics such as average miss penalty (AMP), miss rate (MR) [11], and memory-level parallelism (MLP) [7] provide insight into specific performance characteristics. Some metrics commonly evaluate comprehensive computer performance, including IPC, FLOPS, and BOPS. [11–13] However, they do not reflect the overall memory performance of the system. Multiple metrics' comprehensive evaluation can help us understand a system and make more informed decisions, especially in multi-vendor and complex cloud-based environments. Roofline model fuses the FLOPS and bandwidth to calculate operation intensity metric to guide us to conduct bottleneck analysis [14]. WSMeter metric aggregates IPC metrics to make comprehensive performance evaluation of data center [15]. Some MCDM methods help to make decisions for cloud services based on quality of service criteria [16]. These well-known methods include TOPSIS [17], SAW [18], AHP [19], VIKOR [20] , etc. We have yet to discuss these methods in this work because these methods are not suitable for memory performance evaluation. For example, TOPSIS and VIKOR are subject to rank reversal due to positive and negative ideal solutions changes. AHP also has the potential for inconsistency in the pairwise comparison.

2.2   Memory Performance Benchmarking

Modern memory benchmarks support the generation of various test scenarios incorporated from memory access patterns. Several commonly used memory microbenchmarks include Stream [21], Stream2 [22], Lmbench3 [23], Intel's Memory Latency Checker (MLC) [3], pChase [24],and X-Mem [2]. Benchmarks enable the assessment of loaded latency under various memory access patterns by concurrent control parameters, such as read-write ratios and spatial-temporal localities, etc. For example, the spatial locality characteristics of memory behavior are depicted through random and sequential access patterns. The injection delay value controls the system's stress level. Other potential pattern parameters encompass working set size, CPU and NUMA node affinity, stride size of load traffic-generating threads, etc. Loaded latency indicates the average total main memory latency under different bandwidth utilization. By concurrently measuring bandwidth and latency, the Bandwidth-Latency curve can be constructed to represent the memory system's comprehensive performance across various load intensities. Occasionally, the curve comprises three distinct stages: constant, linear, and exponential [25]. To compare performance, we often average summarized metrics within a single dimension of metric [4,5]. However, these methods fall short when handling a comprehensive bandwidth and latency comparison, primarily due to their comparing conflicts. In this paper, we propose Hmem, which evaluates main memory performance holistically through a meaningful fusion of bandwidth and latency metrics across different test scenarios to provide a more comprehensive representation of memory performance.

2.3 Dimensional Analysis

An appropriate holistic performance metric should be interpretable and physically meaningful to represent some of the system's performance characteristics. Dimensional analysis is a method to analyze and evaluate the general laws of physical quantities based on their unit and dimensions [26]. Dimensional analysis streamlines information by elucidating the relationships between various physical quantities in the metrics. In any equation that precisely depicts the laws of physical phenomena, the term's units on both sides must be the same. Dimensional analysis is widely applicable in various fields, such as mathematics, finance, engineering, etc. In computing and telecommunications, the most commonly used unit of information is a bit used to measure the capacities of other systems and channels. Other metrics derived from bit, including Byte, KB, MB, etc. In tackling complex problems involving multiple variables, eliminating redundant information and differentiating relationships among diverse physical quantities become beneficial and essential.

3   Cloud Server Selection Framework

We present and illustrate the application scenario of comprehensive memory performance evaluation through the cloud server selection framework in Fig. 1. The detailed framework is described as follows:

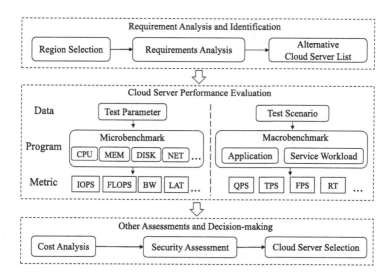

Fig. 1. Cloud server selection framework

– **Requirement Analysis and Identification.** Cloud consumer access to cloud resources is network-based. Choosing an appropriate server deployment location based on the user's needs can maximize service quality protection and reduce performance problems related to geography. By analyzing the requirements, we can comprehend the user's needs for various resource types and performance requirements. We can choose the alternative list of cloud servers for evaluation based on the specific requirements.

– **Cloud Server Performance Evaluation.** Benchmarks can be categorized into microbenchmarks and macrobenchmark according to their program scale. Microbenchmarks consist of specific functions or code snippets that can be used for preliminary and efficient system performance evaluation. Typically, microbenchmark programs reflect specific system performance aspects requiring short execution time. Macrobenchmarks are programs that are extracted from real workloads, including application and service workloads, unlike microbenchmarks. Executing macrobenchmarks takes more time and is more expensive than microbenchmarks.

– **Other Assessments and Decision-making.** Based on the performance metrics of the performance evaluation, we can further evaluate the cost, security, and so on. Ultimately, we synthesize multiple factors to make cloud server selections.

In performance benchmarking, holistic memory performance metrics support us in drawing preliminary cloud servers' performance comparison conclusions. Holistic memory evaluation metrics can help users measure memory performance in cloud server selection.

4   Motivating Example

We present an example of a conflicting comparison of memory performance benchmark results from four mainstream cloud servers under different test scenarios, frequently compared by cloud consumers. These four servers' hardware and software configurations are listed in Table 1.

Table 1. Hardware and software configuration.

Computer	A	B	C	D
Processor	AMD EPYC 7K62	Ampere Altra	KunPeng920	Intel Platinum 8255C
Number of Cores	8	8	8	8
Core Frequency	2.6 GHz/3.3 GHz	2.8 GHz/3.0 GHz	2.6 GHz/3.0 GHz	2.50 Hz/3.1 GHz
Memory Capacity	2 × 16 GB	2 × 16 GB	2 × 16 GB	2 × 16 GB
Memory Frequency	DDR4-2933 MHz	DDR4-3200 MHz	DDR4-2933 MHz	DDR4-2933 MHz
Kernel	4.18.0	4.18.0	4.18.0	4.18.0
Compiler	GCC 8.5.0	GCC 8.5.0	GCC 8.5.0	GCC 8.5.0
	Glibc 2.28	Glibc 2.28	Glibc 2.28	Glibc 2.28

We utilize the memory performance benchmark [2] to measure the bandwidth and latency metrics. The comparison results for these four computers are shown in Table 2. These test scenarios consist of different memory access patterns described in detail in Sect. 6.1. For each scenario, it is apparent that computer B delivers the best performance in terms of bandwidth, while computer D excels in latency across most scenarios. However, we cannot definitively conclude which computers perform best when attempting to draw a comprehensive comparison conclusion from the ranks in each scenario or on average.

Table 2. Comparing conflicts of bandwidth and latency metrics on four computers, BW indicates bandwidth, LAT indicates latency.

Metric	Rank	Test Scenarios					Rank Result
		1	2	3		Avg	
BW	1	B	B	B		B	?
	2	D	D	A		C	
	3	C	A	C		A	
	4	A	C	D	...	D	
LAT	1	D	D	D		D	
	2	B	B	A		B	
	3	C	C	B		C	
	4	A	A	C	...	A	
Best Computers		?	?	?		?	

If we evaluate memory performance only by a single metric (bandwidth or latency), there is a high probability that we will make a wrong evaluation result. For example, to reflect the overall performance of a given workload, we perform two non-parametric correlation tests between the results of different computers on the workload performance and memory metrics to validate this phenomenon in Table 3, including spearman rank correlation coefficient (SROCC) and kendall rank correlation coefficient (KROCC).

The correlation coefficients for both metrics do not show strong correlations (absolute value of correlation coefficients equal or greater than 0.8) on average, indicating that if we were to compare these computers based solely on a single metric (either bandwidth or latency), we would likely produce incorrect ranking results with a high probability because workload performance is affected by both bandwidth and latency. Comprehensive and time-consuming benchmark suites can evaluate overall system performance but do not directly reflect memory performance. Therefore, this paper aims to answer our proposed research question (**RQ**).

Table 3. Spearman's rank correlation coefficient (SROCC) and Kendall's rank correlation coefficient (KROCC) of bandwidth (BW) and latency (LAT) metrics in different workloads.

Benchmark	SROCC		KROCC	
	BW	LAT	BW	LAT
503.bwaves_r	0.20	−0.60	0.00	−0.33
519.lbm_r	0.40	−0.80	0.33	−0.67
549.fotonik3d_r	0.20	−0.60	0.00	−0.33
554.roms_r	0.20	−0.60	0.00	−0.33
603.bwaves_s	0.20	−0.60	0.00	−0.33
619.lbm_s	0.40	−0.80	0.33	−0.67
649.fotonik3d_s	0.20	−0.60	0.00	−0.33
654.roms_s	0.20	−0.60	0.00	−0.33
Average	**0.25**	**−0.65**	**0.08**	**−0.42**

5   Holistic Memory Performance Metric

5.1   MLP Metric

Little's Law [27] is a well-known theory of queuing theory because of its theoretical and practical significance. Little's Law states that the average number of jobs in a stable queuing system (L) is equal to the product of the average arrival rate of jobs (λ) and the average waiting time of a job in the system (W). The form is shown in Eq. (1).

$$L = \lambda W \tag{1}$$

In previous research, Little's Law has been utilized for performance evaluation. Bailey et al. [28] discussed it and related the equation with high-performance computing. Mehta et al. [29] leverage Little's Law to calculate the MLP metric of an application. The observed MLP metric of an application could be compared with the peak theoretical MLP metric computed from hardware parameters, providing valuable insights for performance optimizations and analyses related to program parallelism.

$$MLP = Bandwidth \times Latency \tag{2}$$

According to Little's Law, the average number of bytes transmitted between memory and the processor equates to the product of memory bandwidth and latency, reflecting the level of concurrency within the computer system. This relationship is depicted in Eq. (2). When performing a comprehensive evaluation, we can use the bandwidth and latency metrics from each test scenario to calculate the MLP metric and further aggregate the MLP metric from each test scenario.

5.2 Power Metric

Jain et al. [8] proposed to use the Power metric to comprehensively evaluate different network architectures with throughput and response time metrics. The Power metric, as delineated in Eq. (3), represents the ratio of throughput to response time.

$$Power_{net} = \frac{Throughput}{Response\ Time} \qquad (3)$$

The throughput and response time of two distinct network architectures, A and B, were measured. Although network A has higher throughput, its response time is longer than network B. Upon employing the Power metric for comparison, it became evident that network A surpassed network B in overall performance. However, the original study merely introduced the Power metric without employing tangible experimental results to corroborate the validity of this metric.

$$Power_{mem} = \frac{Bandwidth}{Latency} \qquad (4)$$

Analogously, it is feasible to extrapolate the application of the Power metric to facilitate a holistic evaluation of memory performance, utilizing both bandwidth and latency metrics. This approach is depicted in Eq. (4). For a comprehensive evaluation, we can use each test scenario's bandwidth and latency metrics to calculate the Power metric and aggregate each test scenario's Power metric as a reference for overall memory performance. It should be noted that the power metric does not refer to energy divided by time, and it does not correctly solve the **RQ** problem, e.g. DDR4 has lower power consumption as well as higher transfer performance compared to DDR3 [30].

5.3 Hmem Metric

To address the RQ we proposed, a holistic memory performance metric should fuse bandwidth and latency and be representable to represent the overall performance of the main memory. We propose the holistic memory performance metric, Hmem, defined in Eq. (5). The metric is derived from the average ratio of the relative improvement in performance for both bandwidth and latency. A predefined baseline machine is utilized as a reference machine, allowing the calculation of the performance improvement ratio relative to other computers. The relative weights of bandwidth and latency are equally assigned as 0.5 in this paper representing the portion of each metric contribution to Hmem. The weights are determined based on their importance to Hmem, and we assume that bandwidth and latency are equally important. Generally, the summary of relative weights of metrics should add up to one. The relative weights of different test scenarios also follow the principle.

$$Hmem = (Bandwidth_{ratio}{}^{w_1} \times Latency_{ratio}{}^{w_2})^{\frac{1}{w_1+w_2}} \qquad (5)$$

Algorithm 1. Pseudo Code of Hmem based Evaluation Process

Input: Computer List I; Test Scenarios List J; Bandwidth Weight w_b; Latency
   Weight w_l; Bandwidth metrics for computer i in test scenario j: $Bandwidth_{ij}$;
   Latency metrics for computer i in test scenario j: $Latency_{ij}$; Reference Machine
   Bandwidth in test scenario j: $Bandwidth\_Ref_j$; Reference Machine Latency in test
   scenario j: $Latency\_Ref_j$.
Output: Computers' memory performance Rank.
1: Create Hmem Matrix $HM[I][J]$ and Hmem List $HL[I]$;
2: **for** i in I **do**
3:    **for** j in J **do**
4:       convert $Bandwidth_{ij}$ and $Latency_{ij}$ unit;
5:       $Bandwidth\_Ratio_{ij} \leftarrow Bandwidth_{ij} / Bandwidth\_Ref_j$;
6:       $Latency\_Ratio_{ij} \leftarrow Latency\_Ref_j / Latency_{ij}$;
7:       $Hmem_{ij} \leftarrow (Bandwidth\_Ratio_{ij}^{w_b} * Latency\_Ratio_{ij}^{w_l})^{\frac{1}{w_b + w_l}}$;
8:       assign $Hmem_{ij}$ to $HM[i][j]$;
9:    **end for**
10:    assign $HM[i][0...J]$ summarize results to $HL[i]$;
11: **end for**
12: Rank the computers' based on $HL[I]$;
13: Return the rank of computers' memory performance;

Notably, the bandwidth ratio is computed by taking the system's memory
bandwidth under test (SUT) and dividing it by the bandwidth of the reference
machine, as detailed in Eq. (6). In contrast, calculating the latency ratio involves
dividing the latency of the reference machine by the latency on the SUT, as
outlined in Eq. (7).

$$Latency_{ratio} = \frac{Latency_{REF}}{Latency_{SUT}} \tag{6}$$

$$Bandwidth_{ratio} = \frac{Bandwidth_{SUT}}{Bandwidth_{REF}} \tag{7}$$

The weights attributed to the metrics can be modulated in accordance with
the specific evaluation prerequisites. The pseudo code of the Hmem based evaluation process is outlined in Algorithm 1. We advocate using the geometric mean
to aggregate ratio metrics, primarily due to its consistent rankings, irrespective
of the machine chosen for normalization [31,32]. Despite the vast discussions
surrounding ratio-like metrics in prior research [33], this consistency is vital for
evaluating and ranking cloud servers.

6   Evaluation

6.1   Experimental Setup

We utilize the X-Mem [2] to measure the memory performance of different
(instruction set architecture) ISAs cloud servers. We employ the test scheme of

loaded latency in MLC. We employ seven threads generating load and one thread measuring latency, concurrently collecting metrics. The load-generating threads employ forward-read sequential access patterns with chunk sizes of 32 and 64 bits. The delay value for memory access in nops within the load threads incrementally increases from 0 to 1024, allowing for continuous observation of memory performance under varying pressure. The latency measurement thread utilizes a random read pointer-chasing access pattern. Each load thread is assigned a working set size of one hundred MB within its memory region. The total memory utilized eight hundred MB, with no data sharing occurring between threads.

We selected four mainstream servers covering x86-64 and AArch64 ISAs. These servers are virtualized from physical servers and are often evaluated and compared for memory performance. These four servers' hardware and software configurations are detailed in Table 1. The reference machine is the standard S1 cloud server, the intel E5-2680v4 chips with DDR3, and other hardware and software configurations equal to these four mainstream servers. The reference machine was selected as old generation machines in cloud servers, which refers to the SPEC CPU 2017 reference machine selection standard. We use some workloads that rely heavily on main memory performance in the SPEC CPU 2017 benchmark suites [34] to evaluate the holistic metric, including bwaves, lbm, fotonik3d, and roms [6,35]. For SPECrate workloads, the performance ratio must be multiplied by the number of copies. We chose eight concurrent copies to run each benchmark, testing the workload throughput of the system. For SPECspeed workloads, we selected eight threads to run one copy of each benchmark in a suite, testing the time required to complete a workload. The number of threads and copies equals the number of processor numbers, ensuring full utilization of system performance. Benchmarks were compiled using GCC 8.5 with no flags and employed the reference workload as the input size.

6.2 Physical Meaning Evaluation

For the MLP metric, the result of the dimensional analysis is present in Eq. (8). b represents the dimension of bit and T represents the dimension of time. This equation confirms that the metric represents the average number of bytes transmitted between the memory and processor. The factor of one thousandth that features in the equation emerges from prefix conversions derived from the bandwidth metric, expressed in megabytes per second, and the latency metric, quantified in nanoseconds. The metric is a valid representation of the system's parallelism.

$$MLP = b^1T^{-1} \times b^0T^1 = b^1T^0 = 10^{-3} \times byte \qquad (8)$$

Conversely, the Power metric, as evidenced in Eq. (9), cannot be explained in terms of physical quantities, which could yield unexplained results. The factor of ten raised to the fifteenth power is obtained through unit conversion. While the trend of the metrics shows that the bandwidth metric is reasonable as the numerator and the latency metric as the denominator, the physical meaning of the Power metric remains unclear.

$$Power = b^1 T^{-1} / b^0 T^1 = b^1 T^{-2} = 10^{15} \times \frac{byte}{s^2} \tag{9}$$

The process of dimension analysis for the Hmem is demonstrated in Eq. (10). Although Hmem is dimensionless owing to its relative speedup characteristics, it maintains its practical relevance by signifying the ratio of the average memory performance improvement of the SUT over the reference system. As different metrics exhibit distinct data dispersion and dimensions, Hmem nullifies the dimension's impact through the ratio.

$$Hmem = (b^1 T^{-1} / b^1 T^{-1}) \times (b^0 T^1 / b^0 T^1) = b^0 T^0 \tag{10}$$

In summary, MLP is reasonable for representing the parallelism of memory. Further experimental data is needed to determine how effective the MLP metric is in terms of overall main memory performance. The physical meaning of the Power metric remains ambiguous, structured with the bandwidth and latency metrics serving as numerator and denominator, respectively. Hmem practically represents the SUT average memory performance improvement over the reference machine.

6.3   Proximity of Holistic Metrics and Workload Performance

In order to reflect the overall performance of a given workload, we compute the correlation between our proposed metric and the workload's throughput, corresponding to the SPECspeed and SPECrate metrics of the SPEC CPU 2017 benchmark suites. An appropriate holistic main memory metric for measuring holistic memory performance should correlate highly with the workload throughput. We perform two non-parametric correlation tests: spearman rank correlation coefficient (SROCC) and kendall rank correlation coefficient (KROCC). The mathematical definition of SROCC and KROCC is given in Eq. (11) and Eq. (12).

$$r_{SROCC} = \frac{cov(R(X), R(Y))}{\sigma_{R(X)} \sigma_{R(Y)}} \tag{11}$$

$$r_{KROCC} = \frac{n_c - n_d}{\sqrt{(n_0 - n_X)(n_0 - n_Y)}} \tag{12}$$

$R(X)$ and $R(Y)$ denote the ranks of X and Y, respectively. $cov(R(X), R(Y))$ represents the covariance of the ranks of X and Y. $\sigma_{R(X)}$ and $\sigma_{R(Y)}$ are the standard deviations of the rank variables. n_c and n_d are concordant and discordant pairs, n_0 is the total number of pairs. n_X n_Y are the number of X and Y of concordant pairs, respectively. They assess how well the relationship between two variables can be described using a monotonic function. The values of SROCC and KROCC are between 1 and −1, corresponding to positive and negative linear correlations. Latency should have a negative correlation, and other metrics should have a positive correlation. The SROCC for each memory metric against the workload's throughput is calculated and shown in Table 4. It can be observed that Hmem has the strongest correlation with the workload's throughput, with an average SROCC of 0.85. This correlation between Hmem and the workload's throughput reflects that Hmem is more appropriate to represent holistic main memory performance.

Table 4. Spearman's rank correlation coefficient of different metrics in different workloads, BW indicates bandwidth, LAT indicates latency.

Benchmark	Spearman's rank correlation coefficient				
	Raw Metric		Holistic Metric		
	BW	LAT	MLP	Power	Hmem
503.bwaves_r	0.20	−0.60	0.20	0.40	**0.80**
519.lbm_r	0.40	−0.80	0.40	0.80	**1.00**
549.fotonik3d_r	0.20	−0.60	0.20	0.40	**0.80**
554.roms_r	0.20	−0.60	0.20	0.40	**0.80**
603.bwaves_s	0.20	−0.60	0.20	0.40	**0.80**
619.lbm_s	0.40	−0.80	0.40	0.80	**1.00**
649.fotonik3d_s	0.20	−0.60	0.20	0.40	**0.80**
654.roms_s	0.20	−0.60	0.20	0.40	**0.80**
Average	0.25	−0.65	0.25	0.50	**0.85**

Among the other holistic metrics, the Power metric is the best with an average SROCC value of 0.5. Compared to Power, Hmem improves the correlation value by 0.35. This observation is due to the fact that within these workloads, the Hmem is consistently better than the Power metric. Interestingly, MLP has the same SROCC as BW, meaning that the rank order of BW is the same as MLP. This is probably because, compared to LAT, BW's change range dominates the MLP value. Compared to LAT, BW can be increased exponentially more easily. Among the raw metrics, LAT has the best average SROCC value of -0.65. The main memory performance bottleneck needs further analysis to be confirmed. The SROCC results also indicate that raw metrics measured from benchmarks cannot singly be used to represent systems' holistic main memory performance of systems. The KROCC for each memory metric against the workload's throughput is calculated and shown in Table 5. It can be observed that Hmem also has the strongest correlation with the workload's throughput, with an average KROCC of 0.75. Among the other holistic metrics, the Power metric is the best with an average KROCC value of 0.42. Compared to Power, Hmem improves the correlation value by 0.33. Among the raw metrics, LAT has the

Table 5. Kendall's rank correlation coefficient of different metrics in different work-loads, BW indicates bandwidth, LAT indicates latency.

Benchmark	Kendall's rank correlation coefficient				
	Raw Metric		Holistic Metric		
	BW	LAT	MLP	Power	Hmem
503.bwaves_r	0.00	−0.33	0.00	0.33	**0.67**
519.lbm_r	0.33	−0.67	0.33	0.67	**1.00**
549.fotonik3d_r	0.00	−0.33	0.00	0.33	**0.67**
554.roms_r	0.00	−0.33	0.00	0.33	**0.67**
603.bwaves_s	0.00	−0.33	0.00	0.33	**0.67**
619.lbm_s	0.33	−0.67	0.33	0.67	**1.00**
649.fotonik3d_s	0.00	−0.33	0.00	0.33	**0.67**
654.roms_s	0.00	−0.33	0.00	0.33	**0.67**
Average	0.08	−0.42	0.08	0.42	**0.75**

best average KROCC value of -0.42. In summary, Hmem represents the highest correlation with the workload's throughput. Experimental results indicate Hmem is a more appropriate metric for measuring overall memory performance.

7 Threats to Validity

Internal Threats. In this paper, we have assumed equal weighting for both scenarios and metrics (bandwidth and latency). Depending on evaluation requirements, the weights assigned to scenarios and metrics need to be customized to fit requirements. Besides that, memory capacity impacts workload performance in some scenarios, especially when not enough memory capacity is available for the workload. Current memory benchmark metrics do not represent the impact of memory capacity on performance.

External Threats. Performance testing requires system quiescent to get repeatable and reliable benchmarking results. The unpredicted changes in hardware and software of cloud environments would influence bandwidth and latency measurement results. In addition, due to the impact of test scenarios on Hmem, in order to better reflect the workload performance, the test scenarios should be closer to workload memory access patterns.

8 Practical Experience

Hmem has been adopted in the server evaluation environment of a large cloud service provider. It is automatically calculated on each execution of its evaluation pipeline, which runs hundreds of times a day. We also summarize three points of industrial experience in cloud server selection from the perspective of comprehensive memory performance evaluation.

1. **Holistic Performance Metric Design:** In holistic metric design, analyzing the metric with clear, interpretable physical meaning is necessary. It must be verified in detail to ensure the metric will not produce misleading results in practical applications.
2. **Automated Evaluation for Different Requirements:** The focused test scenarios consist of different memory access patterns according to performance requirements. The precipitation of automated evaluation scripts for different performance requirements can efficiently calculate holistic performance metrics to support decisions.
3. **Efficient Cloud Server Selection:** To guarantee the comprehensiveness of evaluation, we typically conduct both micro-benchmarking and macro-benchmarking to cover real workload behaviors. Holistic metrics of microbenchmarks could be helpful to improve efficiency by filtering the range of servers for engineers before conducting macro-benchmarking.

9   Conclusion and Future Work

In this paper, we define a holistic memory performance metric, Hmem, calculated from a fusion of bandwidth and latency metrics across different access patterns. It can also be applied to different test scenarios for a more comprehensive evaluation. We also conduct a comparative analysis of state-of-the-art memory performance metrics with Hmem. To validate the physical meaning of metrics, we use dimensional analysis to verify that metrics have clear physical meaning. To reflect the overall performance of a given workload, we compute the correlation between our proposed metric and the workload's throughput. Hmem provides the strongest correlation in correlation coefficients compared to other optimal metrics. Experimental results indicate Hmem is a more appropriate metric for measuring overall memory performance. A large cloud service provider has adopted Hmem to evaluate cloud instance memory performance in each execution of the cloud server evaluation pipeline.

For future work, Hmem could also be measured at each level of the cache hierarchy to provide valuable insight. Hmem could also provide reference to other systems evaluated by throughput and latency metrics, such as disk, network, or applications that cross multiple computers. We can also combine cost and Hmem metrics to calculate the memory performance and price ratio to guide us in making better decisions on memory selection. This work also informs future holistic metric design and validation research.

Acknowledgments. This work is supported by the National Natural Science Foundation of China (No. 62272167). We want to thank our lab colleagues and anonymous reviewers for their valuable comments and suggestions. We would also like to thank Chengdong Li from Code Title Poetry (Hangzhou) Technology for his valuable insights during the research process.

References

1. Garg, S.K., Versteeg, S., Buyya, R.: Smicloud: a framework for comparing and ranking cloud services. In: IEEE International Conference on Utility and Cloud Computing (UCC), pp. 210–218. IEEE (2011)
2. Gottscho, M., Govindan, S., Sharma, B., Shoaib, M., Gupta, P.: X-Mem: a cross-platform and extensible memory characterization tool for the cloud. In: IEEE International Symposium on Performance Analysis of Systems and Software (ISPASS), pp. 263–273. IEEE (2016)
3. Vish, V., Karthik, K., Thomas, W., Sri, S.: Intel Memory Latency Checker. https://www.intel.com/content/www/us/en/developer/articles/tool/intelr-memory-latency-checker.html
4. John, L.K.: More on finding a single number to indicate overall performance of a benchmark suite. ACM SIGARCH Comput. Arch. News (SIGARCH) **32**(1), 3–8 (2004)
5. Iqbal, M.F., John, L.K.: Confusion by all means. In: Proceedings of the 6th International Workshop on Unique Chips and Systems (UCAS) (2010)
6. Sun, X.H., Wang, D.: APC: a performance metric of memory systems. ACM SIGMETRICS Perf. Eval. Rev. (SIGMETRICS) **40**(2), 125–130 (2012)
7. Chou, Y., Fahs, B., Abraham, S.: Microarchitecture optimizations for exploiting memory-level parallelism. ACM SIGARCH Comput. Arch. News (SIGARCH) **32**(2), 76–87 (2004)
8. Jain, R.: The Art of Computer Systems Performance Analysis: Techniques for Experimental Design, Measurement, Simulation, and Modeling. Wiley, New York (1991)
9. Liu, J., Jaiyen, B., Veras, R., Mutlu, O.: RAIDR: retention-aware intelligent DRAM refresh. ACM SIGARCH Comput. Arch. News (SIGARCH) **40**, 1–12 (2012)
10. Hassan, H., Pekhimenko, G., Vijaykumar, N., Seshadri, V., Mutlu, O.: ChargeCache: reducing DRAM latency by exploiting row access locality. In: IEEE International Symposium on High Performance Computer Architecture (HPCA), pp. 581–593 (2016)
11. Hennessy, J.L., Patterson, D.A.: Computer Architecture: A Quantitative Approach. Elsevier, Amsterdam (2011)
12. Yi, L., Li, C., Guo, J.: CPI for runtime performance measurement: the good, the bad, and the ugly. In: IEEE International Symposium on Workload Characterization (IISWC), pp. 106–113 (2020)
13. Wang, L., Gao, W., Yang, K., Jiang, Z.: BOPS, a new computation-centric metric for datacenter computing. In: Benchmarking, Measuring, and Optimizing: Second BenchCouncil International Symposium (Bench), pp. 262–277 (2020)
14. Williams, S., Waterman, A., Patterson, D.: Roofline: an insightful visual performance model for multicore architectures. Commun. ACM **52**(4), 65–76 (2009)
15. Lee, J., Kim, C., Lin, K., Cheng, L., Govindaraju, R., Kim, J.: WSMeter: a performance evaluation methodology for google's production warehouse-scale computers. In: Proceedings of the Twenty-Third International Conference on Architectural Support for Programming Languages and Operating Systems (ASPLOS), pp. 549–563 (2018)
16. Sun, L., Dong, H., Hussain, F.K., Hussain, O.K., Chang, E.: Cloud service selection: state-of-the-art and future research directions. J. Netw. Comput. Appl. **45**, 134–150 (2014)

17. Behzadian, M., Otaghsara, S.K., Yazdani, M., Ignatius, J.: A state-of-the-art survey of TOPSIS applications. Expert Syst. Appl. **39**(17), 13051–13069 (2012)
18. Sotoudeh-Anvari, A., Sadjadi, S., Molana, S., Sadi-Nezhad, S.: A new MCDM-based approach using BWM and SAW for optimal search model. Decis. Sci. Lett. **7**(4), 395–404 (2018)
19. de FSM Russo, R., Camanho, R.: Criteria in AHP: a systematic review of literature. Procedia Comput. Sci. **55**, 1123–1132 (2015)
20. Mardani, A., Zavadskas, E.K., Govindan, K., Amat Senin, A., Jusoh, A.: VIKOR technique: a systematic review of the state of the art literature on methodologies and applications. Sustainability **8**(1), 37–75 (2016)
21. McCalpin, J.D.: Stream benchmark (1995). https://www.cs.virginia.edu/stream/ref.html
22. McCalpin, J.D.: Stream2 benchmark (1999). https://cs.virginia.edu/stream/stream2
23. Staelin, C.: Lmbench: an extensible micro-benchmark suite. Softw. Pract. Exp. **35**(11), 1079–1105 (2005)
24. Pase, D.: pChase benchmark (2013). https://github.com/maleadt/pChase
25. Radulovi, M.: Memory bandwidth and latency in HPC: system requirements and performance impact. Universitat Politècnica de Catalunya, pp. 14–20 (2019)
26. Barenblatt, G.I.: Dimensional Analysis. CRC Press, Boca Raton (1987)
27. Little, J.D., Graves, S.C.: Little's law, Building intuition: insights from basic operations management models and principles, pp. 81–100 (2008)
28. Dh, B.: Little's law and high performance computing, NAS applications and tools group, NASA Ames Research Center (1977). https://crd.lbl.gov/~dhbailey/dhbpapers/little.pdf
29. Mehta, S.: Performance analysis and optimization with little's law. In: IEEE International Symposium on Performance Analysis of Systems and Software (ISPASS), pp. 12–23. IEEE (2022)
30. Islam, M.A., Arafath, M.Y., Hasan, M.J.: Design of DDR4 SDRAM controller. In: International Conference on Electrical and Computer Engineering (ICECE), pp. 148–151. IEEE (2014)
31. Citron, D., Hurani, A., Gnadrey, A.: The harmonic or geometric mean: does it really matter? ACM SIGARCH Comput. Arch. News (SIGARCH) **34**(4), 18–25 (2006)
32. Mashey, J.R.: War of the benchmark means: time for a truce. ACM SIGARCH Comput. Arch. News (SIGARCH) **32**(4), 1–14 (2004)
33. Marino, M.D.: Walter: wide I/O scaling of number of memory controllers versus frequency and voltage. IEEE Access **8**, 193874–193889 (2020)
34. Standard Performance Evaluation Corporation: SPEC CPU 2017. https://www.spec.org/cpu2017/
35. Singh, S., Awasthi, M.: Memory centric characterization and analysis of SPEC CPU2017 suite. In: Proceedings of the 2019 ACM/SPEC International Conference on Performance Engineering (ICPE), pp. 285–292 (2019)

Author Index

S. Hunold et al. (Eds.): Bench 2023, LNCS 14521, p. 189, 2024.
https://doi.org/10.1007/978-981-97-0316-6

Printed in the United States
by Baker & Taylor Publisher Services